Viollet
the life of a
legendary goalscorer

by Roy Cavanagh
& Brian Hughes MBE

Foreword by Sir Bobby Charlton

EMPIRE
Publications

EMPIRE PUBLICATIONS
1 Newton Street, Manchester M1 1HW
copyright Roy Cavanagh & Brian Hughes 2001

ISBN 1 901 746 39 9

Photographs courtesy of the authors, Helen Viollet, Eric Baggaley,
Jack Coggan, Paul Windridge
Front cover photograph courtesy of Paul Windridge
Jacket design: Ashley Shaw
Edited by Ashley Shaw and Stuart Fish
Front Cover: Dennis scores another cracker at Highbury, 1961.
Back Cover (top to bottom): Dennis signs for the kids at Pauldens Department
Store; Dennis in party mood at one of his regular haunts; Dennis poses with
Stanley Matthews and teammates in the Stoke dressing room, 1963.

Printed in Great Britain by:
Ashford Colour Press, Gosport, Hampshire.

Contents

Contents

In memory of a beautiful and brave lady,
Monica Greenhouse who died recently of cancer.

1   2

Acknowledgements

Putting this book together has been a personal pleasure. We would like to thank a number of people who helped to make it possible. Foremost among them is Helen Viollet, without whose help, kindness and encouragement this book would not have even got started. We hope you and Rachel will be pleased with our efforts.

Many of Dennis Viollet's schoolfriends and personal friends were gracious and helpful, sharing their memories with us, among them we would especially like to thank are the following: 'Old Margaretian', Eric Baggaley, Alan Wallace, Mr GH Dobie, Alan 'Tiny' Cornforth, Eric Lewis for his help and loan of programmes. A special thanks to Jack Coggan and Mr Arthur Beckett. We would also like to express our thanks and gratitude to readers of the *Manchester Evening News* for their phone calls and help.

We'd also like to thank John Prince, Viv Bowden, Kevin Burthem, Alan Bradshaw, Rick Brent and Geoffrey H Galley. A big thank you to Iain McCartney, co-author of Duncan Edwards' biography and author of last year's Roger Byrne book.

To Eddie Sparrow, Ann Wagster, John Holland MBE, Frank Beacher, Ray Holden, Roy Ladley, Harry Jackson and Ian Niven MBE we'd like to extend our heartfelt thanks.

In addition the contributions of Ken Cuttler and Alex Gaskell have been invaluable in shedding light on Dennis's early days with United. In addition Bernard Bull, Brian Smith, Karl Smith, Peter John, Paul Windridge, David Bronfield and John Heilperns have all contributed while

Graham Bridgwood and John Donagh have added valuable information and photographs about Dennis's Stoke City years.

Special thanks also goes to ex-players such as the late Sir Stanley Matthews, Sir Tom Finney, Sir Bobby Charlton, Albert Scanlon, Ronnie Cope, Ray Wood, Wilf McGuinness, Harry Gregg, Alex Dawson, Noel Cantwell, Ian Greaves, Ken Barnes, Allan Phillpot, Jimmy McIlroy, Bill Asprey and Eric Skeels.

Finally, a big thank you to Ashley Shaw and Stuart Fish of Empire Publications; Paul Hince, Pete Spencer, Tina Smith, Margaret Robinson and others at the *Manchester Evening News* for their assistance.

If there is anyone we have forgotten to mention please accept our apologies, it is not intentional I can assure you.

A Word from the Authors

Brian Hughes MBE

The idea of a book on one of my favourite Manchester United players came when I was working on *The Tommy Taylor Story*, a book I wrote a few years ago. I contacted Dennis in America and sent him a couple of pages of questions. I was pleasantly surprised then when I received a phonecall from him and the promise that an audio tape would be sent within weeks. Dennis was so gracious and sincere and couldn't do enough to help with the book on a player he thought was a magnificent centre-forward.

A week or so later, Jimmy Wagg, the BBC GMR sports presenter and top after-dinner celebrity, was interviewing me at home when there was a knock on my front door. It was the postman, he had the tape Dennis had recorded and sent from Jacksonville. I played it straight away and Dennis's voice came over loud, clear and crisp. Then suddenly as he was describing the events of the Munich tragedy myself and Jimmy sat rigid. Dennis's voice wavered, he stopped, started to speak again, then we heard sobbing. Needless to say we were both distressed.

I turned off the tape and we tried to complete the interview as best we could. I was fortunate to have watched the 'old' Manchester United team, the one referred to as the 1948 team. My older brother was a City supporter and every week he would take me with him to Maine Road, where at that time both City and United played their home games. I was of course much too young to appreciate the wonderful players like Chilton, Aston, Cockburn, Carey, Pearson and Rowley but these players were all pasted into my scrapbook when the Pink and Green evening sports newspapers came out after the matches.

When United returned to Old Trafford, my brother Colin was forced to take me there every other week, much to his annoyance until I was old enough to go on my own. It was here that I saw the seeds of one of the most breathtaking sporting achievements ever seen being sown - the birth of the Busby Babes! Dennis Viollet was one of the first to break through into that fantastic team. I always favoured goalscorers and none came better than this fleet-footed player. It all seemed so easy for him, so effortless. You will read more graphic descriptions of Dennis's exploits in the pages of this book. I can vouch that he was always in amongst the action in the opposition's half. I saw him play as an out-and-out striker and he was a master. As a schemer, there were few better, on the wing he gave me the impression that this had been his position all his life, he was superb, beating full-backs and laying the ball off to other forwards. I also saw him play wing-half with great aplomb and distinction. Fabulous!

Those European Cup ties of the 1950s have remained with me for life. They were unforgettable nights of glory and passion which are impossible to recapture in mere words. There was a tingling in the air leading up to those games. It was an us against them situation, but in a true sporting sense without any thoughts of violent behaviour. The ten-nil drubbing of Anderlecht saw football at its zenith, the team operated like a well-oiled engine. The thrills, spills and passion, along with the undiluted pride that an English club, and young kids at that, could put on such a performance left an indelible memory for those of us lucky enough to have been at Maine Road. Brilliant nights continued: the

Athletico Bilbao tie saw a wonderful attacking spectacle as the Devils came back from two goals down to turn round the tie. I have never heard cheering like it before or since. Then Real Madrid - what a beautiful team they were - where we saw players like di Stefano, Gento and their other stars. But the Busby Babes, although lacking experience, gave them a torrid time.

I must admit that when the present United team won the European Cup and pulled off the treble I shed a few tears. Alex Ferguson has brought back the nostalgia, passion and emotion of those times and he's done magnificently. His players earn vast fortunes and good luck to them. The players of Dennis Viollet's era, however, earned little more than a factory worker . I am certain Dennis Viollet would have endorsed this present team, they play football the Viollet way. He would have been happy for them. I hope this book will let followers of football know what a truly gifted and clever player Dennis Viollet was. I sincerely hope you enjoy reading the book as much as we have writing it. Thanks to everybody who helped us, I am eternally grateful.

Roy Cavanagh

My ideas for this book on Dennis Viollet came from doing *A Salford Lad*, the story of Eddie Colman. A complementary book came to mind using *A Manchester Lad* as its title. A copy of Colman's story finished up with Helen Viollet in America and the seeds for this book on Dennis were sown. I have watched United since 1954 and the Busby Babes were really the first team I saw. To this day, it was them as a team, all eleven, not individuals, that are the memory. Dennis Viollet was part of that team. Dennis Viollet was a complete footballer. Undeniably an outstanding forward in his own right, who could both make and take goals. A great goalscorer, his record is right up there with the records of

Law, Greaves, Rush and Lineker. Added to this, his vision meant he created lots of goals, particularly for his inside-forward partner Tommy Taylor. At first glance, Dennis seemed ill-equipped to scrap with the rock-hard defenders of the day: the likes of Jimmy Scoular, Tommy Banks, Roy Paul and Jimmy Dickinson. In fact, Busby was so concerned that he asked Tommy Taylor to keep his eye on his inside-forward partner.

Dennis was ghostly pale, he didn't look well at times but he had beautiful balance, silky ball control, tremendous acceleration and the brains to use them all. Dennis's partnership with Taylor was almost telepathic, they complemented each other perfectly. Quite why they were never paired together for England is one of life's mysteries. An adroit footballer, quick darting runs were his speciality. Always going for goal, Dennis was a goal maker and a goal taker.

Matt Busby is quoted as saying that Dennis was: "Among the great players I had under my care at Old Trafford. He came as boy, and we brought him up in the Old Trafford tradition. As a player he was whipcord. I admired his skill from the beginning and have always admired it." There can be no finer tribute. Meeting Brian Hughes has been a pleasure. He is a top bloke. To everyone who helped us out - thank you one and all.

Foreword

I first saw Dennis Viollet play in a Schoolboy international match at Newcastle, against Scotland I think, when I was thirteen years old. Two players stood out in that particular game: Dennis Viollet and Jeff Whitefoot. They stood out like sore thumbs. Both of them, I heard older people saying, were destined to sign for Manchester United when they left school. Dennis Viollet in particular impressed me a great deal. He was an inside-forward like myself and took my eye immediately. He was deadly in the box and again, if my memory serves me right, he scored a couple of goals. He was very, very fast off the first six yards and kept remarkable control over the ball while moving at speed. He seemed so confident in everything he did with the ball, and so composed when he received it, he always seemed to be in the right place whenever it was played up to him. He wasn't well built for a forward but the way he used the ball, defenders had little opportunity of clattering him. When they moved in to tackle him he would be gone in a flash. When I joined Manchester United in 1953 Dennis was already at the club and was about to make his debut in the first team against Newcastle. In my early days at Old Trafford I watched his progress as Dennis became a first team regular, even though he was only a young player himself This was a policy our manager Matt Busby made so successful later on with the Busby Babes team.

While in the successful United FA Cup team and the reserves, I had the opportunity to play with or against Dennis on many occasions. He was always friendly and helpful. On the field his ability and goalscoring qualities stood out like a beacon on a foggy night. While on the verge of a first team place, I watched with admiration as he was one of the main reasons why good things were happening with Manchester United during this period. I remember his great performance under the floodlights at Maine Road against Anderlecht in the European Cup when United won by ten clear goals. It was one of the best displays of English football ever seen. Dennis scored four on this occasion and his movement both on and off the ball was a sight to behold. The intelligent way he linked up with the wing-halves and his crisp, inch-perfect passing to his forward colleagues was stamped with class while his unique partnership with Tommy Taylor was something special. They both seemed to have a telepathic understanding - each knowing what the other was about to do. For example, when Tommy went up for a high ball Dennis would move straight away into position in anticipation of Tommyís headed pass. Dennis knew the exact kind of ball Tommy liked to run on to and he would deliver it precisely.

A gracious friend and kind and considerate team-mate, Dennis Viollet was a huge influence when Manchester United were carving a name in Europe in that golden time.

When I broke into the first team I saw how good he was at first hand. Most Friday mornings after training I would sit alone in an empty Old Trafford stand and worry about the following day's game and who would be opposing me. I would go over my previous match and think: "That's the point from which I made my run the other week - did I time it right?" I would relive all the incidents in my mind, to try and work out how I did it, and think how I would do it another time.

"What would I have done if the opposing player had decided to do this or that? Would I have gone to that position or the other?" Many times Dennis would join me.

He seemed to sense my anxiety and help me relax. On the field he was always looking for attacking options and made things so simple. I believe that had it not been for Munich and the injuries he suffered, I am certain Dennis Viollet would have become a more important striker in world terms. I am delighted that this book will convey to readers the personality of a truly wonderful footballer - Dennis Viollet.

Sir Bobby Charlton CBE
October 2001

Preface

Dennis and I were very close friends over the years and I was devastated when his wife Helen informed me that he had passed away.

He had wonderful skills and an all-round talent: great control, subtlety and pace; he was a class footballer and clinical goalscorer. Having played against him on many occasions, I found it very difficult to contain him as a player; to mark him was like looking for the Scarlet Pimpernel, "they seek him here, they seek him there..." This was one of talents, constantly finding the space in which to score his goals. He still holds Manchester United's record for most League goals in a season which, in my opinion, will never be bettered. Off the field Dennis was a modest and comical character with a great sense of humour - always ready for a laugh. When I look back and reminisce, I realise what a pleasure it was to have known and spent so many happy hours in his company,

God Bless Dennis

Ken Barnes
October 2001

Introduction

"No player has gained more pleasure from the great game of football than I have. But as I bow out, there is more than a little sadness for me. I see that the game is changing. The pattern is less colourful, and the individuals grow fewer and fewer. Football is now regimentation. Yet I have been privileged to spend the major part of my career with a club that I have always considered the finest in the world - Manchester United! During those years, and after, I played with the greats like Duncan Edwards, Roger Byrne, Tommy Taylor and the rest. I have also been thrilled to play with the illustrious Stanley Matthews, and against mighty footballers like Puskas and di Stefano. To me these were the football kings, ruling the game with their brilliance and their overwhelming authority. But now, sadly, the kings have gone."

Dennis Viollet

The above was written just before Dennis Viollet hung up his football boots for good and retired from playing the game he loved so passionately. He was in the throes of writing his life story with his friend, the *Daily Mirror* journalist Alec Johnson, the book was to be called *The Kings Have Gone!* Dennis dearly wanted to put his life story into print. Sadly the book was never completed and both Dennis and Alec have since passed away.

We have tried to tell the story Dennis wanted to convey to football lovers all over the country, and we sincerely hope you enjoy reading about Dennis Viollet, who for so long, was captain of Manchester United and Stoke City, filling several positions at both clubs, for he was a gentleman footballer, a family man and a true lover of football. He gave the game not only his skill, and leadership, but also a sense of dignity.

Brian Hughes MBE
Roy Cavanagh
Manchester,
October 2001

Dennis Sydney Viollet (1933 - 1999)

In the modern football transfer market, where strikers are sold for millions and earn thousands a week from their clubs, it is little wonder that football followers from the early 1950s shake their heads in disbelief. This is certainly not a case of nostalgia ain't being what it used to be. No, this is about facts and the statistics, particularly as regards the subject of this book, bear this out today.

Dennis Sydney Viollet is a player many younger Manchester United fans may never have heard of, but long-standing United followers and neutral soccer supporters remember Viollet as one of the original 'Busby Babes'.

The cold facts are these: in September 1950, after two years in Manchester United's junior teams, Viollet signed professional forms with the club. He made his Manchester United first team debut at Newcastle in April 1953. At the same time Matt Busby was rebuilding his brilliant, exciting, and high-scoring 1948 FA Cup winning team, which went onto win the First Division championship in 1952. Viollet later took over the inside-left position from the legendary and ever-popular Stan Pearson, a prolific goalscorer himself. But the cold facts are that Dennis played 261 league games for United scoring 159 goals - an incredible 240 in all games for the club, including an amazing 13 in 12 European Cup-ties and five in 18 FA Cup games.

More than this though was the Viollet style. Dennis was a quicksilver, free scoring inside-forward in the greatest British club side ever assembled. This 'Busby Babes' side was a dream team if ever there was one and Dennis was a wonderfully skillful, intelligent player of the highest order. Not a big man for a forward, he was tall and slender, if anything he looked sick and undernourished and in need of a hot meal. But how Manchester United came to depend on him and his goalscoring exploits.

Viollet's striking partnership with the big brave Tommy Taylor is folklore to thousands of United followers. What a brilliant understanding these two magnificent players had with each other, it was almost telepathic. Their goalscoring records speak for themselves; each player getting well over a hundred goals for the Reds, but it was the way they played together that marked them as an outstanding striking partnership.

However, Dennis was not a temperamental type of player. He would not immediately stand out in a game, he was not prone to dramatics after he was fouled nor would he openly contest a referee's decision. He was a silent, ghost-like kind of forward. All of a sudden he would appear in positions in the opposing penalty area and score goals of simplicity. He was highly regarded by teammates who knew they would always be able to score against the tightest defences with the slim Viollet around. However, there was so much more to his game than mere goal scoring, although it was as a goal poacher that his reputation was largely built.

He was beautifully balanced, a brilliant reader of situations and an astute passer of the ball. He would often drop back into defence if his team were under pressure and, with a deft interception, would send a pass upfield, with all the precision of a missile, turning defence into attack at the swiftest instance.

Dennis certainly did not look like a footballer. He was a real Manchester lad: regal-looking, sharp featured with raven black hair which always looked well brylcreemed and groomed to perfection, he was a smart, conservative dresser. You could mistake him for a tennis player or a man about town, perhaps an office executive. He was a real charmer and known amongst his Old Trafford club-mates as a 'rum' bugger who liked the ladies, a laugh and a sing-song.

Later, Dennis became captain of Manchester United filling several positions for his team. He was a gentleman footballer, a family man, and a true lover of the game. He gave the game not only his skill and leadership but also a sense of caring and understanding that helped many younger players a great deal.

"What a wonderful goal snatcher!" enthused Jimmy Murphy, Manchester United's assistant manager, and the man responsible for grooming Dennis in his formative years with the club. "He would come in on the blind side of those big beefy defenders and nick a goal much to their surprise. Dennis seemed ice cool when going for goal, we knew that nine times out of ten he would score in a one to one situation. He was vital to Manchester United."

The French Connection

Many people have wondered about Dennis's gallic connections; the name Viollet is French. Over the course of his career it was suggested that the football played by Dennis had a marked grace and flair about it which some people characterised as having a continental or Gallic elan or joie de vivre. There certainly appeared to be something of the Eric Cantona in Dennis, a mixture of Gallic flair mixed with Mancunian flashiness. The two United heroes even bore a slight resemblance to each other.

It is interesting that, writing in the days of the Quixall-Viollet- Charlton forward line, Bobby Charlton said that he saw in Dennis the skills and style of Raymond Kopa, then leading the attack for Real Madrid and France. Sir Matt

Busby thought he saw in Viollet a talent grown closer to home, the style and skills of a player whom Busby greatly admired - Hughie Gallacher, centre-forward for Newcastle, Chelsea and Scotland.

In his autobiography *The Way it Was*, Sir Stanley Matthews pays glowing tribute to the skills of Dennis Viollet. For the Blackpool, Stoke and England maestro, however, the closest modern-day equivalent to the style and skills Dennis embodied is Teddy Sheringham of Manchester United, Tottenham Hotspur and England. To be thus likened to Kopa, Gallacher and Sheringham is quite a hat-trick of compliments.

Perhaps the comparison by the late Sir Stanley of Dennis with 2001 Player of the Year Teddy Sheringham shows just how highly Dennis was rated by his fellow players during the two decades or more during which he graced the game of football. Sir Alex Ferguson is certainly correct in believing that Viollet, although one of the best footballers of his generation, remained underrated, and it has been moving and gratifying to stir people's memories of this great player. Hearing and recording the opinions of others on Dennis's extraordinary talent and adding our own, has served to convince us yet more deeply that, as Mike Johnson in Jacksonville attests, 'dignity and class' were the hallmarks of Viollet's career and life.

Perhaps this book will help to bring to further attention one of the greatest players in Manchester United's history. We hope that it does. We hope, too, that Manchester will remain proud of Dennis Viollet, one of her most famous and distinguished sons.

From Moss Side to Old Trafford

Dennis Viollet was born into a typical working-class Church of England household. Manchester was a very poor city in the thirties, there wasn't much money around and any kind of work was hard to come by.

Dennis was born at number 7, Clinton Avenue in an area on the border of Fallowfield and Moss Side, on the south side of the city, a stone's throw from Manchester City's Maine Road ground, on September 20th 1933.

Dennis was brought up in a close, loving and friendly family atmosphere with the typical working class ideals of honesty and doing a hard day's work for your pay. He was the youngest of Mr and Mrs Viollet's three children. His two sisters, Vera and Audrey, doted on him and were always protective towards him. His father, Charles Sydney, was a small, slightly-built man who worked as a telephone fitter for the Post Office, liked his pint of ale but kept himself to himself. His mother, Hannah, was also on the small side but a more outward-going, very friendly and neighbourly person. The Viollet children were noted by neighbours and schoolteachers for their courtesy and friendly disposition.

In the 1930s, Fallowfield and Moss Side were certainly not the intimidating areas that they would later become. Eddie Sparrow was a neighbour, a few years older than Dennis. He recalls a scrawny looking Viollet joining in games of football with the kids from around the district. Apparently young Viollet would follow the older lads to a green near his house and play to his heart's content. He would then tag along with the older boys to Platt Fields where they would play for hours. "What sticks out in my mind about those times, was the caseball," said Eddie. "It was one of those old leather balls with a lace in the middle. When it was wet, that old casey, was like a ball of cement. Dennis was only like a matchstick, but he could control that heavy ball and dribble like Stanley Matthews. I also remember him kicking a little tennis ball outside the Maine Road ground for hours upon end. He was forever practising."

Even at school, Dennis was forever playing with a ball and learning new tricks and techniques. In those times it was not unusual to see teenagers and grown men with their trousers tucked into their socks having a game of football on the street or on waste ground. Young Dennis would join in a game of football wherever he saw such a game. He would badger these older youths and men, who were obviously much bigger and stronger than he was, to be allowed to join in their game. After telling him he was much too little, they would eventually reluctantly agree to let him join in. Afterwards, they would smile and tell him that he was a good 'un - praise indeed!

As a young schoolboy, Dennis had two particular close friends: Eric Baggaley, who lived on Princess Road, and Brian McCormack, who lived around the corner from Dennis. This threesome would ride their bikes down Claremont, Broadfield and Parkside Roads, and all the streets surrounding Manchester City's Maine Road ground. When the lads wanted to play football they would go and play on the pitches on Burdith and Clinton Avenue. They would also go to Alexandra Park, which had a derelict swimming pool, and a strange 'haunted' ruin.

After playing football for hours the lads would then tease the 'Parkies' before heading home. The lads were inseparable. During the war years, Dennis and Brian would walk through darkened streets during the blackout to the

Baggaleys' house, where Mrs Baggaley would get busy making the lads something to eat and drink. They would play darts, billiards or snooker. Dennis, Brian and Eric were great fans of the Ink Spots and would imitate the American group singing: "Oh won't you come along with me? - We'll take a boat to the Land of Dreams - Down the Mississippi to New Orleans." Mr and Mrs Baggaley could be excused for thinking the lads had trapped their fingers in the ringer.

Neighbours commented that whenever they saw him, Dennis was forever kicking a tin can or, if he was lucky, a ball around the maze of back streets, alleyways and crofts of Fallowfield. He was football daft and could be found playing in the school playground at break time and on his way home from school. Then, after his evening meal ('tea') Dennis would join a kickabout with friends - well, 'kickabout' is perhaps the wrong word to describe these occasions, because they were in fact games, with no quarter asked or given.

The kids would pair off into two teams. Usually one side would pretend to be Manchester City while the other side would be Manchester United. It was during these games on those derelict pieces of land and cobbled street corners that young Viollet learned the skills that would make him a world-class insideforward. Those empty pieces of wasteland and cobbled streets were breeding grounds for some of the greatest players ever produced in the British Isles. They were the best coaching sessions any youngster could ever receive and it was those kinds of conditions that helped prepare Dennis Viollet for the battlefields of Europe.

Ann Wagster was a few years younger than Dennis, her family lived around the corner from the Viollet home in Clinton Avenue. Mrs Viollet would often look after Ann while her mother went out to work. Dennis was like a big brother to her and often pulled her leg about her hair and, as she got older, about boyfriends. As the years wore on and

Dennis became a football star the two families stayed in touch although Ann's family had moved to another area.

When Ann was about 20 she applied to join the police. As she was cycling home from her interview, she saw a car pull up in front of her and Dennis got out. After going through the usual pleasantries Dennis suggested Ann sit in the car with him. Leaving the bike at the side of the road she hopped in, and sat beside him. "He was really concerned about me and my mother," remembered Ann. "I told him I was hoping to join the police force and he wished me all the luck in the world. He listened to my tales of woe. You know what I mean when you're only 20: boyfriends and the other things that young people feel are so important. He smiled and assured me everything would turn out right for me and just be patient. Oh, he was a lovely man, so elegant and well mannered and like I said so caring about other people. I don't think I saw him more than a handful of times after that meeting but I followed his career closely. A gold-nugget was Dennis!"

John Holland MBE, a former *Manchester Evening News* photographer, grew up on Russell Street in Moss Side. John's close friend, Alan Watson, who lived on Princess Road, close to Parkside Avenue, was also a friend of Dennis and through Alan, John got to know Dennis quite well. John's home was in a row of terraced houses and in common with that sort of dwelling, had a cobbled passage running the full length at the back. Although as John said, he, Alan and Dennis would sometimes go to nearby Alexandra Park for a kickabout, for some reason John's best memories of that time were when the three pals played in the back entry.

"Alan and I played reasonably standard schoolboy football, but, of course, nowhere in Dennis's class," recalled John. "Playing football in a back entry is a bit different to playing on that lush Wembley turf!" John emphasised his amazement all these years later about how Dennis could control the ball and his coolness in those hectic kickabouts in that back entry. Because of the cobbles the ball would bounce unpredictably, but Dennis never seemed to have any difficulty in controlling it, he had instant reactions.

Dennis introduced his two friends to the skill of using the sides of the walls as additional team members. "To do this, when in possession, he would come at us, pass the ball one way against a wall and run round the opposition the other way, collecting the return pass beautifully!"

After John finished his national service in the Royal Engineers, he lost touch with both Alan and Dennis, but naturally read of Dennis's burgeoning football career with great interest. John travelled all over the country in his job as a staff photographer for the huge newspaper combine at Withy Grove, which was first Kemsley Newspapers, then Thomson Newspapers, eventually becoming Maxwell House, before converting to today's Printworks. In his role as a staff photographer he often attended football matches all over the country including Old Trafford.

"In those days it was customary for photographers to stand at the mouth of the tunnel when the players ran out onto the pitch," said John. He was there one day as United came out and Dennis spotted him instantly. Most other players in similar situations might just give a nod or a wink, but Dennis stopped and had a few words with his old schoolboy friend. And every time John was on duty at Old Trafford, Dennis would make a point of going over to him and speaking to him. These meetings led to their friendship being renewed and Dennis asked John to take photographs of his young family at his home in Kings Road, Stretford.

John said he kept his friend supplied with photographs of him in action for United taken by himself but after a few more years they drifted apart again. "Invariably we speak well of the dead," said John. "I spoke well of Dennis when he was alive and continue to do so now. He was very quiet, but with a determination that was startling and which was reflected in his deep, penetrating eyes whenever he was in conversation. He achieved great things as a footballer but during the time I knew him when he was at his professional peak, he always had time to come over and have a chat, despite the fact that we were often at a 'high-level' function, a school, Manchester Town Hall or wherever. I often think about him in those early days."

In 1946, Dennis's close friend Eric Baggaley decided to become a missionary, and he entered the Salesian Missionary College, at Shrigley Park near Macclesfield. During school holidays they would meet up and knock about together.

Schoolboy Star

In the meantime, Dennis was improving by leaps and bounds. He played for his school team, St Margaret's Church of England Central in Whalley Range and stood out like a beacon on a foggy night. After many dazzling displays and goalscoring feats, Dennis came to the attention of the Manchester Boys selectors, aged only 13. He captained them for two years.

"He had graceful style and dribbling artistry and also, of course, his goal snatching exploits," said Jimmy Murphy, of the schoolboy Viollet. "Dennis most certainly looked the part: neat, wispy, possessing an intelligent football brain with a powerful shot, he was deadly in the 18-yard box. He didn't have a great physique, however this did not bother me too much. He reminded me a great deal of little Jimmy Wilde, the famous Welsh boxing champion. It was said that because Wilde looked so pallid and frail promoters were worried for his safety. Wilde proved he had what it takes to make it to the top of the boxing ladder, and he became known as 'The Ghost with a Hammer in his Hands'. Well, Dennis Viollet was like a ghost with cannonballs in his shooting boots!"

In June 1946, Manchester Boys played Glasgow Boys in an eagerly-awaited match staged at the self-proclaimed showground of the world: Belle Vue, Manchester. In those days, schoolboy football was followed closely and watched by huge crowds. Dennis was selected at inside-right and had a brilliant game. He controlled everything, his play showed an experience beyond his tender years. He passed the ball like a veteran, kept the game flowing on the ground and his shooting was a sight to behold. What stood out was Viollet's unselfishness. Manchester Boys won 6-2 and but for the superb goalkeeping of Lymburn in the Glasgow goal, the Scottish lads would have been beaten by a much higher margin. Dennis scored two scorching goals and team-mates Murray and Yeomans also got a brace each.

Alf Clarke, the *Manchester Evening Chronicle* football writer, described Dennis as a 'Boy With A Future', claiming that he was a future international. "This was Viollet's match," he wrote. "In the full bloom of youthful soccer craftsmanship, Viollet promises to blossom into one of the game's stars."

At 14 Dennis was in the Lancashire Boys side and he captained them for two years. In the Lancashire Schools Cup third round tie, played at Newton Heath Loco, Manchester Boys trounced Newtonle- Willows Boys 4-0. Dennis, captaining the team, played a 'blinder' and scored a hat-trick. The Loco was a well-known venue throughout Manchester for staging important matches such as the Cassidy Cup Final.

It was not unusual to see star players from both big Manchester clubs standing on the old railway logs, cheering for one particular team or other. The pitch itself was notorious for its strengthsapping condition. In truth it was a mud heap and suited big, powerful defenders or forwards. As was usual for such matches, a capacity crowd was in attendance and when the final whistle blew the player on everyone's lips was Dennis Viollet. He seemed to glide over the surface and his intelligent running and passing was magnificent. His poise and ball control was a sight to behold in such conditions and he beat defenders cleanly without a fuss while his shooting had spectators wondering how he generated the power from such a slight frame. Everything he did was stamped with class.

When Manchester Boys played Lancaster Boys in a Lancashire County Cup game on January 17th 1948 at Newton Heath Loco, they gave the Lancaster team a lesson in ball control and shooting. Dennis was immaculate! He oozed class from the top of his head to the tips of his boots. His running off the ball was something to be savoured in one so young and the way he suddenly popped up in the opposition's penalty area was astonishing. He was like an optical illusion, one minute you see him - the next you don't.

He scored four goals and made quite a few as Manchester thrashed Lancaster 12-0. A couple of weeks later, on January 31st 1948, Manchester Boys played Salford Boys at the Cliff, Manchester United's training ground, in Lower Broughton, Salford. Manchester Boys' forward line was superior, thanks to Dennis Viollet and Yeomans on the right flank, these two gave the Salford lads plenty to worry about with their skill and enterprise. Against the run of play, Mallinson put Salford into the lead and Tonge missed a penalty. Murray equalised for Manchester before the interval. In the second half Dennis scored the winner. Once again Viollet, all skin and bones, stood out from the other fine players on view. He never seemed to be in a hurry and he used the ball intelligently every time he received it.

Alan 'Tiny' Cornforth was a member of the Manchester Boys team for two years. He remembers Dennis with fondness. At the age of fourteen he was picked for the England Schoolboys team, he was a proud young man. Incidentally, Mark Jones was also in the same International schools team with him.

Alan first met Dennis when he was selected to play for Manchester Boys against Crosby Boys, at their ground in Liverpool. "I always remember lining up as centre-forward with the great Dennis Viollet playing inside-right," recalled Alan. "We turned out the winners but did not go on to win any trophies that year (1948-49). This was Dennis's second and last year playing for Manchester Boys and my first year. I went on and played the following year (1949-50) when we reached the English Schools Shield Final, but we lost 2-1 on aggregate to Swansea Boys."

Alan said he met Dennis again during his school holidays. He received a letter from his Sports Master at Ducie Avenue School telling him that he had been selected to play for Lancashire Boys at Tranmere Rovers ground and he was to meet the team at 7 o'clock in the morning under the indicator at Victoria Station.

He commented in his letter that Alan would at least know his team-mate from Manchester Boys, the legendary Dennis Viollet. "Dennis was a very good player," said Alan. "He was razor sharp with quickness on the ball and a tremendous shot. He attended St Margaret's High School, Whalley Range, and as far as I can remember there were two other good players from there, Wallace and Heywood. I played against Dennis on a number of occasions for Ducie Avenue and anyone could see how good he was when you played against him. But I did upstage him once in a match played at Maine Road, when I captured the headlines in the *Daily Dispatch*."

The match that Alan refers to was a Lancashire Schools Cup game between Manchester Boys and Salford Boys, played at Maine Road in April 1949. Manchester Boys won 4-0. Archie Ledbrooke, a well-respected football writer, wrote: "For the third goal, the centre forward tipped the ball over the head of the opposing centre-half with a clever right-foot lob. He took the ball with the other foot to run on but found another defender barring his path to goal. He swerved to the left to beat his man by sheer footwork and rounded off this brilliant piece of football with a crashing leftfoot drive. It was generally voted goal of the season. Was this from an international match at Hampden Park? Was it a flashback to Hughie Gallacher, Jimmy Hampson, or maybe the Preston invincibles? No - it happened last night, and the 'man' who pulled out this magnificent bit of football was the smallest of all the players. Cornforth is the lad's name and with his two goals, his general idea of going straight for the target and his all-round ability he even overshadowed England's captain Viollet playing alongside him." That was some tribute. Mr Ledbrooke went on to say that Dennis appeared to have a footballing brain that was in advance of his ability in his feet. "For a youth he has the uncanny idea of when and where to pass, and his penalty goal left Cooper immobile and helpless."

Frank Beacher played for Manchester City's Central League team as a full-back. He was a schoolboy player while Dennis was at St Margaret's. Frank has many happy memories of his tussles with Dennis during the 1940s. Recalling one particular game, Frank said: "We might as well not have turned up! Dennis Viollet ran through us as if we weren't there. When we stopped for the halftime break, Dennis had already scored four goals. Mind you, we felt no shame. Dennis would go on to do this sort of demolition job on many a defence for many years to come. He was like a master locksmith or a cat burglar. Dennis would prod, probe and prompt until he found weak spots and vulnerable areas in the opposition's play. Then he would help himself and his team to rich pickings! Sometimes this would be a priceless one-goal winner, but frequently two, three or even four goals would be plundered for good measure."

At 15 Dennis won the first of his six caps for England Schoolboys. Dennis's proudest moment came on Saturday 15th May 1948 when he played and captained England against Ireland in the Schoolboys Victory Shield at Old Trafford in front of a capacity 45,000 crowd.

Dennis, playing at inside-left, was hailed in all the newspaper reports as the star of the England team. He scored two superb goals: in the 11th minute a swift corner for England saw Dennis rise majestically to score a rare header and added another in the 39th minute. He was the schemer behind most of England's raids. Levitt, at centre-forward and Cliff Birkett also scored to make the final score England 4, Ireland 0.

It was obvious from these early days that Dennis was destined to become a player of immense skill and poise. One could see his potential greatness by the way he conducted himself when he played. Though only skin and bones, he stood erect and his balance, so important in a forward, was superb. Another point was his awareness of situations on the field and through this the way he could direct his passes to colleagues. He was cool and never seemed to be hurried. The biggest asset of all, though, was his goalscoring ability - he was a phenomenon. Some of the schoolboy players he played with for England would go on to distinction as professional players: Jeff Whitefoot, Stan Anderson (Sunderland), Johnny Haynes and Trevor

Chamberlain (both Fulham), George Luke (Newcastle United), Andy Malcolm (West Ham United), Mike Barnard (Middlesbrough) and Mark Jones, who, along with Jeff Whitefoot would join Dennis at Old Trafford.

Newspaper reporter Fred Thorne commented: "Once more Birkett took the eye. He reminds me of Boy Bastin. Matching Birkett for skill was little Viollet, who pushed some of the choicest carpet passes through to Longden at outside-left that I have seen for years in any class of football."

Alf Clarke wrote: "England's victory over Ireland was a match rich in first-class, constructive football, with each goal a gem, with a surfeit of sound and spectacular forward play by England which Ireland could not equal. The craftsman who paved the way for Ireland's defeat was Viollet, whose display at inside-left must have made the many Football League scouts present really envious. Viollet was methodical in all he did. He was unselfish, rarely wasted a pass, and his spoon-feeding of Longden enabled the Rotherham outsideleft to have a most successful game."

In January 1949 Manchester Boys played Newton-le-Willows Boys again and beat them 4-1, Dennis scoring another hat-trick. One of his proudest supporters was his mother, who attended all his games no matter what the weather was like and always encouraged him. On as many Saturdays as possible, often accompanied by her elder daughter Vera, Mrs Viollet would go and watch her son play. She was well known at Maine Road by the Manchester Boys team and officials. Dennis said she was the Manchester Boys team mascot and good luck charm. Years later, a family story tells of Vera and Mrs Viollet at Maine Road during a City versus United 'Derby' game. Dennis broke through the static City defence and was bearing down on the City goal only to be chased and ruthlessly chopped down from behind by that uncompromising and undoubtedly great

1950s wing-half, Roy Paul, the City captain and Welsh international.

Apparently Vera jumped up and down, beside herself with rage. "Paul you dirty *!*?*," she screamed. "I'll get you for that!" She prepared to march down the stand steps, brandishing her umbrella with Mrs Viollet hanging on to her in an effort to stop her invading the pitch to sort out the formidable City captain.

On another occasion, this time at Old Trafford in the early 1960s, a well-known wag (the one who used to take a pet monkey on his shoulder to United's games!) was heckling Dennis something terrible. He was not having one of his better games. "Aye, eye,' the wag bellowed, "What's up, Viollet? Too much nightclubbing again, 'ave yer?" Suddenly, he felt a couple of short, hard raps on his shoulder. He turned round to see a very angry woman wielding an umbrella. "Don't you dare insult my son like that!" shouted a red-faced Mrs Viollet, clearly a feisty lady when occasion demanded!

Dennis loved taking his mum to United games, home and away. He would proudly introduce her to players and managers. He used to tell how the great Liverpool manager, Bill Shankly, would always say, whenever they met, "And how's your mum, Dennis?"

St Margaret's school is sadly gone, demolished in the 1970s to make way for new houses. In its day it was a well-respected school with high standards of discipline and manners. The school was really like something out of a Dickens novel, it was 70 years old when Dennis first attended in 1944. The foundation stone is dated 1872 - Diocese of Manchester, although countless generations gave it another title - the 'Den of Misery.'

As an old schoolfriend of Dennis's, Mr GH Dobie, recalls: "The teaching in those days was obviously as stressful as it is today. In the main, Dennis enjoyed his schooldays and had a good relationship with the teaching staff, though most of them were old stagers as the younger teachers were serving in the forces. However, on one or two occasions he did run foul of the maths teacher, 'Ma' Lowe, a veritable taskmistress. 'It's a good job you can play football Viollet,' Miss Lowe would blurt out after Dennis got a sum wrong. Mr Lucas the headmaster rarely had to speak to him though."

Rick Brent, another of Dennis's school chums remembers how strict the teachers were. "The strap and cane were used quite often in those days. Pupils most certainly knew who was in charge and there was no answering back or disobeying them, if you did you would wish you hadn't." Rick recalled the weekly cartoons which he and another classmate, a lad named Geoff Royle, wrote called the 'Danny Comic'. They would write ideas in comic strip form during lessons and compile it at weekends. First thing Monday morning, Dennis would be the first to read it, approve it and distribute it throughout the class, underhandedly of course. The class would take turns reading it under their desks, in due course faint giggles would emerge from various corners of the classroom. The comic was originally the brainchild of Dennis. he main character in the comic was the history teacher Mr Daniel Wilson, known as 'Danny'. Mr Wilson was about 60, 5 foot 4 inches tall, and very slim. He also had a very large, prominent red nose. The comic was obviously all about Danny Wilson! His glowing red nose was a source of amusement and became the major feature in the weekly comic.

Roy Ladley attended South Hulme Senior Boys School. He played in goal for the school's Cup team. They were once drawn against St Margaret's in a cup game, it was an evening kick-off and the game was played on Burford Road, in Whalley Range.

"We fancied our chances in this competition," said Roy. "We thought we were a lot tougher, stronger and better players than those St Margaret's kids. We were playing quite well but this skinny little rump of a lad kept breaking through our defence and having me diving all over the place. He put five goals past me and we lost 5-3! What a great little player he was. Of course, we were disappointed at getting hammered, but we would have beaten them if it hadn't been for him. Everyone from our school could see he had that something extra that separates ordinary footballers from the potentially great ones. 'What's his name?' we asked our sports teacher? 'Dennis Viollet,' he replied. 'Remember that name because you will be hearing a great deal about him in the future.'"

In 1948 Ray Holden was appointed as a history teacher at St Margaret's during the period when Dennis was a pupil. Mr Holden remembered his first day at the school. "As I was about to start my first class, a knock on the classroom door was heard and in walked Dennis Viollet. He was carrying a can of ink to fill the inkwells on the desks. He walked straight over to where I was standing in front of the class and shook hands with me, this I thought was a very mature gesture from a 14 year old! As I had run the football team at my previous school, I went to watch Dennis playing in a game, St Margaret's versus Didsbury Central. Ted [Wetton, the school team manager] was on the touchline and he approached me to ask if I was interested in running the school 'Shield' team while he concentrated on the 'Cup' team. I agreed, and consequently encountered Dennis during our practice games that were held on Brantingham Road playing fields. In one match I went in to tackle him and I came out worse. Although he was only puny and there was no weight on him I knew he was immensely strong. I was 26 and quite fit but Dennis was something special."

On a separate theme, after Dennis left St Margaret's Mr Holden didn't see him again for a few years. A lifetime Manchester United supporter and season-ticket holder, Mr Holden was delighted when he heard his former pupil had joined United and followed Dennis's career with United closely. In 1956 Mr Holden took his two sons, aged seven and nine to watch United in preseason training. Dennis was running round the track with David Pegg when he spotted his former teacher. He rushed over to Mr Holden and enthusiastically shook his hand and his children's. The teacher asked Dennis if it would be possible to get some autographs of the players. "Call back tomorrow, and I'll have them for you," he said. The following day Dennis presented him with the autographs of the United team. Mr Holden's eldest son, who is now 53, treasures those signatures to this day.

By September 1948, Dennis, now 14 years old, was presented with his England cap, which he had won against Ireland in May. Three hundred pupils at St Margaret's formed a guard of honour as he walked up to the platform in the school hall. His mother and father were as proud as punch, sitting with the teachers on the platform. As Dennis stepped forward to be presented with his cap by Mr G Horsfall, the former chairman of the Manchester Schools Football Association, the hall erupted into a cauldron of noise as the pupils cheered and clapped loudly. Of course they had been told that they could have the rest of the day off school. He was only the second schoolboy international from St Margaret's, the first being HL Whitehead, who played for England in 1914, so it was a proud moment for the school.

Another close schoolboy friend of Dennis was Alan Wallace. Alan would be a guest of Dennis in his testimonial game against England's World Cup winning team many years later. Alan lived in Gorton, attended St Margaret's along with Dennis and played in the same school Cup and Shield teams of which Dennis was captain. Alan said Dennis always led by example and he was amazed at what a strong player Dennis was for his age and physique. "We reached the semi-final in the Shield competition," said Alan when recalling his schooldays with Dennis. "We were drawn against St Gregory's, who were always fierce competitors and produced some great schoolboy football players. However, in this particular match we thrashed them 14-0, yes, fourteen-nil. I scored eight and Dennis got four. He was forever praising me for getting those eight goals, but really it was simple because of the beautiful passes he gave me, they were tailor-made for me. He would move all over the field, suddenly the ball would be in front of me, I aimed at the goals and 'whoosh' - goal! Dennis would tell people we met about my eight-goal spree but he would never mention the time he scored nine in one match, such was his modesty. We won both the Cup and Shield that year, a great double."

In the Cup Final, St Margaret's played Spurley Hey School. It was a cracking game full of attacking football from both teams and loads of excitement. "The difference between the two teams," said Alan, "was Dennis Viollet! He scored our four goals for a 4-1 victory. He was carried shoulder high off the pitch. It was a privilege to have played alongside such a magnificent player."

Going for the double, St Margaret's met Didsbury Central in the Shield final. The score? 4-0 to St Margarets - Dennis hammered in a tremendous hat-trick while Alan got the other goal. "He just took the praise from spectators and teachers in his stride," remarked Alan. "He never bragged about scoring so many important goals or the things he achieved as a schoolboy international. People at the matches, or wherever we went, all talked about what a great player this lad Viollet was. What struck me about him was that whenever he received praise from any source he would turn the attention away from himself and go out of his way to praise his team-mates, yet it was his influence on our teams' play that brought us so much success."

Talking about his schooldays, Dennis said he always believed that any team, whether in the First Division or in the lowliest league, should always try to develop teamwork. "The side which has enough players who can hold and distribute the ball with skill will always triumph over the big kicking brigade," he said. In later years Dennis would find himself in hot water over these kind of comments. He went on to pay tribute to his mentor, Ted Wetton. "What use is it kicking the ball more than 50 yards if it went to an opponent? It was far better to keep possession, even by using flicks and kicks, than to give away possession by using the almighty boot. I am thankful that I came under the supervision of Mr Ted Wetton when I joined St Margaret's. I often think the fans of big league clubs never really appreciate the debt big time football owes to men like Mr Wetton, who spend long hours with schoolboys, showing them how to become better players, helping them to eradicate their faults and fully understand the finer points of the game."

Another influence on Dennis's early years was the headmaster of St Margaret's, Mr Lucas. His personal obssession was America. He was absolutely fascinated by it. He had family and friends living in the States and there was one particular person, Harold Skelmerdine, a former 'old boy' from St Margaret's who had emigrated to New England in the 1920s and had become a historian over there. 'Pop' Lucas always had Dennis and his classmates writing to him to ask him anything they wanted to know about America. Dennis wrote to ask Mr Skelmerdine if football was played over there.

Mr Skelmerdine duly replied. Dennis showed his friend

Rick Brent the letter. Mr Skelmerdine must obviously have been a far-sighted person because he wrote: "English football? No, not yet, but when it does, if it does, you must come over and coach and teach and show these Yanks how proper football should be played!" Obviously Mr Skelmerdine had been informed of Dennis's exploits via Pop Lucas. The headmaster's study was festooned with cups, shields, pennants and trophies of games against other schools that had been won mainly through the efforts of Dennis Viollet.

About four months before Dennis left school at 15, dear old Pop Lucas committed suicide one weekend, he put his head in the gas oven at home. It was obviously quite a shock to everyone, staff and pupils. The pupils were never told why, but much later they learned that he had serious financial problems. It was a very sad occasion. Dennis and the other pupils really liked him. "Every day outside the school gates, Pop Lucas parked his car," said Rick Brent. "It was a 1939 Austin 12. He was the only teacher with a car. One Monday morning as we made our way into school, Dennis and myself noticed Pop's car was not there. Then we heard the sad news of his death."

From scoring four goals against Frank Beacher's school team to scoring four goals against Anderlecht in a European Cup match, Dennis Viollet's career would progress prodigiously. What would never change, but be enhanced, were his superb skills, the complete footballer: speed of foot, eye and brain. What would be honed over the coming years was the ability to bring out the best, not only in his own performance, but in his team-mates too. Press reports of Dennis's play as an English Schoolboy international repeatedly referred to his masterful passing skills, which could slice open the opposition's defence with the precision of a surgeon's scalpel. Dennis was always first and foremost a team player, a player's player. He would certainly go on to score many goals himself but he would also be very instrumental in making many more goals for others.

Dennis was skill personified. This was illustrated when playing once for Manchester Boys at Maine Road. Dennis was on the right wing, moving forward and anticipating a through ball. In fact the ball arrived awkwardly, too high and bouncing behind him. He nonchalantly back-heeled the ball over his head with his left foot and, without breaking his run, trapped, controlled and pushed it forward with his right foot and was already looking up to see who was moving into the goalmouth for his centre or through ball. The 'bad' pass had been made 'good' and Dennis's skill had made the whole sequence into one graceful movement. Making this sort of thing look simple is only possible with a fine sense of balance, joined with consummate ball control. Dennis was, indeed, a very talented footballer, a natural.

During his adolescence, Dennis showed his character. Loyalty was top of his priorities, he had no airs or graces whatsoever, his tastes were simple and he kept the same friends he had grown up with. He conducted himself impeccably at all times, liked wearing fashionable clothes - although he was limited in this department because rationing was still in force for clothes, sweets and food - and always had his hair neatly styled. He was growing into a handsome young man. Young ladies were always giving him sly glances, indeed his only vice seemed to be smoking.

Dennis Viollet, a City Player?

Manchester City were confident that the lad who lived on their doorstep would join them. There was also the fact that the Viollet family were staunch Blues. However, during the war years, Dennis, who was about nine years of age, met a soldier on home leave. The serviceman used to join in kickabouts on the street where Dennis lived. The serviceman was none other than Matt Busby, who played for City before the war.

Matt often visited his close friend Alex Herd, who was a gifted forward. Alex's son David played a great deal of football with the scrawny looking Viollet and they were close friends. Though born in Scotland, young Herd had a broad Manchester accent. It was not uncommon in those days to see adults joining in a game with the kids. Busby had been impressed with Viollet's enthusiasm and undoubted skill from one so young. He put the name of Dennis Viollet in his memory bank for future reference.

Meanwhile, several First Division clubs were hoping to sign the classy youngster from south Manchester, not least the club who thought he should be theirs by right. Not for the last time, however Manchester City's lack of foresight was crucial in their non-signing of the young Viollet.

The Fox family lived next door to the Viollets at number 9 Clinton Avenue. Harry Jackson lodged with the Fox family and was courting one of their daughters, who he later married. Now in his eighties, Mr Jackson tells of how Frank Swift, Manchester City and England's legendary goalkeeper, was a great admirer of Dennis, and had mentioned his name to Manchester City officials indicating that they should sign him. Swift lived on Lloyd Street South, which was near Clinton Avenue. One day he bumped into Mr Viollet and asked if City had been in touch? "No," replied Dennis's father, adding that he had not heard from any other clubs either. Big Frank said he would organise for Mr Viollet to meet the City youth scout. On being told that Mr Viollet's dinner break was between 1pm and 2pm, Frank said that he would make sure to make this the time of the meeting at Maine Road.

On the day of the proposed meeting Dennis and his dad made their way up the steps and into the Maine Road offices. Mr Viollet told the secretary he had a meeting with the scout and he and his son were told to sit down until called. After waiting for over an hour Mr Viollet became agitated and extremely annoyed. He knocked on the office window and explained that he had to be back at work, and what was the delay? Though he was a quiet man, Mr Viollet had a fiery temper when aroused, and when the secretary casually told him the scout had gone out on an appointment and left father and son waiting without an apology or explanation, he lost his temper and gave vent to his feelings. When he finished, he and Dennis marched out of Maine Road.

The following day Frank Swift called at the Viollet house and asked how they had got on at the meeting. When he was told how they had been treated, 'Big Swifty' looked annoyed and promised Mr Viollet that he would get in touch with a close friend and that something would happen very soon. The next day, Matt Busby knocked on the door of 7 Clinton Avenue. The United manager charmed Mr and Mrs Viollet as only he could, although they were died-in-the-wool City supporters they fell hook, line and sinker for Busby's persuasive charm. He left them to think it over but said he would like an answer as soon as possible.

Later, Jimmy Murphy, Bert Whalley and Joe Armstrong called at the Viollet house. Murphy left Mr and Mrs Viollet believing that Manchester United were going to be the greatest football club in the world. There were no half measures with the excitable little Welshman. He wanted Dennis at Old Trafford at all costs. "Don't let young Dennis miss this opportunity of joining this wonderful club," said Murphy. The rest is history.

What the Viollet family didn't know was that in a game Dennis played for Manchester Boys, Matt Busby was in the crowd and with him was Dennis's idol, Stan Pearson. After half an hour, Matt turned to his star inside-left, and asked: "Well, what do you think Stan?" Pearson smiled back at his manager and told him he was impressed with the standard of football on display. "I'll tell you something though," he told his boss, pointing to Dennis Viollet, "that young 'un there is going to become a brilliant player." Busby nodded his approval and smiled - a contented look on his face.

Mr Viollet and Dennis asked Frank Swift what they should do about Matt Busby's offer. "I played with Matt Busby and he is a wonderful fellow," Big Swifty told them. "You won't find a better boss or a better club." Swift's advice finally clinched it. Dennis was joining Manchester United.

Ian Niven, a lifelong City stalwart and now a City life Vice- President, knew Viollet from his schooldays: "I was flabbergasted when I heard Dennis had signed forms with United. I thought it was a mere formality that he would be joining City. It shows you how wrong you can be. Many years later, I'm talking about the 1990s, when Ken Barnes would hold court in City's bootroom Denis Law and Dennis Viollet, (when home from Florida) would sit in the room discussing football. One day I casually asked Dennis why he hadn't signed for City at the beginning of his career, because I distinctly remember that all his family were 'dyed-in-thewool' Blues. He told me that he was waiting for someone from Maine Road to call and speak to him and his parents, but nobody from City came knocking at their door. One day there was a knock on their front door and when Dennis answered it who should be there, with a big smile on his face but none other than Matt Busby himself. Dennis invited the Manchester United manager inside and Busby sat in the front room discussing his plans for United's future. 'I would love you to be part of our future,' he told Dennis. 'My parents were enthralled by Matt's courtesy and charmed by his manner. Really, they were in awe of him. They raised no objections whatsoever about me joining the Reds instead of the Blues. Nobody from City came near our house.'"

Johnny Haynes, the cultured England international midfield player, who for so long was the inspiration for Fulham and England, played with Dennis for England schoolboys. Many years later Johnny waxed lyrical about the virtues of Dennis Viollet. "It's an old clichÈ but Dennis was something special as a footballer and a person. I first met him when we played together for England against Scotland. Dennis impressed me straight away. He was a typical Manchester lad, good manners and showed respect to everybody. As a player he really was outstanding, his balance was akin to that of a ballet dancer. As schoolboys all players are equal, but he stood out from the rest. Why? Because of the talent and football brain he had, his positioning during a game was phenomenal. One minute he would be in our own half, the next he would be in open space to receive the ball. Up and down the field he played and the goals he scored were all different: tap-ins, scorching drives, neat little headers, overhead bicycle kicks, you name it, he could do it. I didn't play against him that often when we became senior players because Fulham were in the Second Division but I saw the Busby Babes team whenever I could and they were a brilliant, young, improving team with truly exceptional players. Dennis was like a lynchpin and at his best in that team. He could scheme, and score goals, yet he also played on the wing and in midfield. He was so unlucky in only getting two caps. Some players get more than they should and others, like Dennis, are very unlucky to only get a couple, he should almost certainly have received a lot more."

Joining The Reds!

Welcome Home' was plastered across the front cover of Manchester United's match programme for the visit of Bolton Wanderers in August 1949. It had been ten years since Old Trafford had staged a football league game due to the damage from Hitler's bombs during the Second World War. The ground, like much of Manchester, was bombed but not defeated - the scars of the conflict were slowly healing as was the turmoil, violence and sadness.

Besides visitors Bolton Wanderers, three members of the previous year's England schoolboy team were welcomed to Old Trafford. Cliff Birkett, Jeff Whitefoot and Dennis Viollet were the three young prospects. These lads were brilliant captures by United's scouting staff because they could have chosen almost any club in the country they fancied. Mark Jones had joined United the previous year. United were determined to secure the best young talent available. Dennis and Jeff Whitefoot were like twins, always in each other's company.

It didn't take Dennis and the other new lads long to realise that they had joined a happy, well run and contented organisation. "I was over the moon with the thrill of it all," said Dennis, describing his first days at Old Trafford. "I felt immediately that I was on my way into a really exciting world. Yet I could never have dreamt just how thrilling it would turn out to be. As I packed my boots and one or two other things for my first trip down to the Old Trafford ground I suddenly felt a little scared. I was joining the club as an amateur but nevertheless I'd be seeing the big names - Jack Rowley, Charlie Mitten and my boyhood idol

Stan Pearson. Yet when I got there and eventually met and actually kicked a ball about in their company I found they all had one thing in common - modesty. There was no room for big heads. That was the first lesson I learned."

These youngsters were soon to appear in 'A' and Colts teams, playing in the Manchester League and the Eccles and District League respectively. A 4-0 victory over the famous Goslings AFC (Henry Cockburn's old club) was an impressive introduction from the new lads, who trained every Tuesday and Thursday at The Cliff under the scrutiny of Jimmy Murphy and the watchful eye of Bert Whalley, the Manchester United coaches.

In November 1949, Dennis made the short walk from his home in Clinton Avenue to Maine Road to watch England play Ireland in a World Cup qualifier. Dennis wanted to watch a player he had admired immensely - Stan Pearson Manchester United's immaculate inside-left, and he certainly wasn't disappointed. Pearson scored twice, and Jack Rowley, United's centre-forward, scored four which helped England to a 9-2 victory, taking them a step closer to the 1950 World Cup. Walking home, young Viollet relived the game through in his mind, he smiled in admiration recalling the nonchalant skills of his idol Stan.

Ken Cuttler was a neighbour of the Viollets and later he would also be an opponent on the field of play. Ken had been aware of the Viollet brand of football from watching Dennis as a schoolboy. Shortly after Dennis joined United, Bert Whalley took the 'A' team to play Stalybridge Celtic Reserves at Bower Fold. Ken was a tough tackling right-half in his early twenties while Dennis couldn't have been more than 16. He was in his favourite insideleft position for this game and in opposition to his older neighbour. "He may have only been a kid of 16 or 17, I was 24, but he certainly showed me a clean pair of heels in this match. He was like greased lightning. I managed to get near him occasionally and win a couple of tackles but he had this wonderful knack of sending you the wrong way and wrong-footing you. He was class! After the game I asked Bert Whalley if he would mind giving me a lift on their coach back to Stretford where I was living at the time. Bert readily agreed to my request. What a wonderful experience it was! I can still remember what a good crowd the Manchester United lads were, singing and laughing and joking. They were like one big happy family. From then on I followed Dennis's great career by watching him play for United over the coming years."

Ken, who now lives in Victoria, Canada ended by saying: "Yes, I remember it all very clearly. Playing against him was a very special moment for me. Dennis Viollet was a very special kind of footballer. I feel honoured and proud to have spent at least 90 minutes of my life opposing the great Dennis Viollet. Believe me, he really was a very, very special player."

September 20th 1950 was Dennis's 18th birthday, a red-letter day as he signed his first professional contract with the club he had began to love dearly - Manchester United. After sampling playing for the colts and juniors Dennis was beginning to get better and better. Two early goals for the 'A' team quickly earned him a regular place in the Central League side. He played with Jack Crompton, Mark Jones, Jackie Blanchflower and Roger Byrne. The reserves had got off to a slow start that season, however the team soon began to climb the league table. At the end of the 1949-50 season, Dennis had played six times for United's Central League side and scored twice. The leading goalscorer was Lol Cassidy with 13. Jack Rowley was the first team's chief marksman with 18.

The 'A' Team

Alex Gaskell was a year older than Dennis but they played together regularly in the 'A' team. Gaskell, a blunt speaking Lancashire lad, was high in his praise for Dennis. "Dennis Viollet was class, a very underrated player," said Alex. "We weren't close friends but you couldn't help but like him. I was more pally with Mark Jones and Geoff Bent, but I used to have a laugh and a joke with Dennis. He seemed very quiet and studious to me, but what a player. He wasn't a dirty player and wasn't that well-built, but he could make that ball do wonderful things. He was well liked and respected by everyone."

Gaskell was a big, strong, strapping lad and played centre-forward for his school team. At 13 he played for Preston North End's 'A' team and scored two goals in a 3-0 victory. It was highly unusual for a schoolboy to be selected for a league club's 'A' team. In the dressing room after the match he was told by the Preston 'A' team manager that he would be in touch with him very soon with a view to joining them. Alex never heard from Preston again. He left school at 14 and worked as an apprentice electrician for ten shillings a week. "I had to do a 42-hour week. I was a hopeless apprentice," admits Alex. "All as I wanted to do was play football and be out in the fresh air." After playing for several local club teams he signed on for Hindsford in the West Lancashire League receiving fifteen shillings a week expenses.

The West Lancashire League was a notoriously tough breeding ground and many of Lancashire and Yorkshire's top clubs had teams competing in this league. A scout from Blackburn Rovers soon spotted him and signed him on amateur forms. Alex played several games in Blackburn's 'A' team while working as an apprentice. During the late

1940s one of his workmates, a big affable Geordie named Mr James, wrote to Louis Rocca at Manchester United and a trial was organised. "I was only an amateur for Blackburn so I could tell them that I had finished playing for them, and this is what I did," recalled Alex. At the trial game he was watched by Jimmy Murphy, Bert Whalley and Arthur Powell, who looked after the Colts. Gaskell was signed on by United as an amateur. After a few weeks, Alex was asked to join the groundstaff. This meant he would receive a weekly wage from United while doing chores around the ground and he readily agreed.

He played in United's 'A' side alongside Dennis Viollet, Jackie Blanchflower, Mark Jones, Billy Foulkes and Eddie Lewis. In the 1950s, Alex was expecting to sign professional forms with United however the club never mentioned anything to him. He hit a lean spell, where on his own admission nothing on the field went right for him. After one particular bad game he was told he was wanted in Matt Busby's office. Walking towards the office, Alex saw Bert Whalley outside and he looked distinctly embarrassed as their eyes met. When he entered, Busby and Jimmy Murphy were waiting. Alex noticed Busby looked extremely uncomfortable at his desk puffing away on his pipe. It was Murphy who told him that United were releasing him with immediate effect - sacked! This meant he had lost his job on the groundstaff as well. Alex was gutted. "I felt my whole world had fallen down around me," said Alex. "I was angry, very angry, and I swore at the both of them and said a few nasty things which perhaps I shouldn't have said. As I stormed out of the office, Bert Whalley tried to console me but I was having none of it. I told him I would come back with another team and ram a few goals up their arses."

Within four weeks of being sacked by United he was called up for his national service and joined the RAF. When he completed his service he signed for Southport and after a few months was transferred to Newcastle United for £6,000. "A lot of brass in those days," says Alex in his strong Lancashire accent. He remembers playing against United's reserves and as he was putting his boots on, Jimmy Murphy came into the Newcastle dressing room and with a big friendly smile walked over to Alex to shake hands and wish him well. Alex glared at Murphy and refused to shake his hand preferring instead to utter some verbal abuse. Murphy was annoyed and walked out.

Back in United's dressing room, Jimmy clenched his fist when giving his team talk and told his defenders what he expected from them when opposing Gaskell. "Before the referee blew the whistle to start the match I had a friendly laugh and a chat with a few of my former team-mates. However, during the game I took some terrible stick from them. All the United lads were having a go at me, tackling me as if their lives depended on it." United won, Alex turned to Mark Jones and asked why they had gone in so hard on him. "We're pals aren't we?" said Alex. "Yes, of course we are," said Mark Jones, "but you're not friends with Jimmy [Murphy] are you?"

Gaskell enjoyed his stay at Newcastle and spoke about their very experienced wing-half Jimmy Scoular. Scoular was a fearsome looking fellow with a shiny bald head and thick legs. He was a Scottish international and later captained Newcastle to their 3-1 1955 FA Cup victory over Manchester City, when he was voted Man-of-the-Match. "Scoular was the only player I can ever remember Bobby Charlton getting annoyed with after Munich," says Alex.

On another occasion when Manchester United played Newcastle at St James' Park in a First Division clash, Alex was selected as twelfth man - there were no substitutes in those days. On the morning of the match Joe Harvey,

Newcastle's manager, pulled Alex to one side and asked him about some of the Manchester United players and who he thought would be the biggest threat to Newcastle. Alex told his coach to get Jimmy Scoular to get stuck into United's teenage left-half from the first whistle and, said Alex, if they kept him quiet they would have an easy passage. The craggy, tough-as-nails Scoular was told to make his presence felt very early in the game. This Scoular did, charging into tackles as if his life depended on the very outcome and he soon confronted the kid Alex had advised to keep quiet. However, 12 minutes into the game Scoular was being stretchered off the field injured. As he was being carried into the changing room Scoular, his face a mask of pain, looked up from the stretcher and snarled at Gaskell: "Next time you've got any effing bright ideas, keep them to your effing self." The kid whom Scoular had encountered was none other than Duncan Edwards! United won 2-1.

Ronnie Cope was a year younger than Dennis Viollet. He had played for Crewe and England schoolboys before joining United at 16 in 1950 and turned professional on his 17th birthday. He played ten years as a pro with the Reds, before leaving to join Luton Town in August 1961 where he spent two unhappy years before going into non-league football with Northwich Victoria and Winsford United. Ronnie played 106 times for the first team and scored two goals, he was a loyal and honest clubman and United's third choice centre-half before Munich.

"When I first joined United I was 16 and Dennis Viollet was one of the first people to welcome me to the club. Though he was only a little bit older than myself, he came across as a very caring person and as time went by our friendship grew. Over the years we became very good friends. Dennis was well liked by everyone at Old Trafford, players and staff. He was a real lad about town, a likeable rascal, with a lovely sense of humour." Ronnie said that he remembered Dennis being a practical joker and always playing tricks on everyone.

After Munich, Ronnie recalled that Jack Crompton, who had taken over as the first team trainer, insisted the players do regular long distance runs. "A great footballer was Dennis, but he hated doing these runs. He would light-heartedly moan and groan about having to do this kind of fitness training. Yet for all this he always seemed to end the session way in front of the other lads. We could never understand how he managed to always finish in front of us when he was so far behind us. One day we found out how he did it. As a milk float passed us, who was sat on the back of the vehicle drinking a pint of milk? Yes, none other than Dennis himself. We later found out that Dennis had paid the milkman a few bob to pick him up along a quiet spot on the run and Jack Crompton never did find out about his little exploit!"

Talking about Dennis the player, Ronnie was in raptures about his ability. "He was a brilliant footballer," enthused Ronnie. "He was only frail and slim but he possessed brilliant ball control and he had searing pace from a standing position. During practice games, if I was marking him, it was a nightmare. One second I would have him in my sight and thinking I could pounce and win the ball off him, but before I could blink my eye he was gone and usually the ball would be neatly nestling in the back of the net. He was a prolific goalscorer and his record speaks for itself but he could also provide them. In my humble opinion Dennis Viollet was one of the all-time greats in the history of Manchester United. He was a legend. Dennis will never be forgotten by the people who were lucky enough to play with him or the fans who watched him play. I could never understand why he only played twice for England when there was nobody as good as him at the time."

Dennis was progressing quite nicely through the club's junior teams. Jimmy Murphy and Bert Whalley were pleased with his development. They experimented with Dennis, as they did with several other players, trying him out in different positions other than his normal inside-forward slot. The youngsters United had at the club were the cr'me-de-la-cr'me. Some developed more quickly than others and got their break into the first team sooner. Jeff Whitefoot, was one example. Dennis was quite friendly with him and he had played with Jeff in schoolboy representative matches. Dennis congratulated Whitefoot when he made his first team debut in April 1950 aged only 16.

On the other hand, Cliff Birkett was regarded as an absolute certainty to make the grade. Busby and Murphy had high hopes for this lad who had played with Dennis in several schoolboy matches. Cliff made his debut a few months after Jeff Whitefoot, just two months after his 17th birthday. Whitefoot and Birkett had reached the first team before Dennis but time would tell whether or not they could last the course. As often happens to many youngsters after a bright start, Birkett's star lost a great deal of its early glitter and after appearing in nine First Division games and scoring twice, plus four games in FA Cup matches (where he failed to score) he was sold to Southport. After only 14 games for them he drifted into non-League soccer.

Whitefoot lasted eight years at Old Trafford. He played in 93 First Division games for United and twice in the FA Cup. At one point he was a first team regular, winning a League championship medal in the 1955-56 season but after losing his place to Eddie Colman he left the club in 1957. Jeff did find success with Nottingham Forest with whom he won a much sought after FA Cup winners medal in 1959 when Forest beat Luton Town at Wembley. Dennis and Jeff remained friends for years afterwards.

Ray Wood began his career as an amateur with Newcastle United in 1948, he then moved to Darlington and in 1949 Matt Busby paid Darlington £5,000 and brought the 18-year-old to Old Trafford. Ray's father insisted that his son complete his apprenticeship as an electrical engineer so the club found him a job at Metrovicks in Trafford Park. Ray soon got to know Dennis Viollet and they became close friends, living near each other and going on holiday together with their wives. Ray was a couple of years older than Dennis but they enjoyed each other's company. Dennis, like Ray, worked during the day and trained on Tuesday and Thursday nights with Jimmy Murphy at the Cliff. This was not unusual in those days: Jackie Blanchflower, Bobby Charlton and Wilf McGuinness also had outside jobs before turning professional at 17. Dennis worked in the office of a Manchester textile company.

"Dennis was a superb player," said Ray when recalling his early days with United. "He was jokingly known as 'Tricky' amongst the other lads because he always seemed to have the latest fashionable items or jewellery. He was affectionately known as a 'rum' 'un and he had a wonderful sense of humour and was always smartly turned out. Being a United player in that period was fabulous. It was like being a member of a very close-knit family where everybody was close and cared for each other. There was a special kind of bond between players and the staff."

But this was not always the case. One day after a training session at the Cliff, Matt Busby informed the players that he wanted a practice game. The first team and the reserves played against each other. During the game there was a great deal of 'needle' flying between Jack Rowley, who was grumpy at the best of times and had a legendary temper, and Brian Birch, a bubbly, outgoing and outspoken

Salford lad who Busby and Murphy had high hopes for.

Afterwards, when they were all getting dressed, the banter was flowing thick and fast when all of a sudden a table was overturned as Jack Rowley, his face a mask of undiluted aggression, reached across and grabbed hold of Birch by the throat. Dennis and the other players jumped in and tried to stop Rowley doing any damage when all of a sudden and quite unexpectedly Matt Busby walked in, the room went deathly silent, you could hear a pin drop.

Eyeing the scene Matt asked what all the commotion was about. A red-faced, very irate and seething Rowley told the manager that he was fed up listening to Birch's sarcasm and boasting. With that Busby looked directly at Rowley and came out with some words of wisdom: "Sarcasm is a sign of an inferiority complex or a childish mind. Now let's have no more of that kind of behaviour." With that the pair were separated. Brian Birch never became a regular first team player and in March 1952 was transferred to Wolverhampton Wanderers.

Murphy the Inspiration

There is no doubt whatsoever that in Jimmy Murphy, Dennis Viollet had met the coach who knew how to bring the best out of him. Murphy would be out on the training ground in all weathers, wearing one of those really shabby, old-fashioned tracksuits, and would spend hours preaching the gospel of simple football. "Give the ball to a red shirt lad," he would tell his protÈgÈs. "Do the simple things well."

Jimmy could get very irate at times and scream and shout, then he would tone his voice down into a whisper. This was all done for a purpose and no malice was intended. He wanted to make the young players in his care world-beaters. He became so passionate about his theories that he would go over the top at times while expressing his ideas that football was a simple game. Dennis admitted in later years that no player could ever accuse Murphy of a lack of commitment or enthusiasm. He never made his coaching sessions boring, nor did he fill his pupils' heads with 'mumbojumbo' as he called it. He made every player feel like they were going to become top-class players, but only after he had smoothed out their rough edges.

"Look son, you are a good player or you wouldn't be here, at Manchester United," he would tell Dennis and other United youngsters. "Let the ball do the work. It can move faster than you can run, so use your brain to send it where you want it to go. - to a team-mate."

In 1950 a chirpy, happy-go-lucky, good-looking red-headed youngster joined United. He had played for St Wilfred's School in Hulme and Manchester Schoolboys. It is at this point that I would like to put the record straight before continuing. In many publications about United it is recorded that Albert Scanlon was a nephew of Charlie Mitten, United's left-winger from the fabulous 1948 Cup-winning side. This is not correct. The only thing they had in common was that they both played outside-left. Albert and Dennis were real down to earth Mancunians. Although Dennis was a couple of years older than Albert or 'Scanny' or 'Joe Friday,' as Albert would later be referred to by his United colleagues, the two Manchester lads struck up a close and lasting friendship.

"Dennis was marvellous, his use of the ball for a schoolboy was fantastic - he stood out like a sore thumb. In 1949 I went to Old Trafford to watch England schoolboys play Ireland and Dennis had a blinder of a match and I'm telling you that you had to be a good player to get capped for England in those days because there were so many great players all over the country. Dennis Viollet was an exceptional player.

All the kids used to talk about what a great footballer he was. What struck me about him, even as a schoolkid, was how smart and immaculate he always was - I was a little scallywag, clothes were the last thing on my mind, but Dennis was debonair.

"When I joined United, Dennis was getting ready for his callup, but I played with him in the Manchester League for United's junior teams. Hazel Grove and Ward Street Boys were among our opposition, these were tough breeding grounds. Dennis was always composed, he reminded me in his style of play of Stan Pearson. Even at this stage of his career Dennis was well respected by all the other players. I didn't really get to know him well in the beginning, we had a laugh and a joke but he lived a lifestyle that would be hard for anyone else to follow, and he never changed. His best pal was Jeff Whitefoot. I became really friendly with Dennis when we went on a club tour to Denmark in the middle 1950s. We had some hilarious times I can tell you. It tickled me when he was introduced to a lady. He would sort of bow and kiss the back of their hand. He was a real Don Juan I can tell you. He loved playing practical jokes and didn't mind when he was the victim of some type of windup. A lovely man."

At the start of the 1951-52 season Dennis was back in United's 'A' team, and he was slowly but surely improving and getting stronger. In September, the 'A' team played New Mills at the Cliff. For some reason United experimented by playing goalkeeper Ray Wood at centre forward. Ray was doing quite nicely, scoring two goals and going for his hat-trick when he pulled a muscle, and poor Geoff Bent had to leave the field at half-time because of a fractured foot. Dennis didn't score in this game but the following week he scored as the 'A' team beat Urmston 8-1. Eddie Lewis, a lad who Matt Busby thought might take over the centre-forward's role in the first team from Jack Rowley, rattled in four goals, Cliff Birkett got a couple and Clempson and Viollet the others. Later, Dennis visited the popular Geoff Bent who had to have his foot encased in plaster for a few weeks. They had a laugh and a good chat and Geoff felt much better.

Dennis was most probably a little envious of the progress his England schoolboy team-mate Cliff Birkett was making at this time. Birkett had made the first team outside-right shirt his own. Meanwhile Dennis was knocking in goals against the likes of Hazel Grove Celtic in the Manchester League. A further match in that competition saw Dennis playing at Macclesfield against their reserves. What was unusual about this game was that United only took ten players with coach Bert Whalley forced to make a brief comeback. A 2-2 result ensued, one of United's goalscorers being Les Olive who was normally a goalkeeper. Another goal from Dennis, in another Greater Manchester outpost, Mosley Common, this time from the penalty spot, put the 'A' team firmly at the top of their league. Winning the Manchester League was Dennis's first trophy as a Manchester United player and further awards swiftly followed.

An appearance for the first team at Reading in a friendly in April 1951 saw Dennis playing outside-right with his idol Stan Pearson playing as his partner in a 4-4 draw at Elm Park. John Aston senior scored twice and Stan Pearson once with a penalty from the captain, Johnny Carey. After the game Dennis told friends how much he enjoyed his run out with the older players and how much he had learned from the experience. He was especially ecstatic when describing Stan Pearson's play and how much he had helped him throughout the game. "He was marvellous," enthused a smiling Dennis when telling his father about the game. "His positioning and movement into open spaces was an education for me.

And he was so loose and relaxed all through the match. He's a great player."

This taster was soon followed by another trophy, the Lancashire Senior Cup. United beat Manchester City 2-1 in the semi-final and the same score won the final at Old Trafford against Bury. Dennis, was again at outside-right and Jack Crompton, Jackie Blanchflower, Mark Jones and Roger Byrne were among his team-mates on this occasion. The game ended Dennis's first season as a professional which produced two medals and his first team debut - a promising start.

For King and Country

In August 1951, just before the season started, Dennis married his girlfriend Barbara Southern. They were mere teenagers and in those days children were still under the jurisdiction of their parents until they reached the age of 21. Their first daughter, Stephanie, was born and in later years three other children, Roger, named after Dennis's friend Roger Byrne, Deborah and Malcolm. So Dennis had extra responsibilities now and his wages were minimal.

In five post-war seasons Manchester United had finished runners-up four times and won the FA Cup. The question on most fans' lips as the season started was: "Could they take that final step and win the League championship?" The lifestyle of the day is illustrated by the fact that following United's opening match at West Bromwich Albion's Hawthorn ground, the United team bus gave six of the West Brom players a lift home. 3-3 was the final score with Jack Rowley netting a hat-trick.

Meanwhile, Dennis was in action for the reserves at Old Trafford and helped them beat Bolton Wanderers 5-1. Johnny Berry, a superb little right-winger, joined United early in the season from Birmingham City, making his debut on September 1st when United went down 1-0 to Bolton at Burnden Park, United's first defeat of the season. Meanwhile, Dennis returned to 'A' team action and it was his equaliser that set United up for a 2-1 victory over local rivals Manchester City. It was also around this time that Dennis was called up for his two years' National Service in the Army. This military service was the real snag to the

FROM THE TOP:
*7 Clinton Avenue,
Fallowfield - Dennis's
childhood home. Dennis
was a fanatical
footballer from a young
age - joining in many
games in the streets of
war-time Manchester.
Dennis is the 5 year-old
tyke holding the ball
(right) and at 6 years old
(below).*

Dennis's practice ground in Burdith Avenue

Dennis with his foot on the ball in another Moss Side team - aged 5

LEFT: *A trio of Moss Side pals: Eric Baggaley, Brian McCormack, and Dennis. On the reverse of this photo Dennis writes: 'Nov. 19th 1944 - had it took in Alexander (sic) Park'.*

RIGHT: *Dennis writes of this photograph 'Same as other'.*

BOTH PHOTOS BY
FRANK BAGGALEY

ABOVE: *A 16 year-old Dennis in the United 'A' team line-up - back row 2nd left. Also in the squad are Bill Foulkes, Mark Jones, Jackie Blanchflower and trainer Arthur Powell*
Below: Dennis sitting on the ground (right)

A pensive looking teenager (LEFT) turned
footballer (BELOW). Dennis in the
England schoolboy strip that picked
him out from the crowd in the garden
at Clinton Avenue, 1949. Dennis is told
to exhibit 'How to kick a ball' by photographer Frank Baggaley.
BELOW: Dennis poses with a match ball
& BOTTOM: lines-up with the England
school boy team at Wembley.

```
                    R E D S
                      1
                    WOOD
        2                           3
       SPIBY                      KILLIN
   4                 5                    6
WHITEFOOT          JONES         BLANCHFLOWER
   7        8          9            10          11
 MOONEY   LEWIS     R. WOOD        POOLE       MURRAY
       Referee :                    Linesmen :
    J. H. ANDREWS                J. LOWE  (Red Flag)
      (Davyhulme)               F. MILLS (Blue Flag)

   11        10         9            8            7
HAMPSON  DOHERTY    CASKELL       VIOLLET      RITCHIE
     6                 5                    4
    EVANS             COPE               ASKEW
       3                              2
    POINTON                         MORTON
                      1
                   GOODWIN
                  B L U E S
```

TOP: *Dennis's United debut in a trial match for the Blues versus the Reds. Dennis down as Inside-Right when he actually appeared at Outside -Right.*

MIDDLE: *Dennis trains at Old Trafford*

BOTTOM: *The Lancashire Senior Cup 1950-1, Dennis's first honour in a United shirt*

TOP: *Dennis and friends*

BELOW: *Dennis's First Team debut at St. James's Park, Newcastle as an Inside-Right, The first of 293 appearances in competitive matches.*

NEWCASTLE UNITED

Black and White Striped Shirts, Black Shorts

Simpson
Goalkeeper

2		3
Cowell		**McMichael**
Right back		Left back

4	5	6
Harvey	**Brennan**	**Crowe**
Right half	Centre half	Left half

7	8	9	10	11
Walker	**Mulgrew**	**Milburn**	**Hannah**	**Mitchell**
Outside right	Inside right	Centre forward	Inside left	Outside left

Referee :
Mr. J. G. WILLIAMS,
Arnold, Notts.

Linesmen
Mr. G. A. Beecroft, Hull.
Yellow Flag
Mr. R. C. Thompson, Stockton
Red Flag

Outside left	Inside left	Centre forward	Inside right	Outside right
Rowley	**Pearson**	**Taylor**	**Viollet**	**Berry**
11	10	9	8	7

Left half	Centre half	Right half
Whitefoot	**Chilton**	**Carey**
6	5	4

Left back	Right back
Byrne	**McNulty**
3	2

Goalkeeper
Crompton

MANCHESTER UNITED

Red Shirts, White Shorts

Selections of music will be rendered before the match and during the Interval by

Westgate Hall Silver Prize Band

FROM LEFT TO RIGHT: *Johnny Berry, Duncan Edwards, Mark Jones, Roger Byrne and Dennis - the youthful joy of the Babes there for all to see. This picture was used on the front cover of Dennis and Ray Wood's brochure entitled 'The Red Devils' published in 1957.*

BOTTOM: *Matt Busby holds court during the close season of 1957.*

BUSBY'S BABES ON
RALEIGH
CYCLES
–CHAMPIONS ALL

Duncan Edwards · David Pegg · Roger Byrne · Dennis Viollet

ABOVE: *An advert of the era sums up the thoughts of United's growing support.*
BELOW: *Dennis beats goalkeeper Merrick at Birmingham's St. Andrews and sidesteps a sliding challenge from Birmingham's Horace Allen*

progress of young players, military training being totally different from football training of course. Dennis could have appealed against his call-up on the grounds that he was a young married man with a wife and baby to support, but he didn't want any preferential treatment and complied with his posting orders.

Quickly on leave, Dennis was among the goals in the 'A' team's 4-0 win over Bury at the Cliff. On the same day Roger Byrne and Jackie Blanchflower made their debuts in the first team's 3-1 defeat at Anfield - United's last defeat in the league for some time.

Talking about his National Service, Dennis said it irked him to be taken away from Old Trafford, but he realised that everyone eligible had to do their two year stint and so he buckled down and just got on with it. "One of my pals in the 17/21 Lancers (a Tank Regiment) was none other than fellow United player Freddie Goodwin. We both played for the Regiment team and it was an injury I got while playing for them that stopped me being posted to the Middle East."

On his weekend leave from Catterick, Dennis would often ride home on the back of Ken Basquill's motorbike. Like Dennis, Ken was doing his National Service. Once in Manchester, the two would arrange to meet at a precise time on the Sunday night in order to get back into camp on time. "You can imagine how cold it was on the back of the bike," said Ken. "We would stuff loads of newspapers down our uniform to keep warm. I often wondered what Matt Busby would have thought if he knew Dennis was getting such a hairy ride across the country on the back of my bike."

Carey - Champion at last

Towards the end of the season United were going like an express train at the top of the First Division, a marvellous run culminating in them having to beat Chelsea at home in the penultimate match. A final game against their nearest challengers Arsenal meant strong hearts were needed when the Pensioners visited Old Trafford. Skipper Johnny Carey, a man with the strongest of hearts, remembered the game well: "With all the near misses, I remember thinking that after all those years it's about time that I got myself a Championship medal," said the quietly spoken captain of United. "Coming up to Easter, we were near the top of the First Division table. We beat Liverpool 4-0 and Burnley 6-1 and had a 2-2 draw against Blackpool set the scene for the vital last two matches, both at home to Chelsea and Arsenal, who themselves were chasing us hard."

"It was the Chelsea match on the April 21st 1952 which will never leave my memory. We just had to win and hope that Arsenal, who were playing West Bromwich Albion on the same night, didn't. Chelsea were a funny sort of team, you never knew what to expect from them. The match had been re-arranged twice because they had been involved in an FA Cup semi-final which went to a replay, so I was worried that they may be more relaxed than our lads. A crowd of around 40,000 turned up for the game that was eventually played on a Monday night. Luckily we got on top and settled into our rhythm. Stan Pearson, who incidentally was the finest player I ever played with, gave us the lead before something happened which will never leave my memory. I got the ball near goal and was moving towards the Stretford End, with all the Chelsea players moving out towards our forwards, leaving me just outside their penalty area inviting a shot. The ball bounced just right for my left foot, which sent the ball high into the Chelsea goal. At that moment the league championship was ours. The crowd were all on their feet cheering us for so long that as Chelsea kicked off again everyone was still celebrating!"

Johnny Carey was too modest to relate that the crowd's cheers were reserved mainly for him. Alf Clarke, the chief football writer for the *Manchester Evening Chronicle*, commented that although he had been watching football for many years, he had never seen such a tribute as that which was accorded to Johnny Carey by the supporters when he scored United's second goal. They rose to the United captain and Carey later told Mr Clarke that he would always remember their gesture. Remember he certainly did, and the crowd's gesture of affection for this genuinely world-class player visibly affected him. Carey also remembered the Chelsea goalkeeper he beat with his winning goal - Bill Robertson. In later years when Carey was managing Leyton Orient during their brief flirtation in the First Division, Bill Robertson was his assistant.

United beat Chelsea 3-0, little Henry Cockburn scoring the third. The result of Arsenal's game on the same night also went United's way leaving them, bar a mathematically impossible defeat, as League Champions.

The Chelsea match was an early evening game because Old Trafford had no floodlights in those days. Even so, after the celebrations, it was still about ten o'clock before the United captain arrived home. In those days very few footballers owned a car so it had been a very brisk walk for Carey to his home in Chorlton. As he walked fans shouted: "Well done!" Johnny was feeling on top of the world when he entered his house but was soon brought back down to earth when his wife told him she was putting the children to bed, and added: "Will you wash up?" So hours after an incredible achievement, having scored his team's second goal and being crowned captain of the First Division Champions, there he was washing pots, pans and cutlery in his kitchen.

While serving in the Army, Dennis met Colin Webster, who had been a part-time professional with Cardiff City.

Dennis had played with Webster for the Northern Command XI. While on leave, Dennis told Matt Busby that he thought Webster, who had been given a free transfer by Cardiff, might be a good acquisition for United. After playing in a couple of trials with United, Busby told the Welshman that he should come and see him at Old Trafford once he had completed his army duty. Webster signed professional forms on the morning of the Arsenal game. Matt gave the Welshman a ticket for the match and told him he would make arrangements for him after the game. Colin was delighted. He watched his new team give the Londoners a 6-1 thrashing, with 'Gunner' Rowley rifling in a hat-trick, Stan Pearson scoring two while Roger Byrne added the sixth.

"It was a fantastic display of attacking football from United," recalls Colin. "Rowley and Pearson were brilliant, absolutely brilliant. I hadn't signed for United expecting to walk into their first team, not at all. But having just seen how good the first team forwards were, and having played with Dennis in the Army matches, even at this time I considered him a class inside-forward. Yes, while partnering Dennis in the Army team and seeing some of the other forwards during my trial period at Old Trafford, I wondered what the hell I was letting myself in for. Nonetheless, the club was great, geared for success from the top to the bottom."

1951-2

The season's opening game was a Reds versus Blues trial at Old Trafford, with Dennis turning out for the Blues. Prior to this match Duncan Edwards and Eddie Colman had made their Manchester United debuts in the junior version. It was quickly back to 'A' team action for Dennis and two goals at Leek Town in the opening Champions versus Gilgryst Cup winners match. He was then switched to right-half for a match with New Mills, but still managed to get on the scoresheet. This was to be Dennis's last appearance at that level for a while as now, at 19, he was to become a Central League regular who, in the first eight matches of the season, had managed just one goal.

A 5-2 victory over Huddersfield, followed by a 3-0 success over Aston Villa, with Dennis among the goals, finally got their season up and running. Injuries and Army life were holding up Dennis's progress at United. Matt Busby was switching players about. For example, Billy Foulkes was given a run in the reserves at centreforward. He was later given his first team debut in his normal rightback position at Liverpool while Dennis was being partnered with his Army mate Colin Webster, in an amazing 9-5 'A' team victory at Hyde. Both men were on the scoresheet. It was back to the Central League for Dennis where he was earning rave notices for his displays at outside-right - commentators believed it was only a matter of time before he was given an opportunity in the first team.

A man soon to have an important part in Dennis's future joined the club in March 1953. Tommy Taylor, signed from Barnsley FC, was a fine physical specimen. Standing just over six feet tall and weighing nearly 13 stones with a head of coal-black curly hair, he looked like a matinee idol and would soon become just that at Old Trafford. Big Tommy signed for the huge fee of £29,999. Matt Busby didn't want to saddle his young star with a £30,000 fee so agreed with the Barnsley chairman Joe Richards to give the tea-lady the pound.

Tommy made an immediate impact by scoring twice on his debut against Preston North End at Old Trafford. A month later the magnificent and incomparable Duncan Edwards was to wear a United first team shirt for the first time, at home to Cardiff. It was soon Dennis's turn to taste senior football.

He made his first team debut at Newcastle on Saturday April 11th 1953, the first of 261 league appearances for the Reds. He was 19 and thrilled to bits at the thought of making the first team. Mind you, he had to get a weekend pass from Catterick Camp for it to happen! He was joined in celebrating that milestone by clubman extraordinaire, Les Olive, who was a footballer and office administrator combined. Les did everything at Old Trafford, he played for the club as a full-back, centre-half, outside-right, insideleft and, on this occasion at Newcastle, he replaced the injured Jack Crompton in goal. In later years, of course, Les went on to become the club's Secretary and a Director after Munich.

Dennis and Les helped United beat Newcastle 2-1, Tommy Taylor scoring both goals. Johnny Berry was injured so Dennis played on the right wing and saw for himself what a wonderful centre-forward Tommy Taylor was. Tommy would soon be nicknamed the 'Smiling Executioner'. United's team that day: Olive; McNulty, Byrne; Carey, Chilton, Whitefoot; Viollet, Pearson, Aston, Taylor and Rowley.

Talking about his debut, Dennis praised the first team players. "Obviously I was on cloud nine being selected for the first eleven. There were so many gifted players at Old Trafford at the time that every player in each of the club's teams had to perform to a high standard every week, if you didn't there were two or three other lads waiting to take your place. What made it doubly difficult for me was I was also doing my National Service. When Matt Busby told me I was playing I was pleased as punch - this was what I had been dreaming of since I first joined United. No, I wasn't unduly nervous, just anxious to play well and let Matt see what I could do in top class company. I cannot thank those experienced players enough for helping me on my debut.

"Of course I had played with Jeff Whitefoot as a schoolboy and he was a good player. Johnny Carey was ever so polite and kind, they all were. They shook my hand and wished me well. Big Tommy eased me through the game and was always available when I had possession in case I wanted an easy option. Lovely men, I couldn't have hoped for such great players to make my first team debut with. My idol, Stan Pearson, talked to me all through the game, telling me what to do and when to release the ball.'

Bernard Bull, a North Manchester lad, had been called up a few weeks before Dennis. Bernard, like Dennis, was in the 68 Training Regiment of the Royal Armour Corps, stationed at Catterick Camp. Freddie Goodwin was also stationed at this camp while another fellow from the north, Ken Goodwin (no relation to Freddie) was also with them. Ken would go on to seek his fame on the Granada TV series The Comedians.

Bernard said Dennis was posted to office duties and sometimes issued the weekend passes for the soldiers. He made sure he, Bernard and the other lads got their passes as well. "We would get the coach on a Friday night and it would drop us off in Piccadilly in Manchester," said Bernard. "We would have a good old laugh and a singsong on the coach. There were no airs or graces about Dennis or Freddie. They were down to earth fellows, smashing company. On the Sunday night, we would all meet in Manchester to get the coach back to Catterick. Dennis would always have a big bag of sandwiches and he'd share them out with everybody. What struck me about him were his manners and quiet nature.

"I saw him play for various Army teams and he was red hot, believe me, brilliant in fact. Dennis was well thought of by the officers and got plenty of weekend leave. We were told we were to be posted overseas, but Dennis didn't want to go abroad. I ended up going to Hong Kong, while he remained at Catterick. I lost touch with him after I went overseas. However, late one night in September 1954, I was walking through Manchester city centre when I heard my name being shouted. I turned to see who was calling me and I was surprised to find out it was Dennis, who was with Bill Foulkes. He came over and shook my hand and introduced me to Bill. I hadn't seen him since our time at Catterick yet he made a big fuss of me. He told me they had just got off the train at London Road station (now Piccadilly) because they had been playing Tottenham who they beat 2-0. Then both he and Foulkes caught the late night bus home. Eh, what about that then, caught the Corporation bus home after playing for United in London. What a lovely fellow he was. I often went to Old Trafford to watch United and he seemed to get better and better with each season. Dennis Viollet was a magnificent inside-forward, worldclass in my opinion, and a wonderful chum."

The following week, on April 18th, Old Trafford had its first view of Dennis in a first team jersey. He'd kept his place and was selected as a right-winger when the Reds played West Bromwich Albion, drawing 2-2. West Brom were near the top of the league table and were tipped by many to become champions. They scored first and the player Dennis was being groomed to replace, Stan Pearson, got the equaliser. Then, in the 29th minute, Dennis got the first of his 159 league goals for United. "I got the ball, beat two men, and looked up," Dennis recalled, "bang in front of me was the goal. For a brief moment I couldn't move my legs. Then I tried a shot, I miskicked the ball but luckily it went into the corner of the net." West Brom scored a late equaliser, but nothing could spoil Dennis Viollet's big day. Playing as a winger, Dennis was reminiscent of George Best

54

when he first broke into United's first team in the 1960s. He had phenomenal speed and his shooting was ferocious, but his dribbling skills were stamped with a capital C for class! He could beat defenders on a sixpence and there's little doubt that in this position he could have been one of the greatest right-wingers ever. However Busby and Murphy wanted him alongside big Tommy Taylor to form a telepathic partnership that would bring honour and glory to United in abundance.

There was an end-of-season tournament to celebrate the Queen's Coronation in Glasgow which included Rangers, Celtic, Aberdeen, Hibernian, and Newcastle United, Arsenal, Tottenham Hotspur and Manchester United. Matt Busby involved Dennis in this tournament, giving him further big-time experience. Having been champions in the 1951-52 season, United dropped down to eighth position the following season, 1952-53. Although Matt Busby and Jimmy Murphy were extremely disappointed, they continued to introduce young players for the future - Dennis Viollet among them.

The Birth Of The Babes

Dennis was determined to try and secure a regular spot in the first team. He tried that little bit harder during pre-season training and was looking sharp and alert. He also had the advantage of not having to worry about his weight. Slowly but surely many of the 1952 championship winning side were coming to the end of their careers with United. They had been loyal servants and over the past few years had brought United success and accolades for their exciting football. They would certainly never be forgotten by United followers.

However, waiting for the chance to break through into the first team were some of the most exciting, talented and breathtaking players ever seen together at one club. Jackie Blanchflower, Albert Scanlon, John Doherty, David Pegg, Mark Jones and perhaps the greatest Manchester United player of them all, big Duncan Edwards, vied with Dennis for first team action. Bill Foulkes, Geoff Bent, Freddie Goodwin, Ian Greaves, Bobby Charlton, Wilf McGuinness and Billy Whelan were not far behind. For these players this would be the breakthrough season. They were quickly labelled the 'Busby Babes' by journalists and sports writers all over the country.

Nevertheless Matt Busby was a fair and patient manager and though he wasn't happy with the previous season's lowly eighth position in the league, he kept faith with the older players. In August 1953 Dennis returned to St James' Park with United's Central League team. He was again amongst the goals, cracking in four for United's second team in a

6-2 victory. This was an even better performance when you consider that Albert Scanlon was injured early in the game and United played most of the match with virtually ten men. This outstanding performance of marksmanship got him back into the first team in September. However, he found himself on the losing side to West Bromwich Albion (2-0) at the Hawthorns, then played in the away 'Derby' at Maine Road in which United were walloped 2-0 by City - Johnny Hart and future England manager Don Revie the goalscorers. This made it six games without a win.

Dennis was disappointed, he always tried that little bit harder whenever United played City, no matter if it was the junior team, reserves or the first team. However, he had something to celebrate: his 20th birthday and demob from the Army.

The wide range of opponents Dennis faced, and the different positions he played in can be seen by the fact that in the space of four weeks, Dennis scored four goals in a reserve match against Newcastle and finished September by scoring goals for the 'A' team against Miles Platting Swifts and Droylsden.

Now back home in Manchester, free of Army life and back in full-time training, his fitness and form started to produce the real end product. Goals came in successive away reserve games at Bury and Blackburn, earning Dennis a trip to Scotland for a midweek friendly at Kilmarnock, which was to prove a turning point in United's history. United won 3-0 with goals from Henry Cockburn, Tommy Taylor and Dennis. It was a happy, youthful United party who stayed the week at Troon before travelling to Harrogate prior to their game against Huddersfield Town. Though most of United's players were feeling on top of the world after their victory in Scotland - this would, to all intents and purposes be Henry Cockburn's final game for the Reds.

"It was only a friendly game in Kilmarnock," said Henry. "Substitutes were allowed, I was playing well and went up for a high ball and the next thing I remember, I'm on the ground with my jaw broken. Matt sent on young Duncan Edwards to replace me and I was finished. I only managed three more games in the first team before I moved to Bury in October 1954." Talking about Dennis, Henry said he was impressed with his ability on the ball and the way he could pack power into his slight frame. "Matt Busby was very high on him," added Henry, "he seemed to do things effortlessly. We would all be chasing around trying to impress and he would look like a prince inspecting the troops as he majestically strode through a game. He was a quiet fellow, never joined in our banter. After I left United I obviously watched them develop into a Championship winning team. Dennis became one of the key players in that team. When United played those continentals in the European Cup he was in his element, the way he used to glide unnoticed into goalscoring positions was uncanny and frightened defenders. He had a great touch, vision and passing that people admired. His link-up play with players like Eddie Colman, Duncan Edwards and big Tommy Taylor contributed to United's success." Henry Cockburn concluded: "Yes, he developed into a magnificent player."

Dennis was, for the first time, first choice in the first team at inside-left, replacing his hero Stan Pearson, in an away game at Huddersfield Town and he stayed in the team for the remainder of the season. Dennis recalled the feeling he had when replacing his idol: "Stan Pearson was one of those special type of insideforwards. He never seemed to have a bad game. I didn't think the day would come when I would be the player to succeed him in the United team. But it happened. The first team had got off to a poor start in the 1953 season so Matt Busby decided to throw a load of younger players into the team and thankfully I was one of them."

When Dennis joined United from school he stood a mere 5 feet 6 inches, tipping the scales at just over 8 stones. When he became a regular first-team player he had only grown two inches to 5 feet 8 inches, while his weight was 10 stones 10 pounds. Interestingly, he stayed the same weight throughout his entire football career. He was by no means a giant, other than in ability.

When United took the field against Huddersfield, Busby launched his youngsters: Ray Wood, Billy Foulkes, Roger Byrne, Duncan Edwards, Jackie Blanchflower and Tommy Taylor. They all joined Viollet in the team - the Busby Babes had arrived!

Dennis would keep his place in the team, injuries aside, for the rest of the season. He played in 29 games and scored 11 goals. He was always quick to praise the older players for their help and advice: "Who could ever forget the United 1948 FA Cup winning team, or the 1952 First Division champions? They were great individuals playing in a marvellously exciting and flamboyant team. They will always be part of Manchester United's history. I could certainly never forget them."

Players like Allenby Chilton and Jack Rowley helped him settle into the first team by encouraging him. Tommy Taylor, although young, also went out of his way to smooth things out for Dennis. "If you feel like you need a breather," Tommy told his 18-months younger colleague. "Just bang the ball up to me." Roger Byrne also helped Dennis settle into the first team and acted as Viollet's protector. "When I first got into the first eleven on a regular basis and being on the small side, I had quite a few big, strong defenders always ready to let me know they were there," said Dennis. "I wasn't one for retaliating, my philosophy was beat them with skill, but

Roger Byrne always seemed to feel that it was his duty to
fight my battles for me. I don't think the bulk of football
fans ever appreciated that Roger was not only England's best
left full-back but he was also a formidable and courageous
captain to play under. He fought tooth and nail for all the
team."

The Busby Babes drew with Huddersfield and gained
another draw against Arsenal 2-2. Busby and Murphy were
pleased with the way the youngsters had adjusted to the pace
and toughness of playing in the First Division and decided
to keep faith with the kids, sink or swim. Their faith was
repaid when they eclipsed Cardiff at Ninian Park 6-1. Dennis
scored twice, Johnny Berry, Jackie Blanchflower, Jack Rowley
and Tommy Taylor getting a goal each. Four more goals
followed a week later at Old Trafford against Blackpool
with Dennis's goal complementing a Tommy Taylor
hattrick. With the forward line functioning like clockwork,
Dennis was becoming a vital part of the structure of the
team and goals continued to flow. There were a couple of
drawn games before a 3-1 defeat at Chelsea. It was after this
game that Jimmy Murphy assured Matt Busby that all would
be well with the young players. He knew each and everyone
of them inside out. "Stick with them, they'll come good," he
told his boss.

Now a regular first team player, Dennis certainly didn't
let success go to his head. His old schoolboy pal Alan Wallace
had followed Dennis's career since leaving St Margaret's
School. Alan would go down to the Cliff or Old Trafford
as often as he could in order to watch his friend's progress.
Dennis would always take time to go over to where Alan was
and ask how he and his family were doing. He would give his
pal complimentary tickets to watch the game and tell Alan
to wait for him afterwards. After the match Dennis would
walk to the bus stop with his friend and they would ride

the 53 bus home; Dennis would get off at Princess Road while Alan continued on to Gorton.

"He was becoming a famous player by this time," said Alan. "Supporters would scurry up to him and ask him to sign their match programme or a bit of paper. He was so kind and jovial with them and signed while thanking them in the process. There was certainly no trait of big-headedness or arrogance with Dennis, I can vouch for that. His manners to people were impeccable."

In the next home match against Liverpool the young Reds went all out, dishing out a 5-1 hammering, with two goals apiece for Blanchflower and Taylor and Dennis getting on the score sheet again. Sheffield Wednesday were thrashed in a double victory 5-2 at Old Trafford, where Dennis notched another goal to add to the goal scored by Blanchflower, and Tommy Taylor's hat-trick. In the away game that followed at Hillsborough Dennis scored the solitary goal that gave United a 1-0 win.

Dennis's form and goals continued in his FA Cup debut away at Burnley. United were two goals behind after ten minutes but Dennis set United on their way. Nevertheless it was still 3-3 with only minutes remaining before Burnley sealed victory with two late efforts. "Inexperience, that's what cost them the game," said Matt Busby.

The performances of United's youngsters wasn't going unnoticed. Dennis and Bill Foulkes were selected as reserves for England's under-23 friendly international in Italy, while Ray Wood, Jeff Whitefoot and Duncan Edwards were selected to play, emphasising United's youthful strength in depth.

Four of United's young players: Ray Wood, Jeff Whitefoot, Mark Jones and Dennis used to do the football pools. One Saturday they realised they had won a second dividend. They were gloriously happy and planned how they were going to spend their windfall. While lapping around Old Trafford the following day, Matt Busby suddenly appeared in the centre circle and shouted the four pools winners over.

"I believe congratulations are in order," said Matt. The players thanked him and looked sheepish. "Have you decided what you are going to do with your winnings?" They told him they hadn't thought about it. "Well, you must keep playing, don't let this money go to your heads." Matt then walked briskly back to his office. To celebrate, they planned an expensive meal at Manchester's famous Midland Hotel. However, when they received their winnings they were shocked, they wouldn't have paid for the first round of drinks - £28. Needless to say the celebration was hastily cancelled.

Meanwhile, Stan Pearson's move to Bury meant that Dennis could feel more comfortable as United's regular number 10. Mind you, he couldn't relax too much with Billy Whelan and Bobby Charlton waiting in the wings.

Another of United's stalwarts, Allenby Chilton, was now captain. Dennis had great respect for the big, affable Geordie and spoke warmly of his role with the younger players. "I don't feel enough credit was given to Allenby Chilton for the change in the first team's fortunes. With so many immature, inexperienced players around him, he had to put in a tremendous amount of work. He was a constant inspiration to us and held the team together. He told us exactly what was wanted - he didn't mince his words - but never held off-field inquests."

Dennis scored his seventh goal in 22 appearances against Huddersfield Town in a 3-1 Old Trafford victory. Jackie Blanchflower and Jack Rowley the other scorers. This victory was followed by a slight slip in form from United's kids, nevertheless Dennis ended the league season in style, scoring goals in each of the last three matches at Old Trafford: a 3-2 defeat to Cardiff City, a 2-0 victory over Charlton Athletic and a 2-0 win against Portsmouth.

The last away match was at Sheffield United, and it proved a thriller. Dennis delivered an inch perfect cross for Johnny Aston to nod home but Brook, the Blades captain, equalised within a minute. Blanchflower put United in the lead again just before half time, and in the 48th minute, Aston backheaded for Dennis to score a gem: he stepped between two defenders to drive a powerpacked shot past Burgin in the Sheffield goal.

At the end of the season Jimmy Murphy pulled Dennis to one side and told him he should analyse how he had performed. "How do you think I've done?" Dennis asked Murphy. "You should feel proud," said Jimmy. "You have made the big breakthrough into the first team, and scored 11 in 29 games. And, what you should remember is that you went into a team that was at the crossroads because the FA Cup and League Championship players were getting older and Matt was re-structuring the whole team. You are one of their replacements, and you and the other lads will get better and better." Busby's Babes had arrived.

April 30th 1954 was FA Cup Final eve, and Arsenal's Highbury Stadium was the venue for a fixture between Young and Old England. Alongside Dennis were Roger Byrne and Duncan Edwards. Most club managers did not like their players involved in this type of fixture, in fact they frowned upon it, regarding it as a meaningless waste of time, especially after such a hard, gruelling season. But Busby always believed that his players could learn a great deal and to young players like Byrne, Edwards and Viollet, this was a chance to catch the England selectors' eyes with a view to the future.

Old England won the match 2-1, but far from

being disappointed at being on the losing side, Dennis was in raptures about the two Old England inside-forwards, Wilf Mannion and Len Shackleton. Mannion, the blond-haired Middlesbrough player and Shackleton, the 'Clown Prince', were absolutely brilliant - they gave a classic inside-forward display. Dennis had nothing but praise for these two wizards of football and spoke about them constantly to colleagues and friends.

"This was my first major representative game," said Dennis. "Both teams had a great deal of incentive to win - the experienced players to prove they were still the best in the game and we younger ones were trying to move further up the ladder of fame. Although my team lost 2-1 I never felt it was a disgrace to be on the losing side. As an inside-forward, I naturally had a particular interest in the two players occupying similar positions for Old England - Wilf Mannion and Len Shackleton. What a display these two gave! Their wonderful tricks, skill and defence-splitting passes brought home to me just how much I had to learn. Their exhibition was something I had never seen before, and have not seen since. They were absolute masters of their profession, they gave our defence a real grilling and taught me more than I could have learned from another dozen games."

This was a season of change at United: Johnny Carey retired to become manager of Blackburn Rovers, Stan Pearson left for Bury, while later in the year Allenby Chilton moved to Grimsby Town and Jack Rowley went to Plymouth Argyle. These players had formed the spine of Busby's great post-war teams.

However, he now had the players to take his next great side forward. In reality, during these two seasons (1953-54 and 1954-55) United just about held a reasonable place in the league table. However football was changing. The players who had dominated after the war were now veterans; Hungary had beaten England 6-3 at Wembley in 1953 with a brand-new type of football based on sublime skills, lightning speed and devastating passing. England were no longer the invincibles and Busby was the first to realise the fact. Over the next three seasons his Babes would blossom into the greatest British club side ever assembled and show those in English football the standard required.

Busby's Finishing School

A defeat was followed by three victories as United began the new campaign at the top of the First Division. Though hampered by the loss of Tommy Taylor through injury Dennis, now partnered by Colin Webster upfront, scored twice away at Sheffield Wednesday (4-2 win), once at Bloomfield Road against Blackpool (4-2 win) and again in the return fixture with Wednesday (2-1 win) before Tommy Taylor returned in the Reds' 3-1 home romp against Charlton. Big Tommy scored in that game but missed the following two matches against Tottenham at White Hart Lane in a 2-0 win (Johnny Berry and Colin Webster the goalscorers) and a 1-1 draw at Burnden Park, Bolton. Dennis had notched seven goals in the opening nine games.

In the 1-1 home draw with Huddersfield Town on the 18th September 1954, Dennis scored a splendid goal against the toughest defence United had faced so far that season. A minute before half-time Johnny Berry centred the ball and as Tommy Taylor went up to meet it in the penalty area he was clattered by two Huddersfield defenders - the crowd roared for what looked a stonewall penalty. But referee Mr Beacock ignored the shouts, the ball ran loose and Dennis, pivoting on his left heel, drove an unstoppable shot into the far corner of the net to give the Reds the lead. Huddersfield equalised later, in a game spoilt by ruthless tackling and bad tempers.

Dennis's disappointment at being held to a draw was tempered after the game when he received a cheque for £750 from Matt Busby. Mark Jones, Jeff Whitefoot and

Jackie Blanchflower also received the same amount of money. None of them were yet 21, never in the history of the game had any club been in the position to award maximum benefits, at the same time, to players as young as these four.

The rules allowed United to count a player's service with them from the time he signed as an amateur as long as his service was unbroken. The two-year National Service that Dennis and Jeff Whitefoot had just finished was counted as unbroken service, so they met up in the city centre and celebrated in style.

A couple of defeats at Manchester City (3-2) and Wolves (4-2) put a stop to United's early season form. Dennis managed to score a picture goal at Molineux but he took no delight in a United defeat. In their next game the Babes hammered Cardiff City 5-2. Dennis had a truly great game and helped Tommy Taylor score four while he got one himself. In this match Dennis showed the full range of his superb skills. He was majestic! He carved out beautiful openings for his team-mates, while his elegance on the ball and the manner in which he brought the ball under instant control was immaculate. What pleased Matt Busby more than anything was his movement without the ball.

There was more good news for United as veteran captain Allenby Chilton recovered from a shoulder injury and prepared to make his 150th consecutive league appearance for the Reds in their away game at Stamford Bridge - a marvellous achievement for a vastly underrated centre-half.

In the same week Bobby Charlton signed professional forms while Bill Foulkes, who was 22 and recently capped against Ireland, decided to give up his pit job and become a full-time professional footballer. This meant that Bill would now have to complete two years of National Service, because as a miner he had been exempt from it. When this was pointed out to him he merely shook his broad shoulders and replied: "I will do whatever I have to do."

An aspect of Dennis's personality that comes through in conversations with those who knew him was his fashion sense and, of course, anyone who was a follower of fashion needs a good tailor. In this respect Dennis had Jack Coggan, who besides owning a tailor's shop, was also director of Stalybridge Celtic and chairman of the Referees' Association.

During the early 1950s, Dennis used to visit Jack's tailors with Duncan Edwards, Tommy Taylor, David Pegg and later, Bobby Charlton and Wilf McGuinness. Jack used to supply the lads with the latest fashions: suits, cardigans, slacks, casual jerseys and other popular items of the 1950s. "They were great lads, they really were. I know it must have been said thousands of times, but they were so down to earth. Dennis was always smartly turned out when he called to visit me. He had a lovely disposition about him and would speak to my mother as if he had known her all his life.

"He used to call with Duncan who was very shy and they would try on everything that caught their eye. If they had seen a suit or shirt or whatever while on their travels they would ask if I had it in stock, if I didn't I would go to wherever they made the item and get it for them. They offered to pay me for the clothes but I would never take any money from them; their friendship meant more to me than money. Of course I was a lot older than them but they treated me like I was one of the lads. I used to get invited to go for a drink after the games and especially midweek games. I also went to a lot of functions as their guest. I suppose I was like a father confessor to them because they would unburden their worries and anxieties to me. After Munich, Dennis would sometimes call round with Shay Brennan and Nobby Stiles. Before his first venture to America, Dennis and I promised to keep in touch which we did.'

On October 16th 1954, United were away to Chelsea, the pride of London. In one of the most memorable, exciting and breathtaking football matches ever witnessed United beat Chelsea 6-5! Over 55,966 spectators were royally entertained by two wonderful footballing sides who attacked each other for the entire 90 minutes producing an eleven goal feast. Everyone present agreed that it was games like this one that would keep fans rolling through the turnstiles.

Dennis scored his first senior hat-trick for United and his pal Tommy Taylor got two with 'Blanchie' (Jackie Blanchflower) notching the other. This really was an incredible match in every respect with the crowd limp with excitement. "If any music hall comedian ever tries to win another cheap laugh at the expense of 'Poor Old Chelsea' - he'll deserve the bird," said Matt Busby after the game.

Seamus O'Connell, Chelsea's England amateur international, made his debut in this game and like Dennis Viollet he also scored a hat-trick. Johnny Berry was in world class form and laid on five of the goals for his colleagues and was unanimously named 'Man of the Match.' Roger Byrne commented, "I have never played in a game as exciting as this one. All our goals were well taken, and the moves leading up to them were in the Hungarian class for sheer brilliance. No sooner had we scored than Chelsea were battering away at our defence trying to balance things out. The crowd set up a continual roar. We all felt very exhilarated, due no doubt to our win." Despite United's victory at Stamford Bridge the Londoners finished the season as League Champions.

United's performances earned representative recognition. Dennis joined Tommy Taylor in the FA XI, to play an Army side at Hillsborough. John Charles, Leeds United's Welsh International who was a magnificent player,

whether at either centre-half or centre-forward and Albert
Quixall, the blond-haired, silky insideforward, playing on
his home ground, were both in the Army team.

On November 16th, Dennis was back on the scoresheet.
United were playing Preston at Old Trafford - the pitch
was like a quagmire, absolutely waterlogged and after ten
minutes Preston went one up when Baxter scored a good
goal. Quickly Tom Finney was all over the pitch urging his
forwards to keep up the attack on United's defence and
the Reds were struggling, the pitch not favouring their
pass-and-move style when, after 33 minutes, Jack Rowley
took a corner, there was a scramble in the penalty area
and Dennis, with his back to goal, fell and scored with a
truly amazing overhead bicycle kick. With less than fifteen
minutes to go, Tommy Taylor chested a high ball down,
flicked it delicately to Dennis who was on to it like a
greyhound and dispatched the ball into the North End net.
Despite all Finney's efforts United hung on to collect both
points. Another victory (2-1) over Arsenal at Old Trafford
kept the team near the top of the table.

The Babes were in good mood and, following their
annual players' dance at the Assembly Rooms, Broughton,
(tickets just 3/6 or 17p), United prepared themselves for an
important series of Christmas fixtures.

Unfortunately Yuletide proved disappointing. A double
defeat by Aston Villa caused concern at Old Trafford, but
then Reading held United to 1-1 draw in the third round
of the FA Cup at Elm Park. In the replay, Dennis scored in
United's 4-1 victory setting up a Manchester 'Derby' for the
fourth round at Maine Road.

The wheels then really came off United's season. Two
defeats by City, 2-0 in the Cup and 5-0 at home in the
league, put supporters in a melancholy mood. Wolves came
to Old Trafford for a midweek afternoon match and, in

front of just 15,679 spectators, went home with a rousing 4-2 victory. Busby experimented, moving Dennis to inside-right and giving Duncan Edwards the number ten jersey. United's woe was compounded by another defeat, this time 3-0 at Cardiff.

This further downturn in form meant changes. Dennis was dropped in favour of Billy Whelan and played for the reserves at Bury in a scoreless Manchester Senior Cup match before making a reappearance in a couple of Central League games. A goal against Sheffield United reserves brought a return to the first team for Dennis against the same side at Old Trafford. Viollet celebrated in style, United romping home 5-0: Taylor (2), Johnny Berry, Billy Whelan and Dennis all on the scoresheet.

United completed the season with a flourish. Victory at Highbury (3-2), was followed by a 2-1 home victory over the newly-crowned First Division Champions, Chelsea. This game was a memorable match for Roy Cavanagh, co-author of this book. Aged eight, his late father took him to Old Trafford to watch his favourite team. After the game Mr Cavanagh attempted to obtain the autographs of the new champions and somehow managed to get aboard the Chelsea team coach. Unfortunately the coach drove off with Roy's father still aboard, leaving little Roy forlornly by the wayside! Happily, all ended well and Roy walked home over Trafford Bridge admiring a full autograph book.

Having completed the double over the champions, United finished the season in fifth place. Dennis had scored 20 goals in his 34 league appearances. Busby had juggled his resources well and only inexperience and a crucial loss of form had cost them a higher finish and more glory. Nevertheless, United were on the verge of success and the supporters and players felt it as the team embarked on a close-season tour of Scandinavia.

A Passport to Glory

For the second year running, Tommy Taylor picked up an injury at the start of a new season, pulling a thigh muscle during the opening game at Birmingham City. Nevertheless, Dennis was in sparkling form, his movement was sharp and intelligent and despite the handicap of Taylor's loss, Dennis scored both United goals in a 2-2 draw.

The same score greeted the Old Trafford opener against Tottenham, which saw Berry and Webster open their goal accounts for the new season. Another goal from Dennis secured a 3-1 victory again at Old Trafford. Eddie Lewis and Albert Scanlon the other goalscorers. In the return match against Tottenham at White Hart lane, United won 2-1 Duncan Edwards bagging both goals, before Dennis picked up an injury that sidelined him for four games.

Viollet's importance to United was emphasised by three defeats in his absence, so it was a welcome return for Dennis when United played Preston North End at Old Trafford. The Reds were victorious 3-2, David Pegg, Tommy Taylor and Dennis getting the goals. This was Viollet's fourth goal in five games but in what was proving to be an injury-prone season, Dennis sustained a foot injury in a scoreless draw with Burnley. This injury kept him out of two home victories over Luton Town and Wolves which took Busby's Babes to the top of the table.

Dennis missed the following three games (a spell in which United won two and were held to a draw in the third) but returned for the home fixture with Huddersfield, United triumphing 3-0 with Berry, Pegg and Taylor the scorers. The following week, United returned to the top of the league table after Tommy Taylor's lone goal saw them defeat Cardiff. Dennis also played in a 1-1 draw against Arsenal but missed the next game, an away fixture with Bolton Wanderers.

The Lancashire club were something of a bogey side as far as United were concerned. They were big, tough, rough and never stopped trying. As co-author Roy Cavanagh explains: "It was with a bit of trepidation that as an eight-year-old, my father took me to Burnden Park for my first away match as a United supporter. Being from Salford it was extra special to see local hero Eddie Colman make his debut but despite an early Tommy Taylor goal, United continued their dismal form against the Wanderers going down to a 3-1 defeat."

In these days of capacity crowds at Old Trafford, it is perhaps interesting to reflect that Chelsea's visit to Old Trafford in November 1955 produced a gate of just over 22,000. They were the lucky ones though, watching United thrash the reigning champions 3-0, Tommy Taylor getting two and captain Roger Byrne the other. Dennis came back for this game and didn't miss another league match for the remainder of the season. The Reds then drew a top of the table clash 0-0 away at Blackpool before beating Sunderland 2-1 at home with Dennis's striking partner Tommy Taylor scoring both goals. A 3-2 defeat at Portsmouth was a set back but in the next home game against Birmingham City the Reds won 2-1, with a rare goal from big Mark Jones before Dennis got the winner. It would turn out to be Mark Jones' only goal in over 120 first team matches for the club, while it was Dennis's sixth in 14 games. Again, even allowing for the closeness of Christmas, the match drew a crowd of only 27,704.

Dennis enjoyed Christmas 1955, doubling his goal tally in the four matches played over a seven-day period. It started on Christmas Day at the Hawthorns where he scored a hat-trick, helping United to a 4-1 win. This was increased on Boxing Day when Charlton Athletic, despite a wonderful performance from legendary Charlton goalkeeper Sam Bartram, received a 5-1 hammering in front of 44,000. Dennis netted twice, Byrne, Johnny Doherty and Taylor getting the other goals. In those days the teams played home and away at Christmas so after the Boxing Day game, both teams boarded the London-bound train, Christmas dinner en route, to face each other the following day at The Valley.

As was usual with these return fixtures form went out of the window and Charlton won 3-0. This didn't deter Dennis however, as he scored his sixth Christmas goal in a 2-1 home victory over Manchester City. His first goal, and the winner, against the team from his side of town gave him huge satisfaction. His pal Tommy Taylor scored the other in front of a 60,956 New Year's Eve crowd.

Moving into 1956, United were four points clear at the top of the league table as they prepared for a third round FA Cup-tie at Eastville against Bristol Rovers. They were trounced 4-0, a result that caused shock waves throughout the world of football. Older United supporters claimed that the Reds were not really interested in a long, hard, tiring FA Cup run and consequently were pleased to be out of the cup as they could now give their full attention to winning the league championship. Be that as it may, the players were bitterly disappointed to be eclipsed in this manner.

Once back into league action United had two contrasting results against Sheffield United and Preston North End, winning the first 3-1 and losing the second by the same score at Deepdale. They then put their foot down and moved clear at the top of the league table thanks to five successive victories: 2-0 wins at home to Burnley and away at Luton Town, Dennis scoring against both teams. Then

Wolves were licked 2-0; Tommy Taylor netting both goals, followed by a 1-0 home win against Aston Villa and a 4-2 win at Chelsea, Dennis showing his particular liking for Stamford Bridge by scoring twice.

The press dubbed United's forward line 'Will-o-the-Wisps', because of their brilliant interchanging during a game. Chelsea, the current league champions, looked at one stage as if they were going to give the youngsters from Manchester a football lesson. Veteran Roy Bentley looked to put the Londoners on the road to victory when he got the opening goal. Dennis had other ideas however and he and Billy Whelan ran riot. Dennis lost his defender Brian Nicholas completely during a ten-minute spell when he scored the equalising goal and then put United ahead. His goals were a masterpiece in execution. United's forward line was working to clockwork precision and the Chelsea defence found themselves chasing phantoms. David Pegg and Tommy Taylor got the other goals.

Mind you, Dennis knew he needed to be on his toes as a certain youngster by the name of Bobby Charlton was beginning to make his mark at Youth and Central League level. Charlton had already scored 30 goals in 31 Central League appearances and was starring in the FA Youth Cup, for which United drew a then record crowd of over 26,000 for the fourth round tie against Newcastle United. In the fifth round United thrashed Bexley Heath, a nursery side of Charlton Athletic, 11-1 - Bobby scoring five times. Don't for one minute think that Bexley Heath were just a little amateur outfit, far from it, they were a good side with a few outstanding individuals. During this game news came over the tannoy system confirming that Dennis Viollet's goal had consolidated United's lead at the top of Division One with a 1-1 draw. As Easter approached, Tommy Taylor's goal was enough to earn a 1-0 win over local rivals Bolton Wanderers, before Dennis grabbed two more to help United inflict a Good Friday 5-2 walloping of Newcastle United at Old Trafford - with Doherty, Pegg and Taylor also on the scoresheet. A 0-0 draw at St. James' Park the following Monday was followed by a 2-0 victory at Leeds Road, Huddersfield, to set United up for a championship showdown.

The Championship Decider

The only team in with a chance of catching United were Blackpool, and it was they who provided the opposition on the first Saturday in April 1956. It seems hard to believe, considering the stature of the two clubs today, how highly regarded Blackpool were during this period. The Seasiders were a very good side with internationals Jackie Mudie, Stan Mortensen and, of course, Stanley Matthews.

There were incredible scenes outside Old Trafford; the gates were closed half an hour before kick-off with thousands unable to get in and, with over 62,277 delirious fans jammed inside the ground, the atmosphere was electric. Roy Cavanagh takes up the story: "My Uncle took me along to the match and we were lucky because we only just got in before they locked the turnstiles, it was about 2-15pm. Mounted Police were trying to keep order. We were standing at the back of the Stretford End which meant that I saw very little of the game, turning round to watch Glovers Cables play on a pitch where the souvenir shop was at the back of the Stretford End! Blackpool's mascot was a live duck, leading them out with a minder dressed like an Eastern Prince!"

Jimmy Murphy was in charge of United because manager Busby had to travel to Glasgow following a family bereavement. Matt couldn't have wished for a better man in charge during his absence, Murphy was a winner through and through. He had trained the majority of United's team from schoolboys and knew exactly what to do and say to get the best out of them.

The teams - United: Wood; Greaves, Byrne; Colman, Jones, Edwards; Berry, Doherty, Taylor, Viollet and Pegg.

Blackpool: Farm; Frith, Wright; Kelly (J) Gratrix, Kelly (H); Matthews, Taylor, Durie, Mudie and Perry.

Ian Greaves had taken over at full-back from Bill Foulkes earlier in the season. "My vivid memory of this match was when big Dave Durie headed Blackpool into the lead in the early minutes," recalls Ian Greaves. "It was a terrible blow, we were nervous and Busby would certainly not have been pleased at the slack marking by our defenders."

Jimmy Murphy was out of the dugout shouting to his players to forget the goal, compose themselves and settle down. Easier said than done in a highly emotional game like this. Stan Matthews could sense the United youngsters' frustration and roamed across the forward line in an effort to get another goal. He set up chances for Bill Perry and Jackie Mudie. Then Johnny Berry, the most experienced member of United's team, started to turn on the magic, he set the example for the youngsters to follow. "But try as hard as we did, the equaliser just wouldn't come," remarked Ian Greaves.

Fittingly this championship decider was a classic, although a nasty clash of heads between Tommy Taylor and Blackpool's fullback Jackie Wright saw both of them forced from the field to receive medical attention. "When Tommy Taylor was led off I thought our chance of sealing the title had gone," Ian Greaves recalled.

Suddenly United received a lifeline when George Farm, the Blackpool keeper, brought down Johnny Doherty in the penalty area. Captain Roger Byrne was the normal penalty taker, but he had missed a couple during the season so he asked Johnny Berry to take it. Little Johnny didn't bat an eyelid and rammed the ball home to equalise, giving Farm no chance. Inside Old Trafford it was bedlam, the noise could be heard for miles around. The two injured players came back, typically Tommy Taylor was soon in the thick of the action, his injured head no longer troubling him at all. Ian Greaves can't praise Taylor highly enough, comparing him to the great Tommy Lawton and Nat Lofthouse as a header of a ball.

United could afford a draw in this game but Jimmy Murphy was shouting for his players to win the game and leave no doubt. Ten minutes before the final whistle, Berry, United's best forward, crossed for Tommy Taylor, who was almost on his hands and knees but managed to scramble the ball past Farm. As the ball trickled over the line a wall of noise hit the evening air - United were champions. Jimmy Murphy jumped from the dugout laughing and crying, his little seeds had blossomed into glorious life and reaped the ultimate reward.

The championship trophy was presented at the end of the final league game, at Old Trafford, against Portsmouth. Perhaps surprisingly, after the post-war record Old Trafford crowd of 62,277 for the decider against Blackpool, the attendance for this match was only 38,417. Dennis finished the season on a high note getting the only goal for the new champions in a 1-0 victory, it was his 20th league goal from 34 appearances. Incredibly these figures precisely duplicated his statistics from the season before but now included a prized Championship winner's medal.

There was a championship reception party at Manchester Town Hall later that night. It was a great season for all United's teams: the reserves were champions of the Central League and the FA Cup Youth team had beaten Chesterfield, who had a youngster named Gordon Banks in goal, in the final of the FA Youth Cup.

However the real prize, at least as far as Busby and Murphy were concerned, was the imminent assault on Europe. In preparation for this, Dennis and the team embarked on another tour of Scandinavia, helping United to repeat the previous year's feat of winning all four matches. Dennis scored in three of the games, while in the last match in Sweden he reverted to outside-right, giving a Matthewsesque display - he completely mesmerised the Swedish defence. It was now all systems go for the Busby Babes, as they planned an English club's first European Cup campaign.

Dennis the Devil?

In his book *A Strange Kind Of Glory* former Manchester United player Eamon Dunphy wrote: "The new champions were called the Red Devils. It was an apt description, for their vivacious roguishness was one of their most attractive qualities. Dennis Viollet, who scored twenty goals that season, brought another distinctly Mancunian dimension to the side. Dennis was devil: a rogue, smooth, elegant and sophisticated, as were the Manchester nightclubs he loved to frequent. Dennis was a Manchester lad to his marrow. Not for him the coffee-bars or ice-rinks or the innocent cavorting of Sale Locarno. The Cromford Club, perhaps, preferably the velvet promise of the Queens and Continental Clubs where the real action was. He was a loner. Liked by the lads and liking them, but to them he was elusive, mysterious, Town, after the last bus had long since gone. And that's the way he played his football, beautifully balanced, subtle, a gliding, powerful presence, composed and deadly when the opening came."

Meanwhile in Joe Lovejoy's rivetting biography of George Best, *Bestie - Portrait of a Legend*, Dennis is described as: "The forerunner of George Best - a great player with a drink problem. Even when it was common knowledge that he was living it up and letting it affect his performance on the field, Matt did nothing." Mr Lovejoy goes on to write that Dennis, just like George Best, could do what he pleased off the field. He continues to say that in the period that Matt Busby himself played, "If players liked a drink so what? As long as they did their stuff when it mattered on a Saturday afternoon."

Was Dennis really like the person that Eamon Dunphy and Joe Lovejoy described in their books? Was he a devil and a hard drinker? There is no denying that like the vast majority of footballers, Dennis liked relaxing with a drink, although it must be said that we spoke to several of his playing colleagues and friends who denied strongly that Dennis had any kind of drink problem.

There is also certainly no denying that Dennis enjoyed the atmosphere of nightclubs and the company of the opposite sex. He was known as a real Don Juan, while his marriage at an early age did not appear to curb his evening activities. Dennis's second wife Helen has admitted that there is enough evidence of Dennis's nocturnal activities for another book.

His success with the ladies is underlined by his relaxed behaviour around them. He wasn't boisterous or loud in their company, he was a real smoothie, with a ready smile and a twinkle in his eye that would have done justice to James Bond - Sean Connery later became one of Dennis's friends - he could literally charm the birds off the trees.

First hand evidence of Dennis's pulling power came from Brian Smith, a regular visitor to the *Dennis Viollet Record Bar*, next to the old Tatler Cinema on Whitworth Street in Manchester city centre. Brian often spoke to Dennis and found him really helpful and extremely knowledgeable about music (Brian was partial to rock'n'roll). But the most striking feature of Dennis's shop, according to Brian were the customers: "There was always a bevvy of nubile woman hanging around. He was a handsome sod! It was often joked at the time that Manchester Magistrates' Court printed their paternity orders with his name already on!"

Voyage of Sinbad

Dennis burst into the new 1956-57 season in terrific style, scoring both goals in an otherwise disappointing 2-2 draw against Birmingham City to begin United's title defence. You could have described this game as the 'Water Polo' match of the century, Manchester's notorious climate excelling itself for this game. Torrential rain fell throughout and the inclement weather kept the crowd to a mere 32,000, with those on the open sides of the ground receiving a soaking. It was impossible to play football in these conditions but both teams tried. In the 30th minute Dennis put United in front before Mark Jones scored an own goal. Govan put the Brummies into the lead but ten minutes before the final whistle, Dennis latched on to a wayward backpass from Birmingham's Smith, rounded keeper Gil Merrick and equalised.

Two excellent away victories at Preston North End (3-1) and West Bromwich Albion (3-2) showed the new champions were again going to be a force to be reckoned with. In the match at the Hawthorns, Dennis scored a late equaliser then, moving into the West Brom penalty area, he unleashed a right-footed rocket of a shot which rebounded off the goalkeeper for Billy Whelan to grab an injury-time winner.

Dennis scored a magnificent hat-trick in the home win over Preston by a 3-1 scoreline followed by a 3-0 Old Trafford victory over Portsmouth - Dennis joining Johnny Berry and David Pegg on the scoresheet. This was followed by a 2-1 win over Chelsea at Stamford Bridge, and a 1-1 draw at the other end of the country at Newcastle. In the seven opening games of the new season, the Reds were undefeated and topped the First Division table. Dennis was in sparkling form, scoring seven goals, adding a new dimension to his game - ideal preparation for United's assault on European honours.

The football United played in this period was different from the average English standard. They played more like the continentals or South Americans, the difference being that as opposed to the subtle, probing, slow build-up of European and South American teams, United packed plenty of 'punch' near goal. To their sublime interpassing and technical skills the Red Devils added the quicker passing and attacking play of the British method. The Reds had almost perfect teamwork - their exquisite short passing could be switched when needed to the old English long ball style.

Busby and Murphy had honed players to be comfortable on the ball. They were taught that it was a friend, mastery of which would frighten defenders and, eventually, grind them down.

The Babes tactics were simple. Colman and Edwards would outpace and out-manoeuvre the opposition and supply United's five man forward line with plenty of ammunition. Viollet and Whelan would often drop back, pick up the ball in midfield opening up more options. United could play the ball on the floor or in the air and, with Foulkes, Byrne, Jones and Edwards, plus Taylor up front they had steel to go with the silk.

But the real beauty of this young United team at this time was that they were still improving and promised so much not just for United but for English football. Players like Dennis, Bobby Charlton, Duncan Edwards, Albert Scanlon and Kenny Morgans were developing nicely and were going to be a force to be reckoned with for years to come, not only in this country, but more importantly in Europe.

It is now well known why United defied the might of the Football League and set sail on their 'Voyage of Sinbad'. The original idea for the European Cup competition went back as far as 1927 when Henri Delaunay, the secretary of the French Football Federation, was one of its keenest supporters. A proposal was put to FIFA but the problems of arranging extra fixtures stopped the venture. However, after the Second World War and with the advent of improved air travel and floodlighting, it became more of a practical proposition. In 1954 the French Sports magazine L'Equipe kick started the idea again and the first competition was held in 1955. Chelsea, as champions, were first offered England's entry but the Football League told them in no uncertain manner not to compete and the Chelsea board did what they were told, and refused the offer. Matt Busby and his chairman, Harold Hardman, however, were all in favour and when they became First Division Champions they informed the FA that, despite opposition from the Football League, they would accept UEFA's invitation to compete in the European Champions Cup.

We must remember that the European Cup came into being only a couple of years after Hungary had embarrassed English football with a breathtaking display 6-3 display at Wembley. Busby was a visionary. He realised that English footballers needed to play the best Continental teams if our football was to reach the Hungarian level.

United's entry into the European Cup was to become a truly wonderful adventure, giving supporters and fans around the country some of the most unforgettable, enjoyable and exciting nights that will live in the memory of those lucky enough to be present at these games until the day they die. It would also link the club with romance, tragedy and sporting conquest. It opened up the world to football United-style. Manchester United Football Club would never be the same again.

In Manchester meanwhile, times were hard. Living conditions for working-class supporters were dour and poorly paid, people were treated harshly and although authority was sometimes challenged, obeyance without contradiction or question remained the order of the day.

On September 11th 1956, United travelled to the Belgian capital Brussels, for the preliminary round first leg, of the European Cup the following day. Royal Sporting Club of Anderlecht were their opponents. The club and the players were excited at the prospect of measuring themselves against foreign opposition in a competitive match. British clubs had, of course, played friendly matches against teams from Europe before but this was the real thing. The Belgian people treated the United players and officials with friendliness and respect - they couldn't do enough to make the club and the few supporters who had made the journey, more welcome.

The Anderlecht supporters were very knowledgeable about the team from Old Trafford. Of course, this was before many United fans were able to travel to foreign away matches. However, the few Reds who made the trip people were well behaved, courteous and well mannered.

Astrid Park, Anderlecht's floodlit stadium, was a wonderful setting. It was a small, neat ground, far removed from the antiquated monstrosities found at home. The playing surface was exquisite, like a bowling green and made for good football - the game itself had been advertised locally as 'Le Grand Match International en Nocturne.'

Despite the loss of Duncan Edwards through injury, the Reds produced a fine performance, winning 2-0. Jackie Blanchflower took Duncan's place and played a 'blinder'. Anderlecht's most famous player and captain, Jeff Mermans, who had been capped 57 times by Belgium, caused danger in the opening minutes but Viollet made history when he became the first ever Englishman to score in the European Cup midway through the first half.

Dennis set off on a long silky run before firing a fierce shot that hit the Belgian net like a rocket. A penalty save in the second half by Ray Wood preserved the lead and shortly afterwards Tommy Taylor increased United's advantage when he met David Pegg's beautifully floated cross to head home.

United had won their first competitive European match in style. The whole team played to a high standard in a good, sporting fashion. Supporters at home were overjoyed with the result. The average Manchester United follower simply could not afford to take the time off work or incur the expense of going to Belgium. Many were lucky if they could afford a week in Blackpool or North Wales - this was regarded as a foreign land to many - for their summer holidays. Nonetheless, they were one hundred percent behind the team in thought and spirit.

Once home, Busby's thoughts turned toward the next league game at Old Trafford against Sheffield Wednesday in three days' time. Matt and Jimmy Murphy knew that a sloppy performance following their impressive result in Europe would bring scorn from FA and Football League officials and criticism from members of the press not in favour of the European Cup. The players were feeling great and full of beans, ready to keep up their good form.

Inevitably there was newspaper talk that United's players would be tired and weary after the jaunt in Europe. But Sheffield Wednesday would not have agreed with them following a comprehensive 4-1 United win. Johnny Berry, Tommy Taylor, Dennis and Billy Whelan were United's goalscorers. That answered the critics. The following week, the Reds faced Manchester City at Old Trafford. There was a great deal of speculation doing the rounds that United would be taking it easy against their local rivals because of their imminent second leg tie the following Wednesday night against Anderlecht. Dennis and Billy Whelan put paid to that nonsense in a 2-0 blitz of the Blues.

Manchester was buzzing in the days leading up to the return game with Anderlecht. The match was played at Maine Road and as fans rushed straight from work through the rain, it was as if they sensed something special was about to happen.

Indeed it was one of the most memorable games of football any Manchester United team has ever been involved in. They beat the Belgians 10-0, yes, ten goals to nil! United displayed a standard of football that could be compared to the greatest seen anywhere in the world.

To make two comparisons, those lucky enough to remember November 25th 1953 when the great Hungarian team, the 'Magical Magyars', came to Wembley and beat England 6-3, a defeat which ended England's 45-year unbeaten home record against continental teams. The Hungarians gave England a lesson in 'pure footballing magic'. Ron Greenwood, a Chelsea player and later England manager, said it was the most exciting day of his life: "Tomorrow's world was suddenly opened up to us." Attacking football and breathtaking goals, with individual skills that seemed out of this world.

The only other comparison to United's attacking brilliance against Anderlecht would be Real Madrid's destruction of Frankfurt at Hampden Park in May 1960, when the fantastic Real team of di Stefano, Puskas, Gento, Del Sol and Santamaria beat the Germans 7-3 to win the European Cup for the fifth successive time. That was how well United performed on this night of footballing splendour.

The roar of the crowd was deafening. Every Mancunian was proud, this was what Matt Busby had been preaching to them about - broadening theirs and United's horizons. Although the pitch was wet and greasy, with pools of water on various parts of the turf, five goals in each half represented one of the club's finest displays.

Tommy Taylor opened his account with a stunning downward header after just nine minutes. Both teams were serving up a feast of football, the Belgians couldn't seem to master the soaking wet surface and many of their attacks broke down because of the conditions. Taylor got a second, followed four minutes later by Dennis, sharp as a winning greyhound, scored his first from a poor clearance when De Koster, the Belgian centre-half, made a hash of his clearance. Viollet intercepted the ball, waltzed round the goalkeeper and smashed the ball into the rain-sodden net. De Koster was still shaky and was even more red-faced when he played a back pass to his keeper only to watch Dennis move like greased lightning, latch on to the ball and plant it into the net: 4-0. Dennis completed his hat-trick when he received the ball just outside the penalty area and, before the goalkeeper could blink, delivered a rasping left-footed drive into the corner of the goal. 5-0 at half-time in a European Cup match!

This was brilliant football from United, there was no way they were going to ease up and go through the motions. For the next forty-five minutes their thirst for goals became insatiable. The forwards were like sharks that had tasted blood and were going after their prey to complete the job. The build-up play and interpassing from United was almost unbelievable. Taylor made it six and gained his hat-trick, Billy Whelan scored his first then Dennis got another goal, his fourth, after a brilliant run from Roger Byrne. Johnny Berry also got in on the act before Whelan scored his second and United's tenth. Phew! What a performance! Dennis and his team-mates were disappointed though, because they desperately wanted David Pegg to add his name to the scoresheet. Pegg's left-wing partnership with Viollet was becoming one of United's most potent weapons and it was a surprise that England hadn't called them both up for the forthcoming International against Ireland.

The following morning many critics claimed that Anderlecht were a mediocre side. These people were wrong, to beat any team by ten clear goals takes some doing. Many failed to mention that on their previous visit to the British Isles Anderlecht had defeated Arsenal. They were also managed by Bill Gormley, an Englishman, who had played for Blackburn Rovers and they had won the Belgian championship seven times since 1946-47. Jeff Mermans, the Anderlecht captain known in Belgium's 'Mr Soccer', paid United the greatest tribute when he told the press: "They should pick this United team for England. They are that good!" He went on to say that in his opinion the Busby Babes had the craft of the Hungarians and were as fit as the Russians. Mermans, capped 57 times for Belgium, added: "I have never played against a team so adept at the best continental style of football. It was an education to see the kind of football I never expected it from an English side."

Naturally, many thought the Belgian captain gave United lavish praise as an excuse for his team's huge defeat. However Anderlecht played fast and spirited football that would have beaten most teams. It was merely that United rose to this tremendous occasion.

The referee, Mervyn Griffiths said: "United were absolutely awesome! I have refereed teams all over Europe but I have never seen football like United displayed and the precision of their passing was remarkable. Even after they had scored their tenth goal, they were still running as if the game had only just started."

After their first taste of competitive European football the United supporters wanted more. They couldn't wait for the next game to come around and the new competition became the main talking point in pubs and factories, it also raised eyebrows in Europe such was the margin of victory. As Busby had predicted, Mancunians were broadening their horizons, discovering a newfound international presence through the club. Many had only vaguely read about different cities and countries in Europe and they most certainly could never have afforded to travel to these destinations. So it was with great pride and anticipation that they read every morsel of information in magazines and newspapers about United's fantastic voyage to these lands across the sea.

Dennis was called up for the Football League match against the League of Ireland in Dublin as replacement for the injured Johnny Haynes. After scoring nine goals in nine league games and five goals in two European Cup matches, it was a worthy honour for this quiet, unassuming player. It seems hard to believe nowadays, but clubs had to continue with their fixtures despite their players playing in international games in the late 1950s.

For the visit of Charlton Athletic in October 1956, United lost four players: Byrne, Edwards and Taylor were in the England team, while Jackie Blanchflower was playing for Northern Ireland against England in Belfast. Can you imagine clubs and managers standing for this sort of thing today? Mind you, those international call-ups opened the door for the debut of a future footballing legend, Bobby Charlton. United won the game 4-2, Bobby scoring twice with Johnny Berry and Billy Whelan getting a goal apiece.

In his season and a half in the first team Dennis had developed a truly unique partnership with Tommy Taylor.

Their understanding of each other's play was almost telepathic, they seemed to know where each other wanted the ball and where each would run at certain points in a game - team-mates joked that they'd find each other in the dark. Later in his life Dennis went out of his way to praise Tommy. Busby and Murphy knew that Dennis was at his best with a big, powerful leader at the side of him, Dennis loved playing off such a character and scored plenty of his goals because of big Tommy's unselfish service in the air and on the ground.

Defenders didn't like the well-built, curly-haired front man charging toward their goal. Yet what made centre-forward Taylor different from most strikers of the period was his ability to roam out to the wing, a tactic which caused the centre-halves of the 50s no end of problems. The centre-half and his other defenders were used to dealing with a centre-forward who stayed in the middle, a character who would battle with them for the ball, leap for high centres and enjoy a battle with them. Tommy Taylor could play that role but he also had a touch of the continental about his play, he didn't just react but thought his way around the field, pulling defenders out of position, allowing players from midfield and the wings space to play.

Dennis once said of Taylor: "I knew instinctively where to run whenever I saw him going up to head the ball. Sometimes he would just glance his header down to the side of him which enabled me to run on to it. He could get up so high from a standing position - it was amazing really. I enjoyed playing with all the United lads but I had a special sort of bonding with Tommy. When he made those decoy runs out to both wings I used to anticipate where the ball would be delivered and I often managed to get a goal or two from Tommy's intelligent play. He also had great awareness about his play. People said I was at my best when

I played alongside him, well that's true, but any inside-forward would have been able to play well with Tommy alongside them. Reporters didn't, or I should say, couldn't appreciate the way Tommy played. He worked tremendously hard for his Manchester United and England colleagues, always ready to receive the ball and ready to take defenders on a tiring run in order to leave space for me and other players. And he was so brave. Like many others, Tommy was a vastly underrated player and in my opinion a magnificent centre-forward."

Having easily disposed of Anderlecht, United were drawn against West German champions Borussia Dortmund. Once again the home leg had to be played at Maine Road and 75,598 fans packed the ground for the occasion. Once again Manchester was hit by European Cup fever with people in pubs, clubs, factories and shops all discussing United's chances against the teak-tough German outfit. Following the Anderlecht performance expectations had grown to almost ludicrous proportions. Initially, the Germans were dismissed as veterans, but though a great deal older than Busby's team they were also a great deal more experienced.

It was a mild October evening when the two teams lined up to thunderous applause. United, full of youth and zest, tore into their opponents just as they had against the Belgians. However, the Germans in their golden satin shirts and black shorts attacked ferociously and the United defence was quickly under extreme pressure. Nevertheless, after 27 minutes United were two goals in front, Dennis the scorer each time. This was Viollet at his brilliant best. Using short, crisp and fast close passing movements, the Reds sent him through the strong Borussia defence like a hot knife through butter and Dennis didn't fail on either occasion.

Kwiatowski, the German goalkeeper, who had borrowed

a green goalkeeper's jersey from Manchester City goalkeeper Bert Trautmann before the game, was very agile and threw himself around in his goal area like a breakdancer. However, despite his efforts, within seconds of Viollet's second goal, Bursmuller, while trying to control a shot from David Pegg, helped the ball into his own net to put United 3-0 in front leaving the huge Maine Road throng screaming themselves hoarse.

Dennis was like an electric eel, darting all over the German half in an effort to get more goals and make the tie safe. He then had a nasty accident, as he turned quickly he banged heads with the Dortmund right-half. He had to leave the field not returning until early in the second half. He was quickly back into action and both he and Tommy Taylor were blasting the Borussia goalkeeper with shots and headers, Dennis's slim outline could be seen weaving in and out of the dazed and dazzled German defenders.

A second European hat-trick from darting Dennis, looked almost certain to follow and, with United 3-0 up, the game seemed over. However Dortmund twice produced the famed German fighting spirit to score two late goals. These goals could be blamed on United's inexperience. Roger Byrne breasted the ball down and instead of clearing it upfield, passed back to Ray Wood. Kapitulski latched on to it, ran forward and shot past a helpless Wood. A few minutes later, the Germans scored again from another defensive error. In the end the German team could feel hard done that they hadn't got an equaliser. The tie was back in the balance.

After the game, two coaches waited outside Maine Road to whisk the players and officials into the city centre for a banquet at the Midland Hotel. As Dennis stepped outside the dressing room he spotted his old school chum Alan Wallace, on leave from the army. Dennis shouted Alan over and sat him on the official Manchester United coach. The two pals had a good old chinwag while the other players made their way onto the bus to go to the reception.

Alan, Dennis and the rest of the United lads gave the German team and officials a beautiful banquet in the Midland Hotel in the city centre. The players from both teams attended the reception. Sometimes these occasions were irksome and the United players would sneak away after the speeches and presentations were completed, heading for the nightclubs to have a quiet drink and relax while chatting about the night's game. Dennis loved this aspect of the European games. He could certainly feel pleased with himself because he had played excellently. These were the kind of games where Dennis was at his best. However, whenever he was congratulated on his performance, he would make a point of praising his colleagues for making the goal chances for him but on this particular night he had been the goal snatcher supreme!

Karl Smith first heard the name Dennis Viollet in the mid-1950s as a boy of eight. His mother and father ran the Thatched House Hotel on Market Street in the centre of Manchester, where the Arndale Centre now stands. The *Manchester Evening News* was also close by and several of the reporters used to congregate in the hotel for a pint of ale to discuss the fortunes of the teams they covered. Karl heard plenty about Dennis. "He [Viollet] is the main man," Karl heard one particular reporter say. Another connoisseur was heard to say announce: "The United team revolves around him. He's like quicksilver." Karl badgered his older brother, who was a United follower, to take him to a game and, after a great deal of persuading, the older Smith reluctantly agreed. "I enjoyed it immensely and from then on I had a hero," said Karl. His hero was Dennis Viollet! One particular game which stands out in Karl's mind was when

Voyage of Sinbad

United played Blackpool at Old Trafford. "I watched Dennis play and I was in awe of him, the neat way he headed goals, his accurate and powerful shooting. I remember George Farm, the Blackpool goalkeeper, fumbling a corner at the Stretford End, the United players were all running out of the box, except Viollet. He paused and back-heeled the ball into the net. The crowd rose to him. I can picture him even now, just sauntering back to the centre, no fuss or hand waving, just a cheeky smirk to the crowd."

A first-half goal by Dennis for United against Sunderland at Roker Park paved the way for a splendid 3-1 victory, which gave them breathing space at the top of the league table. Billy Whelan got the other goal along with an own goal. Of more concern for Busby was Dennis's groin strain, which would continue to cause him problems all season.

Records are meant to be broken, but sometimes it is a surprise when it happens. Everton's visit in mid-October seemed a foregone conclusion when judging the form of the two teams but United fans were shell-shocked as the Babes were on the wrong end of a 5-2 thrashing at Old Trafford. Dennis missed this game because of the injury he picked up against Sunderland and the defeat ended a 26-match unbeaten run in the league. Everton even fielded young debutant Albert Dunlop in goal, although it must be said he had a magnificent match. Bobby Charlton took Dennis's place in the forward line and scored. Perhaps the significance of Dennis Viollet to United's play was illustrated by the result.

Matt Busby felt his young team needed a break and a change of environment for a few days so he took the team, Dennis included, to Blackpool. After breathing the clean sea air and enjoying a spot of light training on the sand, the team felt nice and relaxed before the Derby against City at Maine Road in the FA Charity Shield. United won 1-0, but

95

for Dennis this was a very special moment. "Scoring this goal probably gave me more pleasure than any other goal I can remember scoring," he said. "My mum and dad were City fans really so to go back home and win such an important game made it a very special occasion for me." 15-year-old David Gaskell was thrown into action due to an injury during the match to Ray Wood. Gaskell played brilliantly, so much so that a television commentator thought Wood had returned to action in the second half.

Wood was also forced to miss the next game away to Blackpool, which ended in a 2-2 draw thanks to two Tommy Taylor headers. Dennis again suffered from his groin injury and it was this injury that forced him to pull out of a Football League appearance up at Newcastle the following week. He also had to miss a few United games, including the vital second leg of the European Cup tie in Germany. Matt Busby decided he would put Duncan Edwards in Dennis's place, with young Wilf McGuinness playing at left-half. United, with their backs to the wall, clung on to a respectable 0-0 draw in Dortmund and qualified for the European Cup quarterfinals.

For this latest European tie, a proper club trip was organised for supporters. Fans were flown from Ringway to Bilbao, spent two nights in a hotel, were transported to and from the match, and had centre stand seats before winging their way back to Manchester. The total cost? £29.

The late Sammy Smythe, landlord of the Swan Hotel in Crumpsall, north Manchester, organised the trips. Sammy, a lifelong United fan, did a great deal of voluntary work for United over a number of years. These travelling reds quickly became known as 'Globetrotting Fans'. But the continental engagements of United gave supporters the chance to prove that they would follow the Busby Babes to the end of the earth. After the success of the German trip, a

36-seater aircraft was booked to go to Spain to watch United play Bilbao.

Dennis missed the next five matches due to injury, but was back in time for the away fixture at Aston Villa on December 8th, which United won 3-1 with goals from Taylor(2) and Dennis. The Reds were still leading the First Division and Dennis was in great nick, a fact emphasised by him scoring in successive victories against Cardiff City and Portsmouth. The match against Portsmouth at Fratton Park was United's first victory there since the 1947-48 season. They made hard work of it: Henderson scored a 'gift' goal for Portsmouth just before the interval; after 48 minutes David Pegg got the equaliser; Duncan Edwards playing at centre-forward in place of the injured Taylor put them in front; four minutes later, in the 69th minute, Edwards delivered a beautiful pass through for Dennis to score a picture goal.

Puskas Wants To Join United

Ferenc Puskas is one of the greatest footballers of any era. He ranks alongside the greats: Pele, di Stefano, Maradona, Matthews, Finney. Indeed if any great player can lay claim to being a legend, then this squat, tubby little inside-forward with the magical left foot would stand comparison with any of them. Known as the 'Galloping Major' he was the master craftsman of the great Hungarian team that went unbeaten for four years, became Olympic Champions in 1952 and widely known as the 'Golden Squad'.

When the Hungarians came to Wembley Stadium in 1953 and thrashed England 6-3, many English sceptics believed this was a fluke result. A few months later, in Budapest, they walloped us again, as if to prove the point, this time 7-1. The architect of both victories was Puskas: a tactical genius and maker and taker of goals. In 84 matches for Hungary he scored 83 times - he remains the most prolific international goalscorer of all time.

After the Hungarian Uprising in 1956 Puskas turned 30 and many observers reckoned that he was finished, yet he made these critics look foolish when he began a second phase of his illustrious career. He joined Real Madrid and made them into the greatest club side in the world, yet Manchester United could have had him for nothing.

By 1956 Puskas was a political refugee and he and a couple of his team-mates were over in England trying to join an English team when he told journalists he would love to play for Manchester United. Matt Busby was flattered that one of the greatest footballers in the world thought so highly of his club, but told the press that he wasn't interested in signing the great Hungarian.

"You can count me out," he told them. "I am building a young team, and the last thing I would dream of doing would be to sign any continental players, no matter how big their reputation. In a year or two's time, some of my young 'uns will be as good if not better than any players in the world." He later told journalists that in Dennis Viollet he had a brilliantly gifted inside-forward who he forecast was a near certainty to play for England on a regular basis. He also mentioned Billy Whelan and told them not to forget Bobby Charlton: "A boy you are going to hear a great deal about." Puskas went on to sign for Real but it shows the calibre of the young players United had on their staff that Busby was willing to forego such a gifted genius for the opportunity of keeping the Babes on track.

After Christmas, United embarked on two wildly contrasting cup games: away at Hartlepool in the FA Cup before travelling to Northern Spain to play Atletico Bilbao. In the end the weather was better in Hartlepool than in 'sunny' Spain!

Dennis was a little distracted at this stage however as

his wife Barbara was expecting their second child while conditions at the Victoria Ground, Hartlepool didn't help - it was pouring down.

However United, with Edwards and Colman in brilliant form, cruised into an early 3-0 lead with goals from Whelan, Berry and Taylor, before a tremendous fightback by the Third Division side saw them embarrass United and draw level midway through the second half. A late winner by Billy Whelan put United into the hat for round four, where they drew another away tie, this time at Wrexham. Three days later Barbara presented Dennis with a beautiful bouncing boy, who the couple christened Roger after Dennis's friend, Roger Byrne. He was overjoyed, the father of a daughter and a son.

As if to celebrate the new arrival, United limbered up for Spain with a convincing 6-1 over Newcastle - Dennis, Billy Whelan and David Pegg scoring a brace each.

Not so Sunny Spain

Boarding the old Dakota at Ringway, the United players were in a happy mood, laughing and joking with each other - after all, they were leaving cold, rainy Manchester and were on their way to the sunshine of Spain, or so they thought. Mind you, Billy Whelan and Mark Jones, not the best of travellers at times were airsick and chairman Harold Hardman, who was 75, suffered a stroke en route and when the aircraft landed he was rushed to hospital and missed the game.

To make matters worse the pilot, Captain Riley, asked everyone to keep their eyes open for the runway. "When the captain made this announcement over the tannoy, we all looked at each other," remarked Dennis. "Can you believe it, the passengers being asked to keep a look out for the runway?" Duncan Edwards, his face green, looked as if he would be sick at any moment. The airport had been closed because of heavy snow, when the plane eventually touched down it was freezing cold and the team disembarked into a blizzard.

To add to the perilous journey, the food served in the hotel was not to the players' liking and Tommy Taylor had an upset stomach. Walter Crickmer, the club secretary, went into the hotel kitchen to speak to the chef about the food, but he couldn't understand him. Despite everything, the team made the best of the situation and had a laugh and joke among themselves. The weather showed no sign of improvement though and prospects for the game looked doubtful. This was a big worry for Matt Busby, he knew that any kind of postponement would bring trouble from the FA.

The following day, after several pitch inspections, the referee declared the game could be played and Busby offered a silent prayer. However, when the players went to inspect the pitch they couldn't believe how bad the playing surface was - in any other situation this game would not have been played.

Nevertheless, despite the dreadful weather over 45,000 spectators stood with their berets on their heads and umbrellas up trying to fend off the rain inside the San Mames Stadium and, as the players made their way onto the field, the heavy rain turned into snow. The pitch, already pathetic, turned into a mudbath. Playing in unfamiliar blue shirts, United soon got into action; Dennis nearly scoring but seeing his shot go wide. Bilbao, playing in their usual red and white stripes, quickly settled down and adapted much better to the worsening conditions, so much so that they were 3-0 in front by half-time.

In the second half United fought back brilliantly and within eight minutes had pulled a goal back, Dennis passing for his partner Taylor to score. The noise of the Spanish crowd was frightening at times - they were certainly very vocal. Five minutes later Dennis made it 3-2 and the crowd went silent. The German referee gave some mysterious free kicks against United later and it was no surprise when the Spanish champions scored another two goals. Some of the play resembled a pantomime because of the conditions, but the lads from Manchester fought back furiously.

Five minutes from time Billy Whelan made it 5-3 with one of the greatest individual goals ever seen on any ground. Whelan was waiting just inside his own half when Edwards spotted him unmarked and delivered a beautiful pass. With Viollet and Taylor moving at speed on either side of him, Billy ignored them and went on a dribbling spree through the mud and the heart of the Bilbao defence, dodging the Spanish defenders who were charging at him like snorting bulls. Jimmy Murphy was jumping up and down shouting for Billy to pass, Matt Busby could hardly watch and the strength of the slimly-built Irish lad must have been ebbing away after running an incredible distance with the ball apparently glued to his boots. This kind of magic didn't deserve to end in failure and it didn't! With the energy-sapping mud taking its toll Billy let fly into the top left hand corner of the Bilbao net for a really fantastic goal. Poor Billy was nearly drowned in the sea of mud as the Babes converged on him to celebrate a truly memorable wonder goal. Meanwhile the United officials danced, clapped, and yelled deliriously in the mud, even Busby and Murphy were laughing and crying with joy. What a brilliantly taken solo effort from the quietest member of the team - 5-3 the final score and Manchester and the rest of England were proud of these fighting Busby Babes.

The journey home proved another nightmare. The Dakota that United had flown into Bilbao had been left on the runway because the hanger was full and it was covered in thick snow and ice. The engineer who had been flown out from England to service the aircraft did his job but the pilot refused to fly. Busby was worried because United's next game was away to Sheffield Wednesday the following Saturday. So the players and officials got busy with brushes and shovels and freed the aircraft. Could you imagine this sort of thing happening today?

Billy Whelan, no doubt still exhausted from his amazing goal, sat out the excavation of the plane and with a big grin on his face took photographs of his hard-working team-mates. When they finally received permission to take off, the flight proved worse than the outgoing one. The plane ran into a gale and the United party and officials were petrified. Going into Jersey to refuel, the aircraft dipped alarmingly and bounced on the runway. Flying was in its infancy and nothing like it is today, hence the refuelling. Once back in Manchester Dennis and his pals were very relieved indeed.

All the newspaper talk was about the mammoth task United faced in the return leg at Maine Road on 6th February. For the time being at least it was a case of getting on with league business the following Saturday. United were bound to be tired and jaded after the horrific journey and heavy conditions in Spain. Sheffield Wednesday their opponents at Hillsborough showed them no mercy and United lost 2-1.

Then United played twice in in four days at Maine Road, beating Manchester City 4-2 in a league game: Edwards, Taylor, Whelan and Dennis scoring the goals before the return leg against Bilbao. Could they pull three goals back? Everybody had an opinion about that issue. The United players and management most certainly believed they could achieve what appeared to be an impossible task.

A crowd of 65,000 crammed into Maine Road for what

would turn out to be one of the greatest nights of European football. The noise of the fans was phenomenal and this was before the kick-off. All through the game the devoted and loyal United supporters screamed, yelled, clapped, used their rattles and bells and made the biggest volume of noise ever heard before at a football match.

Dennis was razor-sharp, so too were all the team, however the match was still goalless just before half-time when a Duncan Edwards rocket was blocked by a Bilbao defender, only for the quicksilver Viollet to nip in and slip the ball into the net. Once again the sound that greeted the goal made the hairs on the back of your neck stand on end.

Could United get the other two goals required? That was the question everybody was again asking. Dennis believed that he had answered that question twice, but both goals were disallowed. Dennis swore that he was onside for the first while the second was disallowed because the referee said the ball had touched Billy Whelan who was offside.

Meanwhile Tommy Taylor was at his majestic best. This was one of his greatest ever games for United. It was big Tommy who scored the second goal and levelled the tie, then, with six minutes remaining, Tommy went on a powerful run, squared the ball for Johnny Berry who rammed home the winner to send United into the semi-finals of the European Cup. This remains one of the club's greatest victories, ranking alongside other great nights in the Nou Camp in 1999 and Wembley in 1968. Maine Road erupted into a volume of deafening noise - the score was flashed onto Cinema screens throughout Manchester to loud cheers. The scenes of jubilation all over the city were reminiscent of VE day.

Harry Gregg, at the time a Doncaster Rovers player, remembers being caught up in the excitement of United's victory, even in Yorkshire: "I was a big star in a small pool at Doncaster Rovers. I was in my digs with a few of my team-mates watching the highlights on one of those old 12-inch black and white television sets. The following day all the Doncaster players were in the dressing-room talking about the great Busby Babes, when our manager the greatest Irish player I have ever seen, Peter Doherty, came into the dressing room. He told us he had been at the game and that the finest player on the pitch hardly got a mention: "The boy Viollet. He was the finest player on the pitch." I always remembered this, and when I joined United, Peter was proved right. Believe me, Dennis Viollet was a genius, one of the best all-round players I ever saw or played with. He wasn't big in stature, but he had a lovely build. Dennis could play anywhere, he was a great, great player, in a wonderful team."

Harry said that when he joined Manchester United in December 1957 he roomed with Dennis on United's away trip to Luton. "He was a real genuine character," said an enthusiastic Gregg. "I got taught lessons. I came from the sticks, as green as grass, I was as happy as can be when I joined these superstars, and here was Dennis teaching me about life. The word 'great' is a word that is overused in my opinion, but I have no hesitation in using it when describing Dennis Viollet. He made the Busby Babes team function like a Rolls Royce engine. He had the quality to be a striker and a schemer, there is no doubt about that, no doubt at all. The nearest player I could compare him with believe it or not is Denis Law! Both were outstanding strikers, both had that sizzling pace over short distances that made them special. And both had what is called a 'football brain', they were able to size up situations before anybody else, and they were the greatest in their use of the one-two pass, absolutely brilliant.

"I can remember playing against Preston North End, one

of our defenders got injured and Dennis dropped back to right full-back and he was magnificent. Dennis didn't make a lot of noise about it but he could take care of himself on the field, he was quiet but he could look after himself. Another great attribute he possessed was that he never mouthed off on the pitch, ever. Later, when he captained United, he led by example, by his own God-given talents. And now, all these years later I realise that Peter Doherty had never been so right, Dennis Viollet was the gem in the crown of that great Busby Babes team."

Dennis himself spoke very glowingly about his forward striking partner Tommy Taylor after the Bilbao game: "Tommy and I worked really well together. He was the perfect foil for me. Many's the time he would fool defenders into following him, letting the ball run on and leaving me in the clear for a shot at goal. In the Bilbao match he ran rings around Garay, probably the best centrehalf in the world. Off he would go with his beautiful, graceful movements."

Wilf McGuinness was born in Collyhurst, on the north side of Manchester. Later his family moved to Blackley where Wilf attended Mount Carmel School. He captained Manchester, Lancashire and England Schoolboys and played in 81 League games for United. He was also a Youth and England Under-23 international, was capped twice for the England first team before a broken leg ended his promising career at the age of 22 in 1959. He later joined United's coaching staff and then became manager for a brief spell.

Wilf is Manchester United through and through and is one of the best ambassadors United could have: "The game against Bilbao was Dennis Viollet at his very best," said an enthusiastic McGuinness. "Tommy Taylor had a fantastic game, but Dennis was absolute class. His control of the ball was great, no matter at what angle the ball was played up to him he would have it under control in a split-second. What defenders never understood when marking Dennis was his uncanny knack of being in the right place at the right time. He needed just three steps and he was in front of goal, he didn't rush or run at full speed to get into a goalscoring position like other forwards do. It was effortless for him. All the older players at Old Trafford and also at other clubs called him a pro's pro. In the Bilbao match it was an education to watch his movement off the ball. He easily glided into open spaces to receive the ball, Dennis was a footballer, a creator, always thinking two or three moves ahead and his intelligent use of the ball to big Tommy and out to the wings was beautiful to watch."

Wilf smiled broadly when talking about Dennis away from football. "He was so unassuming, lovely manners, always smiling and caring. He was about four years older than Bobby, Duncan, Eddie Colman and myself and we looked up to him. Before Munich if we had any problems we would go to Roger Byrne, and he would sort things out for us but Dennis was always considerate and helpful. He had this air about him, he looked distinguished: intelligent and sophisticated. We used to attend quite a few supporters' club dances and the crowning of Miss Manchester United - Dennis would be selected to put the crown on the young lady's head.

"I learned a great deal about things other than football from Dennis. For example, when we were teenagers and went to the Plaza or the Ritz and met a girl we fancied, we would let them buy their own drinks then sit next to them. The conversation would be about the pictures or a new record in the hit parade, nothing topical or serious. If we fancied taking them home we would arrange to meet them at the bus stop in Piccadilly where all the night buses left for destinations throughout the Manchester area. Then we would wait until they got on the bus, get on behind them, and sit next to them after they'd paid their fare. Only little things, certainly unromantic, but remember this was in the fifties, we were all innocent.

"Compare Dennis to our feeble attempts at wooing the ladies. There is no comparison really. He was a real smoothie! He would gently kiss a lady's hand and engage women in conversation, listening to them intently, making them feel so important and beautiful. Compare his method at ordering drinks, to our cackhanded attempts! Dennis would order a bottle of wine, followed by a rose. Wow! What a charmer; he never boasted, gloated, used coarse language or was aggressive to them, he was sophistication personified and they adored his methods."

Manchester United were flying high in all competitions. They'd reached the semi-final of the European Cup, a 5-0 victory at Wrexham put them in the fifth round of the FA Cup and a 6-2 home victory over Arsenal left them well clear at the top of Division One. Schoolboy chums were in opposition, Dennis for United and David Herd for Arsenal, with Herd amongst the goals in that match. A thundering shot from Duncan Edwards settled the fifth round FA Cup match at Old Trafford against Everton. Dennis was injured in this game and was forced to miss the match at Charlton in midweek. Mind you, the quality of United's squad was seen by Bobby Charlton replacing Dennis, and showing his liking for his namesakes by scoring a hat-trick in a 5-1 win. It also emphasised what Busby meant when he said he was not interested in signing Puskas a few weeks earlier.

Dennis's groin injury was still causing him discomfort and despite regular treatment it just would not clear up, forcing him to miss vital matches as United's season really came to the boil. Home defeats by Blackpool and Bolton, for which the Old Trafford floodlights were officially opened, showed Viollet's importance to the team and that importance was intensified by an injury to Tommy Taylor.

For the vital FA Cup semi-final against an experienced Birmingham team at Hillsborough, Dennis returned to the side. He wasn't one hundred percent fit by any means. However, Matt Busby decided to play him at centre-forward, with Bobby Charlton at inside-left. United had gone to Blackpool to prepare in the days before the vital cup-tie.

Birmingham were a big, powerful side who had lost to Manchester City in the FA Cup final just twelve months before. They were confident of a return to Wembley and intent on avenging the memory of that defeat. Birmingham were known as a hard-working side capable of inspired performances, particular in cup-ties. Their defence boasted the stylish England international goalkeeper Gil Merrick, another England international, Jeff Hall at full-back and tough tackling skipper Roy Warhurst, who would later join Manchester City.

Though Dennis wore the number nine jersey, he played in a withdrawn position. He used his intelligence to roam and create openings for his colleagues. Berry put United into the lead against his old club, Charlton got the vital second goal, a scorcher. United's youngsters played superb football. Their fluency and interchanging left the big Brummie defenders chasing shadows. Yes, United were still in with a chance of the treble.

Alec Johnson, a prominent sports journalist and close friend of Dennis, was at the semi-final against Birmingham to report the match for his newspaper. After the game, Tommy Taylor asked if Alec would mind if he travelled back to Manchester with him. Alec readily agreed. On their journey back over the Pennines they discussed the game and Tommy was in raptures over Dennis's performance: "I'll have a job getting my place back in the team," Tommy told the journalist. "Wasn't Dennis brilliant today? The way he drifts into space and makes it easy for other players to give him the ball is marvellous. He wasn't really match fit but he played a blinder." Alec said that all the way back to Manchester Tommy was praising his striking partner.

Incidentally, Karl Smith recalls seeing Dennis Viollet on the Monday after the Birmingham game. Dennis was booking some driving lessons and Karl's brother was running the Manchester School of Motoring while the owner was away and he was filling in Dennis's application form. They got talking about the game and Dennis told Karl's brother about the semi-final.

The Brummies had a big, gruesome centre-half, named Trevor Smith, who could put himself about a bit. During the game the referee blew the whistle because somebody was hurt. "It was very muddy," Dennis told Karl's brother. "I heard Trevor Smith shouting me. I thought now there's going to be trouble. Just before the whistle blew, we had both gone down in the mud after colliding into each other, and I thought he was angry with me, instead he told me he had lost his set of false teeth and asked if I would help him find them. So there we were on all fours in the penalty area searching for them!" They laughed about the incident. "Did he find them?" asked Karl's brother. "Yes," Dennis laughed aloud, "the teeth were buried in the mud!"

Dennis was out injured again after the semi-final victory and it was a race against time to get him fit for the eagerly awaited match against Real Madrid in Spain on April 11th. After intensive treatment both he and Tommy Taylor were declared fit and were back in the team for this important game. Both Dennis and Tommy Taylor had played in a midweek Central League fixture against Derby County at the Baseball Ground. The pitch was icy and rock hard but both of them were soon on the scoresheet, Tommy getting a rivetting hat-trick and Dennis scoring twice. Matt Busby and Jimmy Murphy were delighted with the way the two players had performed. Both played in a scoreless draw at home against Tottenham on the Saturday before flying off to Madrid for their Wednesday encounter with Real.

Real Madrid were a fabulous side in every respect and they were vastly more experienced than the young United players. They had world-class players in the great Argentine Alfredo di Stefano, the classy Frenchman Raymond Kopa, Gento, Madrid's flying left winger Rial and their defenders were all big tough fellows who took no prisoners. Madrid were the holders of the European Cup. The game was played in the magnificent Bernebeu in front of a capacity 130,000 crowd.

Despite United's defensive heroics, Madrid won the match 3-1. United kept the rampant Madrid players at bay until the 60th minute, when Gento, the fastest footballer the British press had ever seen, scored. Tommy Taylor had almost put United in front minutes earlier but missed the best chance of the match. Ray Wood played a 'blinder' and kept United in the hunt. In fact the entire United defence put on a wonderful performance to keep the Real forwards at bay. Taylor finally scored to make it 2-1 before they conceded a late goal.

David Pegg had a good game and was always dangerous darting down the left wing. It has to be said though that Madrid used strong-arm tactics when there really was no need. They roughed United's forwards up and Dennis was kept quiet by the ruthlessness of the Spaniards' methods. Poor old Tommy Taylor seemed to be fighting a lone battle up front, but he never stopped trying.

The British press wrote the following day that Real had got away with murder. George Follows of the *Daily Herald* said he had never witnessed such crude and violent tackling as that seen in the Madrid display. He singled out Marquitos, the centre-half, as the worst culprit. It was the general consensus of the British press that Dutch referee Leo Horn had been far too lenient with the Madrid players and allowed skulduggery to continue without taking any kind of action. There really appeared to be no need for the Spaniards to use such foul and intimidating methods, however, their attitude was a mark of respect for United who they clearly saw as a real threat to their European Champion status. Nevertheless foul means spoiled a great game and United couldn't handle it, Madrid were the better team on the day there was no disputing that it was another lesson learned for the youngsters.

The second leg would be played under the Old Trafford floodlights on 25th April. United were so desperate to get Dennis fully fit, they nursed him over the Easter fixtures, only playing him at home against Burnley when they fielded eight reserves. Only Dennis, Ray Wood and Bill Foulkes of the regular team played.

The Real Thing

Before United took the field against Real, they had confirmed that they were First Division Champions for the second successive year. They were also in the final of the FA Cup to be played at Wembley Stadium two weeks later. So to all intents and purpose they were still in with a chance of a unique treble! The question on everybody's lips was: "Could they repeat their magic of Bilbao against Real Madrid?"

Sadly Dennis was not fit to play, having played on the previous Saturday at Old Trafford against Burnley when United won 2-0. United had made eight changes for the league game and given a debut to 17-year-old centre-forward Alex Dawson, who scored the first. Though Dennis played against Burnley he had looked far from his usual razor-sharp self and seemed to be nursing himself through the game. He had, of course missed the previous two matches because of his groin injury and desperately wanted to be fit for both the Madrid game and the cup final coming quickly after.

Meanwhile, newspaper gossip surrounded the swarthy youngster filling in for Tommy Taylor, Alex Dawson. Alex weighed in at 12 stones and had only recently signed professional forms with United. He had made his debut in the Central League at Everton as a right-winger but after scoring 21 times in 26 appearances in the Central League he was given his chance.

Real Madrid put on a soccer spectacle under the floodlights of Old Trafford, the first European Cup match played at United's home. The Reds tried to match them but lacked experience. Nevertheless it was a cracking match with brilliant football and world-class individual performances from both teams. If noise could have won the game then United would have had no problems - the supporters did their team proud. They encouraged them with non-stop chanting, singing, hand clapping, bugleblowing, stamping and anything else they thought might help the team.

Jimmy Murphy later praised the fans for their continued support throughout the entire ninety minutes. Taylor was tripped twice and kneed in the back in the opening minutes. Jackie Blanchflower had a brilliant game against di Stefano. Both sides played hard and fast, it was a thrill a minute. The referee incensed the crowd with some mysterious decisions and Taylor was blatantly flattened in the Madrid penalty area only for it to be ignored. Di Stefano showed his brilliance and world class skills, Duncan Edwards played like a man possessed, he was here, there, everywhere.

Kopa got the first goal, engineered by di Stefano. Eight minutes later United were two goals down when Gento centred and put so much power and spin on the ball that it slipped from Ray Wood's grasp for Mateos to score. Ominously for United, Madrid then moved up a couple of gears and displayed the breathtaking skills which made them the best team in the world. Even the United supporters had to admit that this was the kind of excitement and football they would like to see more often.

United's young team never knew when they were beaten though and they tried to pull off the impossible. Taylor in particular tore into the Madrid defence and only the giant Marquitos kept him at bay. The Spanish defence was rock solid, only a special kind of magic would prise it open.

Eleven minutes after the interval Taylor scored and the level of noise increased. Five minutes from the final whistle, Bobby Charlton, deputising for Dennis, got the equaliser and the crowd went berserk. The chants of "United, United, United," could be heard for miles around. It was 5-3 on aggregate to the Madrid masters, could the Reds pull it back? Sadly they couldn't but no team could have tried harder. To give a world-class team like Real Madrid a two goal start and pull back to draw 2-2 was remarkable in itself. Dennis was bitterly disappointed to have missed the game but he, like everyone else who saw it, recognised the different techniques of the Madrid side. The United team were young and inexperienced at this stage of their development and they could only get better. There was little doubt in the Busby and Murphy minds that they were in charge of a team that would eventually win the European Cup. In this first season in the competition they were the only team to come close to Madrid and with players like Bobby Charlton, Albert Scanlon, Wilf McGuinness and Kenny Morgans vying for regular first team action, they were certain to win it within a few years.

Dennis played in the last two league games, the first a 3-2 victory away at Cardiff - Albert Scanlon scoring twice and Alex Dawson again on the score sheet, to take United's final tally of away points to 32 out of a possible 42. It was also their 11th league double of the season, smashing the record previously held by Arsenal in 1935. It was to United's credit that they were able to achieve this distinction with a team that included five reserves and played with only ten men for most of the game. Jackie Blanchflower had been injured in the opening minutes and there had to be a defensive reshuffle, depriving Dennis of a full 90 minutes in his favourite inside-left position because he dropped back to play wing-half and had a storming game. Bill Foulkes moved to centre-half and acquitted himself well. Bill was never flashy or spectacular but was one of the most consistent players in United's team. Young Alex Dawson had another good game and scored. Colin Webster, keen to impress the Welsh selectors after being one of twenty nominated for a Welsh cap in the World Cup series, helped Albert Scanlon to get two goals with his astute passing.

On Monday April 22nd, the Leeds fans mobbed the Welsh giant John Charles after he had scored two goals as Leeds beat Sunderland 3-1. It was his last league match before joining Juventus. The two goals brought big John's goal tally to 39 for the season. There was a great deal of criticism regarding Charles moving to Italy. He was the first really well-known star to move overseas and several managers expressed concern that Italian clubs would bribe our best players to Italy with big money. There was mention that the Italians were after Duncan Edwards and Tommy Taylor as well as other United players. Busby was livid at these suggestions and said outright that no United player would be leaving Old Trafford under any circumstances. "We are building a young team that can only get better with

experience. Also, we are grooming younger players in order
to keep Manchester United at the top, it's not right for the
Italians to come along and sign our players."

The last game of the season was played at Old Trafford, a
1-1 draw with West Bromwich Albion. With the Cup Final
in mind, Mark Jones came through the game without the
slightest doubt about his injured knee, which had kept
him out of first-team action since early March. For Dennis
however, the game brought mixed fortunes and failed to
shed any light on his fitness for Wembley.

United were crowned First Division champions with a
record 64 points, the best in the First Division since 1931
when Arsenal got 66. They had made certain of winning
the championship with a 4-0 win against Sunderland five
days before the Madrid game at Old Trafford. The trophy
was presented to skipper Roger Byrne by Mr H Shentall,
the vice-president of the League, and Mr N Brooks. All the
regular first team players were present.

One big point which did emerge among the injuries
towards the end of the season was the potential of United's
great centreforward prospect, 17-year-old Alex Dawson.
He took the honours in an exciting attacking display and
the newspapers were of the opinion that he was destined
to follow Tommy Taylor (England) and Colin Webster
(Wales) by becoming yet another United player to win an
international cap, this time for Scotland.

Alex joined United in 1956 straight from school.
Born in Aberdeen he had played for the same Aberdeen
schoolboy team as Denis Law. When Alex was 11 his father,
a trawlerman on the deep-sea fishing boats, moved the family
to Hull. Young Dawson became a Busby Babe and a prolific
goalscorer. He recalled as a homesick youngster the kindness
shown him by Dennis Viollet: "Dennis always had a big
smile on his face and asked if I'd settled down in my digs,

he encouraged not only me, but all the other newcomers at the club. Those first team players like Dennis, Tommy Taylor, Eddie Colman and Duncan Edwards were like Gods to us apprentices, let alone the supporters. They were great people.

"Dennis was an immaculate player, an artist, as light-footed as a ballet dancer. He had an eye for goal and was as quick in thoughts and movements as a cobra. Dennis did something while most of his opponents were thinking about doing something and his speed created many openings for other players. One of the reasons for his success was that he knew the exact moment to release the ball. Tommy Taylor and the other lads I am sure would be the first to admit how much they owed to his assistance. A great, great player."

At 16 Alex was promoted into United's star-studded Central League team where he played with the likes of Bobby Charlton, Geoff Bent, Wilf McGuinness and Ronnie Cope, who were a little older and more experienced than him but Dennis's injury gave him his first team debut against Burnley in April 1957 aged just 17. "When I got into the first team I was only 17 and people have often asked me if I was nervous or overawed? Well I wasn't! I was in the Central League team at 16 and so I had got used to playing against older, more experienced and tougher players and in a way this experience toughened me up rather quickly. And playing with the class players United had in their first team made it easier for me. Dennis, Duncan, Eddie, Roger, Jackie and Mark. They were all so helpful and considerate. It was a wonderful feeling being part of United during this period. There was this wonderful atmosphere about the whole place. A togetherness that I never experienced again after I left the club. When I was told that I was in the first team I was overjoyed."

United were odds-on favourites to win the double, a feat

last achieved in 1897 by their FA Cup final opponents Aston Villa. United went to Blackpool to prepare for the final. Both Tommy Taylor, who had missed the last three games of the season and Dennis, were receiving constant treatment - neither player wanted to miss out on such an important occasion. They knew of many well-known players who had never had the opportunity of playing in an FA Cup final, so both were hoping that their injuries would heal up in time.

Dennis was the most concerned, he knew he had not been at his sharpest for quite some time and had not scored since February 2nd against Manchester City. Twenty-four hours before the cup final, Busby and Murphy gave Dennis a rigid fitness test in an effort to see if he could play at Wembley - Taylor had already been declared fit to play in the final. Dennis was obviously frustrated when he failed the test, but wished young Bobby Charlton, who would be taking his place, the very best of luck. He was heartbroken and felt absolutely devastated at missing out on every footballer's dream, to play in an FA Cup final on the hallowed turf of Wembley Stadium. His name appeared in the cup final programme, but he never played.

The groin injury had troubled Dennis for quite some weeks and he had aggravated it in the semi-final victory against Birmingham. "My injury was still troubling me right up to the week before the final," he said. After training in Blackpool Dennis was getting changed when Tom Curry the trainer told him that Matt Busby wanted to see him in his room: "As I knocked on his door and entered, Matt smiled and told me to sit down. 'Tom tells me your leg is still sore, Dennis,' he said quietly but firmly. 'What do you think about your chances for Saturday?' It was one of the worst moments of my life. Every player will tell you what a sickening moment it is when you know in your heart of hearts that you just can't quite make it. I gave the Boss my answer by saying nothing but merely looking rather miserably at the carpet. After a brief silence Matt Busby coughed, he was obviously not looking forward to telling me I was not going to play at Wembley. 'You know,' said Busby firmly but kindly, 'You'd never forgive yourself if something went wrong out there at Wembley.' I waited a few moments before replying. 'Yes, I think you'd better count me out, Boss.' So that was my Wembley dream gone up in smoke."

On a boiling hot day, May 4th 1957, United's hopes of winning the double also went up in smoke after just ten minutes, when Aston Villa's outside-left Peter McParland charged into United goalkeeper Ray Wood, shattering his jaw and virtually putting him out of the match. Whatever way one looked at it, this was a quite vicious charge on poor Ray Wood. The ambulancemen came running onto the field and he had to be stretchered off. Charging the goalkeeper was an accepted part of football and in very few circumstances did referees deem it a foul. To compound Wood's loss there were no substitutes and centre-half Jackie Blanchflower went into goal and played magnificently. Wood did return in the second half as a passenger on the wing. The 1950s saw quite a few finals marred by serious injuries and these injuries often affected the outcome of the games. This was certainly the case in this game, United played their hearts out and produced some wonderful football, but that man McParland scored to put Villa 2-0 in the lead. In an all-out attack, Edwards took a corner for United in the 82nd minute and Taylor went up high and nodded a brilliantly into the net. In the last few minutes of the game, Wood was sent back into goal as United went at it hammer and tongs in a last ditch effort to draw the game but it wasn't to be. United and their supporters felt that they'd been robbed - Aston Villa's nickname 'The Villains' never seemed to be more apt.

At a reception a couple of days later captain Roger Byrne told clubmates and officials: "Manchester United really have done exceptionally well this season. We were in the running for a treble of trophies but managed to win only one." Then he thanked every player and the United backroom staff and Matt Busby. "We were very unfortunate not to bring the FA Cup back to Manchester with us, but mark my words we will be back at Wembley next year!"

In the 1950s, the FA would only award medals to the eleven players who actually played in the Cup final. However, as Dennis had played in every round of the FA Cup, Matt Busby and the United directors applied to the FA for permission to present him with a medal and the FA reluctantly agreed. So Dennis did, after all, receive an FA Cup runners-up medal for the 1957 FA Cup final.

There followed a close season tour of Denmark and Dennis, though still injured, was taken along. He had to replace the injured Roger Byrne in one of the two matches played. It had been a mixed season for Dennis. He had played in 27 league matches, scoring 16 goals, five FA Cup games, scoring nine goals and six European Cup games netting nine times. However he hadn't scored since February, thanks to a loss of form through injury. He had also missed two of the biggest games of the season against Madrid at home and in the Wembley final.

Nevertheless there was no doubting that Dennis was a star in the making. Before pre-season training began, Ray Wood and Dennis were walking through Manchester when they passed a car showroom and gazed through the window. Dennis spotted a beautiful car that instantly took his fancy, it was a Riley. They both went inside to have a closer look at the vehicle. After a bit of a bartering Dennis said: "Right, I'll buy that." Ray looked at him and laughed, he knew Dennis couldn't drive and to his knowledge had never had a driving lesson in his life. After filling in the necessary paperwork Dennis turned to the salesman and said: "Will you deliver it to my house in Urmston, please?" The salesman looked startled, here was Dennis who had just bought a car and he was asking if it could be delivered to his house like a piece of furniture. Later, Ray and Dennis decided with their wives to go on holiday to Switzerland and drive there. Ray bought some learner driver plates and allowed Dennis to drive on the continent. They had loads of fun and some hair-raising experiences.

One evening while in their hotel in Switzerland the two players decided they would give their wives a surprise and take them to a dinner dance. They arranged to meet at a pre-arranged time in the hotel lounge. Dennis, because of his connections in the clothing industry was able to get all the up-to-date fashions: suits, casual sweaters, cardigans, slacks and ladies clothes particularly evening dresses. He would often take orders from the other players and turn up at training with a suitcase full.

When they met down in the lounge Ray and Dennis were enjoying a drink when first of all Ray's wife came and sat down with them wearing a beautiful dress. A few minutes later, Barbara, Dennis's wife joined them. The two women looked at each other and discovered they were wearing the same design. Dennis had obviously got both dresses and neither would change. Instead they looked menacingly toward Dennis and there was an icy atmosphere throughout the evening.

A Collector's Item

Today there is a huge market for memorabilia concerning the Busby Babes. The 1957 brochure *The Red Devils*, is a particularly rare item and worth a great deal of money today but it is all the more valuable because its authors were Ray Wood and Dennis Viollet.

As if to illustrate how naïve players were in this period, before the FA Cup final against Aston Villa the players decided they would have a souvenir brochure printed to commemorate their Wembley appearance. Dennis and Ray Wood were asked to organise this out of the players' pool. They spoke to Eddie Clarke, a friend of Matt Busby's, about getting the brochure published. Bookmaker Johnny Foy was another of Matt Busby's friends who helped out by getting advertising for the publication. When Dennis and Ray sat down with Eddie and Johnny to discuss the venture, Eddie asked the two players how much they were going to charge for an advert in the book? Dennis and Ray looked at each other and turning to Eddie said meekly, "What about £10?"

Eddie pulled his face, picked up the telephone and dialled the owner of a big business concern. "Hello," said Eddie, talking to the owner. "Listen, your staff and customers are mainly United supporters, do you agree?" The hurried reply was a resounding "Oh yes!"

"Well I've put you down for an advert in the players' brochure for a hundred pounds." The two players gulped and looked at each other - they thought a tenner was too high a price. Dennis and Ray then spoke to George Follows, the *Daily Herald* journalist. He agreed to put the 38-page brochure together and his newspaper helped by advertising it in their paper, shops and through their newspaper lads. It cost 2s 6d.

After the Cup Final Dennis and Ray went to the *Daily Herald* offices just off Oxford Road to collect the money. The money was all in coins: threepenny bits, sixpences, shillings and half-crowns and had been stored in one of those big newspaper bags that the sellers used to wield around town at the time. "It was blooming heavy I can tell you, we couldn't lift it," said Ray. Startled onlookers watched in amazement as the two well-known players dragged the bag down the steps, onto the pavement and into a taxi. "Johnny Foy had organised for his bank to let us go in by the side entrance where they counted the money for us. But only about 6,000 copies of the brochure were ever sold. We incinerated between thirty and thirty-two thousand copies. I wish we'd had the foresight to have saved them. What would they be worth today on the memorabilia market?"

The full *Red Devils* brochure from 1957 was reproduced inside the match programme for the Munich Testimonial match in 1998. "I think there were 50,000 of the Testimonial programme sold," Ray added. "That's nearly nine times as many as we managed, on a single night!"

The Calypso Kids

The Busby Babes were becoming legends. They even had a Calypso song written about them:

If they're playing in your town
Be sure to get to that football ground
If you do, then you will see
Football taught by Matt Busby
At Manchester - Manchester United
A bunch of bouncing Busby Babes
They deserve to be Knighted.

Manchester was still adjusting after the horrors of war, where many families lost fathers, brothers, uncles, cousins and friends. The greyness of the immediate post-war years was being lifted, not least by a young, successful team challenging the best in Europe. Manchester didn't look so grey anymore, the vivid flash of the Red Devils' jerseys were adding colour to the times.

Entertainment was also changing. Alongside the hundreds of cinemas in the city centre: the Gaumont, the Odeon, and the Theatre Royal there were also new places for younger people (teenagers as they were being called) popping up: The Plaza, with top DJ Jimmy Savile in charge, was packed solid every session; as was The Ritz with the Phil Moss band. For the slightly older crowd there were jazz clubs such as the Bodega and the Café Royal. As for Dennis, he frequented the Sportsman on Market Street and the famous Cromford Club owned by Matt Busby's close friend, and former

Collyhurst boxer, Paddy McGrath. Dennis liked his nights out and was a bit of a devil - he was known as a 'rum' lad, always impeccably dressed and full of class and charm, like the clubs he frequented. Not that there was much money flowing around at United: wages in 1957 stood at a £15 maximum, plus £5 appearance fee and £3 win bonus. You certainly wouldn't get rich on that amount of money, especially if you were a family man like Dennis. Being a United player brought instant recognition in Manchester. The Babes enjoyed a growing reputation in the rest of the country but superstar status in their home town.

A normal week for a United first team player began with a a day off on Monday when the players would sometimes play at Davyhulme Golf Club. On Tuesday the players would report at 10am for training which consisted of a warm-up and a practice match. Wednesday would see them lapping the ground, usually at Old Trafford, then running up the stands before a trip into the gym which in those days was situated under the main stand, near the dressing rooms, close to the central tunnel where the teams would emerge on match days. Inside the gym some players would skip and others would punch the speedball like boxers, this was eye co-ordination and reflexes. There was also medicine ball work and exercises. This kind of preparation was obviously far different from the kind carried out at Carrington today, but nevertheless it produced results for United. Thursday would see them doing much the same as the previous day but perhaps with a five-a-side game while Friday would see the team limbering up before a a team talk from Busby and Murphy.

Property prices in the Manchester area fluctuated. A threebedroomed semi-detached house in a nice area on the south side of the city would cost you about £1,750. Television was in its infancy, very few ordinary working class families could afford one, however, for those that could they would be captivated by the $64,000 *Question, Sunday Night at the London Palladium, I Love Lucy* and a weekly dose of *Robin Hood*. The wireless was still the more popular medium.

The main topic of conversation in Manchester's pubs was whether United could retain their title for a third year and go on and win the two trophies that had eluded them the previous season, the FA Cup and European Cup. Having got used to close season tours, the pre-season variety was introduced this year, with a short tour of Germany. Dennis was now fully fit, and showed it in Berlin. A comfortable 3-0 victory ensued with two goals from Dennis and one from his partner Tommy Taylor. The team was running like a well-oiled machine. The same team played in Hanover and gave a magnificent display to win 4-2, again Viollet and Taylor scoring all the goals. The other member of United's inside forward trio, Billy Whelan, showed his colleagues he was up for the new season by getting a hat-trick in the opening league match at newly-promoted Leicester City's Filbert Street ground. When Everton were beaten by the same three goals to nil scoreline, and Manchester City demolished 4-1 at Old Trafford in quick succession the champions were off like a house on fire. Dennis showed his liking for the team from across Manchester by scoring in a 'Derby' match yet again.

Ken Barnes, the Manchester City wing-half and captain, was one of the most skillful players in the First Division and like Dennis he had been consistently overlooked by the England selectors. Ken had a close friendship with Dennis, in those days it was not unusual for opposing players to be friendly with each other and socialise together. "I often played against Dennis Viollet in the Derby matches," said Ken. "Yes, I was a great admirer of Dennis as a player and as a person. He had a wonderful awareness on the field, beautifully balanced and a tremendous burst of speed from a standing position. He scored his goals through guile and skill. His football brain telling him when to make his move into the danger zone or to pass the ball to a team-mate. For defenders he was very difficult to mark, you could be watching him carefully or trying to mark him closely but he would wander all over the pitch, lose you, only to pop up unexpectedly and score or set up a goal for Tommy Taylor or another forward. We all tend to wax lyrical about players from our own playing days as being great, and better than current stars, however that's certainly not the case when discussing Dennis Viollet. He would have been a great footballer in any era, notice I said footballer. Why? Because of the way he played his football! Dennis was first and foremost a team player, a player's player. He would certainly score many goals himself, but he could also make many more for other players. In his record-breaking season (1959- 60) he scored 32 goals, but United scored a total of 102 goals."

There were goals aplenty for United in 1957: 22 in the season's first six games yielding five wins and a draw. Dennis had netted six of those goals including two against Leeds in a 5-0 Old Trafford scoreline. The Manchester public were beginning to appreciate the magnificent side it had on its doorstep with over 172,000 watching the first three home matches. Whether the first signs of complacency began creeping into United was soon a subject for supporters as two shock defeats followed the opening successes. The fact that Bolton Wanderers beat United was not that much of a surprise, they seemed to have a jinx over them, but a 4-0 hiding was taking things a bit too far. When Blackpool reversed a 4-1 home defeat by United, to win 2-1 at Old Trafford more questions were being asked.

They were quickly answered: Arsenal were put to the sword 4-2 at Old Trafford, before the first leg of the European

Cup at Dublin's Dalymount Park against Shamrock Rovers. This produced an emphatic 6-0 victory for the Red Devils. Fittingly, Dublin-born Billy Whelan scored two of those goals in front of a crowd of over 46,000.

Britain was hit by a flu bug at this time and Dennis was one of four players, along with Byrne, Colman and Whelan who were ruled out for the trip to Wolverhampton Wanderers which United unsurprisingly lost 3-1. Dennis was fit again for the second leg against Shamrock Rovers at Old Trafford. There was a carnival-like atmosphere inside and outside Old Trafford as throngs of Irish supporters made their presence felt. They had come to Manchester to enjoy themselves for an occasion that looked a mere formality for United. Inside the opening five minutes Dennis missed a sitter, before bursting into life with an explosive goal. The Irish team and their fans were far from disheartened and created a wonderful atmosphere. They were disappointed that Duncan Edwards and their own 'boyo', Billy Whelan, were missing from United's team, but were impressed by young Wilf McGuinness taking Duncan's place on the night.

David Pegg, running on to a beautifully timed through ball from Dennis, scored a good goal before Rovers took the game to United and had quite a few near misses. Mark Jones was having a great game, it was a good job because Peyton, the Rovers insideright, was rampant. In the 55th minute he scored to make it 2-1 on the night, receiving thunderous applause not only from his own supporters but United's fans as well. Dennis answered back for United when he scored a truly magnificent goal. Berry gave him the ball low and fast within a split second Dennis had it under control and it shot it into the net before goalkeeper D'Arcy could move. A brilliantly executed goal! Rovers struck again when Hamilton netted and within seconds the same player almost scored a second. It ended 3-2 to United, but it was a far from satisfactory victory.

By this time Wilf McGuinness was making one or two first team appearances. Wilf, like Dennis Viollet, was a former Manchester and England schoolboy international and captain. Speaking about the qualities of Dennis Viollet many years later he said: "Dennis was a world class player and I don't say that flippantly. He really was. You could give him a bad pass and you knew yourself it was a bad pass because you would realise straight away, but Dennis would turn it into a good one because of control."

Wilf recalled a typically thoughtful gesture by Dennis in the post-Munich era: "I missed out on another United trip because of injury. This time the club were visiting Italy and included in the tour was an audience for Matt Busby and the team with the rotund, jovial and warmly human Pope John XXIII. Dennis, not a Catholic, knew that I would dearly have loved to have been there, so he brought me back some Rosary beads that had been blessed by the Pope as a memento. A smashing lad!"

Two matches within three weeks at Old Trafford against FA Cup final foes Aston Villa increased the temperature. There were worries that the United supporters would give Peter McParland a hard time because of his charge on Ray Wood in the final - a challenge that many observers regarded as a blatant foul. The newspapers claimed that United players would target McParland in their first meeting since May, however, these theories were illfounded as the Reds decided to take their revenge by beating Aston Villa fairly and squarely - 4-1 in the league and 4-0 in the Charity Shield, a game in which Tommy Taylor scored a brilliant hat-trick.

A 2-1 away win over Nottingham Forest followed in front of a then record league attendance at the City ground. Dennis and Billy Whelan were the goal scorers, giving Dennis his 75th goal in 138 league starts for United.

For the next game, at home to Portsmouth, United lost Byrne, Edwards and Taylor to the England team to play Wales at Cardiff. Unlike today, United couldn't request a postponement, they had to get on with it and the loss of these three influential players proved too big a handicap - United losing 3-0 - a shaven-headed youngster named Derek Dougan grabbing a hat-trick.

Dennis received a bad ankle injury in this game and this put him out of action for the following six league matches plus both legs of the European Cup against Dukla Prague. Matt Busby told his old friend Frank Swift: "You know, Frank, this lad [Viollet] seldom gets enough credit in newspaper reports, he's the hardgrafting inside-forward who makes the whole forward line click. We are never the same team without him. He's always in the thick of the action and he's the best goal snatcher I know. With Dennis back in the team, I'm confident we shall see United slipping into top gear." Of the six league games, United won three, lost two and drew the other, while the two European Cup matches ended with United winning 3-0 at Old Trafford but losing 1-0 in Prague.

Evidently, Dennis was a vital cog in United's well-oiled machine and after a run out with the reserves, he was back in action for United on December 7th for the away game against Birmingham City - a 3-3 draw in which Dennis scored twice with Tommy Taylor getting the other. His return made such a big difference to United's forward line that hopes were high that the Reds could get themselves into a challenging position in the title race.

Dennis played in the next eight league games. However, following a 1-0 home defeat to a late goal by Chelsea, Matt Busby was extremely angry. He and Jimmy Murphy got their heads together and decided a shake-up was needed. Harry Gregg was signed from Doncaster Rovers for a record fee for a goalkeeper and Kenny Morgans, Bobby Charlton and Albert Scanlon were promoted on merit into the first team. Busby had decided things had to change.

Leicester City came to Old Trafford with two former United players, John Doherty and Johnny Morris, in their line-up. United showed flashes of their best form walloping them 4-0. Dennis, sharp as a razor, scored twice with Bobby Charlton and Albert Scanlon also netting. The very last Christmas Day game ever played at Old Trafford saw Luton Town thrashed 3-0 - Charlton, Edwards and Taylor the scorers. On Boxing Day, the return saw Luton hold United to a 2-2 draw, Taylor and Scanlon the scorers. Two days later United played out a memorable 2-2 draw in the Maine Road derby in front of 70,000. As supporter Brian Smith relates: "The best goal I ever saw Dennis Viollet score was against Manchester City in a Maine Road thriller. Cutting in from the right, he took a pass from inside him in his stride, flicked it forward (looping it up, almost over his head) and volleyed it into the net. I can still remember going crackers over the sheer breathtaking skill of that particular goal."

United welcomed in 1958 with optimistic expectation. Though they had lost a great deal of ground in the league, their form meant they could easily make up ground on the leaders. However the first game of the New Year took them to Borough Park, Workington Town's neat, compact little ground for an FA Cup third round tie.

21,000 spectators filled the tiny stadium to capacity with gate receipts of £2,236 destined to remain a record for the Cumbrian club until they left the league in 1977. Joe Harvey, the former Newcastle captain, was the Workington manager - could the old Newcastle player, who had enjoyed great cup success with the Magpies in the 1950s, spring a surprise against United?

The pitch was semi-frozen, deep in mud, the perfect

conditions for a giantkilling act. A shock looked likely when after five minutes of play the Cumbrian minnows swept into the lead. Following a long high ball inside forward Robson shot powerfully and the ball hit Harry Gregg and before he could recover fell at left-winger Colbridge's feet who rammed it into the empty net. The home crowd made a fantastic sound and the Manchester players knew they were in for one hell of a game. It was bitterly cold and the pitch was in terrible icy, bumpy condition. At half-time the Workington team were cheered and applauded back to their dressing room a goal up against the champions - on the balance of play been they should have been two up.

In United's dressing room, Matt Busby preached patience to his players and just before they went out for the second half he told Colman and Edwards: "Get Dennis on the ball." His instructions were to thread ground passes for Viollet to run on to. United pinned the Third Division side back and applied non-stop pressure on their defence. Dennis was like a bomb waiting to explode. In a six minute spell, with beautiful balance on a treacherous surface, he showed why he was an ace marksman. In that six minutes Dennis scored a pulverising hat-trick. His first came when he intercepted Tommy Taylor's shot at goal after Newlands, the Workington goalkeeper, had committed himself to save Taylor's original shot and was wrongfooted, Dennis put the ball in the corner of the net. His second immediately followed with the Cumbrians still shocked by United's opener. Albert Scanlon ran into space, delivered an inch-perfect pass putting Dennis clear of the defence and he didn't miss. Dennis was there again minutes later to record one of United's quickest hat-tricks, receiving a Kenny Morgans cross in his stride which he blasted into the net. Later United settled down and played with the class and assurance of a great team but Dennis had turned the tie around.

Joe Harvey summed the game up when he said: 'What a player! And to think that England are searching the country for a goalpoaching inside forward. This fellow Viollet should be an automatic choice.'

Frank Swift, writing for the News of the World said: "Dennis Viollet, Manchester United's goal-poaching inside-left, will remember this game for the rest of his life. His brilliantly taken hattrick in a dramatic six minutes saved his team from disaster. Dennis was superb. His balance and majestic control of the ball in such severe circumstances stamped him as a craftsman of the highest order."

Back to league business and United travelled to Leeds for a 1-1 draw, Dennis again the marksman. Three days later, the Reds played Red Star Belgrade in the quarter-final of the European Cup at Old Trafford. Thick fog circled the ground and made conditions very difficult. In the opening minutes both Dennis and Bobby Charlton almost scored, but it was the nifty, classy Belgrade insideforward Tasic who got the first goal.

United were playing like strangers - true the pitch was tricky but it was the same for both teams. There was also a great deal of petty fouling by both sides. The Red Star goalkeeper Vladimir Beara, was dressed in black. The former ballet dancer known as the 'Black Panther' was majestic throughout. United's power men, Foulkes, Byrne, Jones and Edwards had to be on top of their game to block the Belgrade forwards time and again.

Finally the tide turned and Edwards made the first goal with a pass to Scanlon who centred for Charlton to score. United needed a touch of inspiration, they also knew they needed another goal to take to Belgrade. With less than ten minutes left Dennis Viollet produced an act of sheer genius. Out on the right flank he beat three Red Star defenders, racing past them in a mazy dribble as if they were statues. He swung the ball into the middle and Eddie Colman scored. The last ten minutes were all United but try as they might they couldn't increase their lead. Referee Lesquenes blew the final whistle. He had blown his whistle for 41 fouls: 24 for United; 17 for Red Star.

Beating the Bolton bogey

As has already been explained, United always seemed to struggle against local rivals Bolton. In this era they seemed to be United's main rivals while Liverpool, the team modern fans regard as the sworn enemy, languished hopelessly in the Second Division. Bolton's record was impressive in this period and fans regarded them as a bogey side. In the 1950s they were a big, rough, robust side that did not take many prisoners. Oh, they could play alright but it was their physical presence that made life hard for most teams in the First Division. With players like England international Nat Lofthouse spearheading their attack and Tommy Banks, Roy Hartle and big John Higgins in defence they really were a force to be reckoned with. Four days after beating Red Star, United played Bolton at Old Trafford. The players spoke about wanting to put the record straight following a 4-0 hammering at Burnden Park earlier in the season when the Reds were playing in fits and starts. United's steady improvement of form was fully demonstrated in a staggering 7-2 victory. Bobby Charlton got a hattrick, Dennis scored twice while Albert Scanlon and Duncan Edwards weighed in with a goal apiece. This was the sixth goal for Dennis since the New Year. More importantly, this emphatic victory closed the gap behind Wolves, who were riding high at the top of the league table to just six points.

Matt Busby had a settled team once more - Gregg; Foulkes, Byrne; Colman, Jones, Edwards; Morgans,

Charlton, Taylor, Viollet and Scanlon. He was particular pleased with his two wingers, Kenny Morgans and Albert Scanlon, in place of the established pair of Johnny Berry and David Pegg. Both these wingers could dribble, cross, shoot and most importantly, they were direct. David Pegg was obviously upset at losing his place in the team, but he vowed to fight and win it back. Johnny Berry however, was so upset he asked for a transfer, which Busby refused.

United played Alf Ramsey's Ipswich Town at Old Trafford in the FA Cup fourth round on January 25th. Newspaper talk concerned United's bid for the treble. Though they were behind Wolverhampton Wanderers in the league championship chase their form suggested they could catch up while the campaign on all other fronts was progressing nicely. What the crowd did not know was that this was the last Old Trafford outing for their beloved Babes.

Scott Duncan, the former United manager, was making a return to his old club, he was now the secretary of the East Anglian club. In front of a 53,550 crowd United, in fluent form, took the lead when an Ipswich defender slipped on the ball while attempting to clear it, Bobby Charlton latched onto the loose ball and scored with a cannonball shot which Roy Bailey - father of future United keeper Gary - in the Ipswich goal had no chance of stopping. With just four minutes of the game left Charlton ran on to the ball and gracefully dribbled his way through the Ipswich defence before sending a blistering shot into the roof of the net for a comfortable 2-0 victory for the Red Devils.

The Best of the Babes

Before flying to Belgrade for the return leg, United had a very important league game against Arsenal at Highbury. The United players loved visiting the capital and always seemed to reserve their best displays for London opposition. This could partly be explained by the big build-up the London based papers would give United's opponents before every visit to the capital. But for once the papers got it right - for once the London opposition didn't lie down, indeed Arsenal were as attack-minded as their illustrious opponents.

The London editions were predicting an all-action, top of the table clash between two attacking teams hell-bent on scoring as many as they could. This was a game eagerly anticipated by the Arsenal fans and the vast posse of journalists covering it. On the Friday before the Saturday match the team moved to London and stayed at their favourite hotel, the Lancaster Gate. After being allocated their rooms the two Salford lads, Albert Scanlon and Eddie Colman, decided they wanted to go to the cinema to watch a Frank Sinatra film, Pal Joey. They were both big Sinatra fans, even going as far as wearing trilbies like their idol. Albert was feeling on top of the world - since he settled into the first team the Reds had not lost. Eddie, his pal, was always a bubbly character.

On the Saturday morning the team received a shock when they were told that one of the Manchester United directors, Mr G E Whitaker, had been found dead in his bed in the hotel. As the United coach made its way to Highbury they passed thousands of fans making their way to the stadium, the atmosphere was already red hot. In the dressing rooms the players heard that the gates had been locked on a 63,000 capacity crowd. United changed into their all-white Wembley strip while Matt Busby passed around black armbands for the players to wear as a mark of respect for Mr Whitaker. The team was bubbling with confidence, they honestly believed they could beat any team they faced.

Duncan Edwards did most to gee the lads up. "Come on lads, we can beat this lot and get closer to Wolves," he bawled, as Roger Byrne went from player to player quietly issuing instructions. Dennis was in his pre-match routine. He was pensive, getting himself mentally fit for the game, rachetting up his concentration to match the crowd's fever pitch. This was normal for him. No injury worries this time for Dennis, he was in tip-top physical condition and impatient to get out onto the pitch.

Tommy Taylor and Mark Jones were chatting away to each other in broad Yorkshire accents that nobody else could understand - they often took some ribbing from the rest of the players about their accents and the need for a translator but it was all good clean fun. Kenny Morgans and Bobby Charlton were busy tying their bootlaces and enjoying the banter. Harry Gregg, the big Irish goalie, was confidently going through a few stretching exercises, while the other players went through their little rituals. They could hear the noise and feel the vibrations of the capacity crowd above them - a knock on the door from the officials and the time for joking was over.

Indeed, the Highbury crowd seemed more tense than the players. As the teams ran out the tannoy blared out the teams. Arsenal: Kelsey; S. Charlton, Evans; Ward, Fotheringham, Bowen; Groves, Tapscott, Herd, Bloomfield, Nutt.

Arsenal had some outstanding players: Jack Kelsey was a Welsh international and a wonderful goalkeeper; David Herd, Dennis Viollet's old schoolboy pal, would eventually go on to become a Scottish international and join Manchester United a few years later. Dave Bowen, Derek Tapscott, Vick Groves and Jimmy Bloomfield were top notch players. United lined-up: Gregg; Foulkes, Byrne; Colman, Jones, Edwards; Morgans, Charlton, Taylor, Viollet, Scanlon.

From the kick-off Morgans and Scanlon were flying, their wings giving Arsenal a drubbing. United were playing vintage football! After ten minutes, 18-year-old Kenny Morgans dribbled at speed past two defenders lunging at thin air, young Morgans slid a marvellous side pass that Duncan Edwards took in his stride and ferociously shot past Kelsey. The Welsh international managed to get his hands to the ball but so powerful was the shot that it whizzed through them and into the corner of the net.

The Arsenal crowd tried to turn up the volume, warming to both teams' entertaining attitude. Minutes after Duncan's goal, Albert Scanlon collected a loose ball in his own half and with power and majesty flew down the left wing leaving several Arsenal players for dead. Even his own team-mates Dennis, Tommy Taylor and Bobby Charlton couldn't keep up with him. "He was like a greyhound at Belle Vue," laughed Dennis Viollet. Only Tapscott and Stan Charlton could eventually manage to get anywhere near him as he headed for the left corner flag, leaving everyone except Albert out of breath. Charlton moved toward the Arsenal goal, Scanlon looked up, spotted him and delivered a beautiful ball into his path. Bobby, gulping for air, let fly and the ball was in Arsenal's net. "What a fantastic run Albert made," Bobby remembers. "The speed and power of him was unbelievable. We were all trying to keep up with him, then he unleashed a magical pass for me to score." 2-0 and United were cruising!

The pitch was soggy and greasy, but both teams were displaying skills and thrills that many pundits thought only the great Hungarian team could employ. Before half-time the young Red Devils were three up. Again the two United wingers were involved in the build-up, supplying Tommy Taylor to make it a happy United dressing room at the interval. Matt Busby was gushing with pride. The first-half exhibition was simply out of this world. Arsenal, a team in contention for the title themselves, had tried to respond but couldn't - the Babes were devastating.

In the second half the home crowd received encouragement as the Gunners pulled two goals back through David Herd and Jimmy Bloomfield. The Highbury crowd went ballistic when Bloomfield scored again to equalise. United had thrown it away, Busby was livid - his youngsters, with one eye on the Red Star game in four days' time, had eased off and paid the price. After conceding a 3-0 lead away from home, many experienced teams would have felt demoralised and folded but these youngsters from Manchester were something special and believed they could beat any team they faced.

Almost immediately Colman and Edwards got a firm grip of midfield and galvanised their forwards, up and down the muddy field these two strove passing, tackling and getting their forwards moving into spaces. Duncan was playing like a demon, defending one minute, passing to his forwards the next, and having a shot at goal, he was phenomenal. In this mood United were unbeatable, they were indeed a great, great team and Edwards was exceptional. Without being too nostalgic, when present day journalists write that Liverpool's Steven Gerrard is another Duncan Edwards, they honestly do not know what they are talking about. Gerrard is undoubtedly a wonderful player and may go on to great feats for both Liverpool and England but without being biased, there is nobody who comes anywhere near to being compared to this truly magnificent player and athlete - Duncan Edwards.

As Albert Scanlon said: "Even when Arsenal pulled us back to 3-3 we were not worried. Big Duncan was shouting at us to get stuck in, Mark Jones clenched his fist and shouted out advice, and Roger was as cool as a cucumber as he steadied us down and kept telling us to keep our passing game going. This was one of those matches you could never, ever forget.

All the team played exceptionally well and we were up and down the pitch non-stop, looking to score goals. These were the kind of games the fans loved and so did us players."

United's wingers singed the turf on the right and left of their respective flanks, they were playing 'blinders'! There is no greater sight for football lovers than to see two wingers flying down the wing - Morgans and Scanlon were doing this and a great deal more. Albert Scanlon dummied, then flew past Stan Charlton and centred for Dennis to nod home United's fourth goal. Later, Morgans passed to Taylor who scored a remarkable individual solo effort at 5-3, surely it was all over. But not as far as Arsenal were concerned, they tore back to make it 5-4. Once again the supporters of both teams were breathless with excitement.

When the final whistle blew both teams embraced each other, they were all proud to have been part of a football match that was something out of the ordinary, something special, very special. The crowd stayed and applauded every player off the pitch. Matt Busby was overjoyed. "Aren't you worried about the four goals you conceded?" a young reporter asked him as he made his way into the United dressing room. Matt smiled at the young man and politely told him: "No, not at all, because we got five! More important, you saw how those sixty-odd thousand people enjoyed the game. This is the kind of football the spectators pay to watch."

Dennis was feeling brilliant and later commented: "This was some game I can tell you. I scored with a rare header, Scanny centred the ball for Tommy who liked it delivered fast, high and hard something Albert could supply with perfection. I somehow got to it before Tommy and glanced the ball into the net - the power of the cross nearly took my head off my shoulders. After that goal Tommy went up even further in my estimation, because he would head those type of crosses umpteen times in a game. It was a very happy, contented team, that made its way back to Manchester. We certainly celebrated on the train."

When the train pulled into London Road station Matt Busby told his players to go and enjoy themselves but to be up bright and early the following morning; he had a twinkle in his eye. Several players headed straight for the Plaza Ballroom where Jimmy Savile was the resident compere and DJ. The place was packed solid with everybody either on the dancefloor or at tables enjoying a drink. Obviously the news of United's brilliant victory in London was the main topic of conversation. Savile, in his inimitable fashion, announced that some of the players were in the audience and he even got Mark Jones and Eddie Colman up on the stage to sing their rendering of the song Frankie and Johnny.

After the Plaza closed most of the players made their way to the well-known nightclubs for a late drink while Dennis made his own way to a different night spot - it wasn't that Dennis didn't like his team-mates' company, he most certainly did, but he preferred socialising with the friends he had known for years.

The season held plenty of promise. United were still in the FA Cup and if they beat Red Star in a few days' time Dennis could look forward to another European Cup semi-final and a test against the best Europe could offer. More importantly Dennis knew that following the Red Star game came a crucial confrontation and potential title decider with Wolves.

The Babes' Last Stand

It was a club rule at Manchester United that any player injured on a Saturday had to report to Old Trafford on Sunday morning for treatment. Wilf McGuinness had been carrying a slight injury for a couple of weeks and had been injured on the Saturday while playing for the reserves. He arrived at Old Trafford on the Sunday morning hoping Ted Dalton, United's physiotherapist, could patch him up so he could travel with his mates to Belgrade. Although no substitutes were allowed, Busby would always take several extra players just in case someone went down with a cold or a dodgy stomach. He also did this to foster team spirit and let the lads know they remained an important part of Manchester United.

Jimmy Murphy was in the treatment room laughing and joking as usual keeping everyone in good spirits. Ted Dalton spoke to Busby and Murphy and it was decided that Wilf would not travel to Belgrade but would remain behind for further treatment.

"They were thinking of the Wolves game the following Saturday," remembers Wilf. "Of course I was upset and disappointed. I knocked about with Bobby Charlton, Eddie Colman and David Pegg and knew we would have a good giggle travelling to Belgrade. I could understand the Boss's decision to leave me behind for treatment, he was thinking that if Eddie or Duncan got injured he would need replacements for the Wolves match." Wilf counts himself lucky now that he never made the trip behind the Iron Curtain: "I still don't know if it was luck or fate that made me miss that journey."

Colin Webster had been told a few days before the Arsenal match to prepare himself to travel. Colin knew he would be playing in the reserves on the day United tackled Arsenal, but was nevertheless looking forward to a trip abroad but he went down with a heavy dose of flu and was told not to go to Old Trafford but stay at home and keep warm. Colin felt shocking, not with his illness but because he desperately wanted to go with the boys to Belgrade. "I was cursing my bloody bad luck at missing out," recalls Colin in his deep Welsh accent. "We always had good fun on those away trips and it made me feel part of the whole set-up at the club. However, it wasn't to be and I remained behind."

Jackie Blanchflower the classy, cultured centre-half, had been a first team regular at the start of the season. He was selected by his country, Northern Ireland, to play in an international and in those days, as has been mentioned earlier, a club could not ask the League for a postponement. Mark Jones stepped into his place and Jackie had to wait his turn to claim it back. This was one of the great things about Busby team, they had an abundance of talent in every position. "It was one of those situations, when you get selected for your country you obviously have to take it," said Jackie. "After all, Mark Jones was terribly unlucky. He was a terrific centrehalf, but because there were so many English centre-halves to choose from - Billy Wright, the Wolverhampton Wanderers centre- half was England captain - Mark never got an opportunity to play for his country. So my good fortune in becoming an international cost me my place in the first team during this period.'

A couple of weeks before the Red Star game, Ronnie Cope had been told by Matt Busby that he would be travelling with the team to Belgrade. He was told to hand his passport

1948 VERY GOOD — 1957 THE TOPS

MANCHESTER UNITED . . . I salute you. I'm thrilled and proud of your wonderful achievements. THRILLED, because you have put British football back on top of the world, and PROUD because of my long and happy association with the club as a player. Over the past dozen years, United teams have all carried the Busby hallmark . . . 100 per cent teamwork, superb confidence, technically - efficient players, well trained and fully disciplined.

It's an onerous task to make comparisons between United teams of different eras, and it is not my intention to minimize the excellent entertainment provided by the United in the immediate post-war years. Yet I am firmly convinced that this 1957 United is the greatest of the many successful combinations Manager Matt Busby has assembled in post-war football. *Yes, greater than United's cup-winning team of 1948.*

I believe Roger Byrne and his men are tops, because they are a better-balanced side. Their play is razor sharp, thriving on the controlled exuberance of youth, with outstanding reserve strength ensuring there is no letting-up by first-team regulars. Sufficient unto me to have had the honour to have captained a team worthy of comparison with the United of to-day.

Take the respective forward lines. Very similar all-action centre-forwards, with Jack Rowley's thunderbolt shooting matching Tommy Taylor's bullet-like headers. But whereas, we had two forceful players in Jimmy Delaney and Johnny Morris on the right, with ball-players Stan Pearson and Charlie Mitten on the left, the present United team have ball-players in Bill Whelan and David Pegg on opposite flanks, with the direct players alongside them. It's only fair to say that the 1948 forward line largely overcame this apparent lopsidedness with fluent interchanging of positions.

Our wing-halves Johnny Anderson and Henry Cockburn were essentially destructive players,

By JOHNNY CAREY
Manager of Blackburn Rovers

Former captain of Eire and Manchester United, Player of the Year in 1948, recently voted United's greatest-ever footballer in a poll of newspaper readers.

and how Johnny Aston and I appreciated these sterling qualities. As we were largely dependent on our positional play rather than on speed, quick-tackling wing-halves were vital to our defensive set-up.

It is here that the present United really gets my vote.

Wing-halves Eddie Colman and Duncan Edwards can move forward with confidence, knowing that the fast recovery of Bill Foulkes and Roger Byrne can quickly retrieve an error. The tall, commanding figure of Allen Chilton was another important link in our defensive armour. Allen got every ball in the air, which left goalkeeper Jack Crompton to concentrate on his remarkable split-second anticipation of the snap shot.

Mark Jones is cast in the Chilton mould, which is high praise indeed. Ray Wood's phenomenal clearances to the educated head of Tommy Taylor invariably cause consternation among opposing defenders. Especially so when quicksilver Viollet is haring through the middle for the flicked-on header.

In 1948, Manager Busby devised his tactics to offset the weaknesses in the team structure. I don't say that no such problem exists to-day. But it is less evident. These are golden days for Manchester United.

★ THEY have reached their exalted position by playing attractive, high-speed, and scrupulously-fair soccer.

★ THEY are feared and respected throughout the football world.

★ THEY are truly worthy of this great honour.

Thanks for the Memory

Thank you, Jack, for those generous sentiments. You and Johnny Aston, Allen Chilton, Stan Pearson, Jack Rowley and the rest of the old gang helped to make Manchester United what it is to-day. You set a high standard of skill, sportsmanship and team-play. You were an example and a challenge — to the youngsters who have so brilliantly succeeded you. — MATT BUSBY

ABOVE: *United's 1948 Cup winning captain makes a favourable comparison between the Babes and his great post-war team.*

RIGHT: *Dennis's partnership with Tommy Taylor was a significant factor in Carey's conclusion that the '57 team were 'The Tops'.*

Top: *The team of the century line-up - Dennis bottom left.*

Above: *Dennis making headlines in the Evening Chronicle Saturday Pink Final.*

Left: *Dennis nearly scores past a diving Bert Trautmann at Old Trafford*

TOP: *Tommy Taylor celebrates his goal in the Bernebeu against Real.*

MIDDLE: *Dennis closes in on the Bournemouth goal in a 1957 Cup-tie.*

BOTTOM: *The Babes celebrate the 1956/7 League title at the Midland Hotel. Duncan Edwards, Ian Greaves, Ray Wood, Dennis, Mark Jones, David Pegg and Eddie Colman charge their glasses*

ABOVE: *An excited crowd of youngsters await Dennis's signature at Paulden's department store, Manchester.*

BELOW: *February 1958: Dennis and Tommy Taylor in ballet pose, attack the Arsenal goal in the Babes' last game on British soil.*

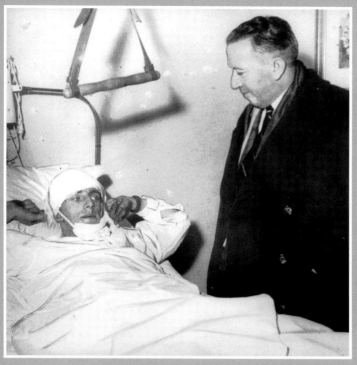

TOP: *Jimmy Murphy calls on Dennis in the Rechts der Isar hospital following the Munich aircrash. Dennis's bandaged head indicates the nature of his injuries.*

BELOW: *Kenny Morgans on left with Dennis and Albert Scanlon as the wives (including Barbara Viollet far left) attempt to cheer their husbands.*

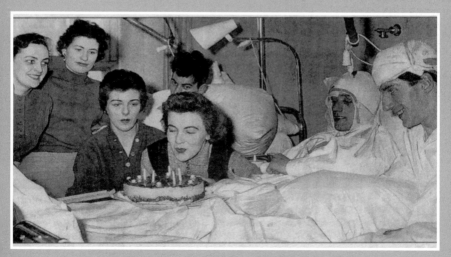

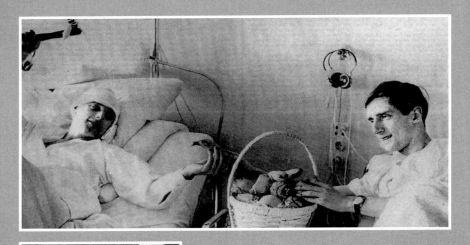

TOP: *Dennis after the fruit following his recovery.*

LEFT: *Dennis's 6 year-old daughter Stephanie presents the doctors with a bouquet of flowers.*

BELOW: *Dennis leaving for England with his wife and Kenny Morgans.*

ABOVE: *the remnants of the Babes attempt to play on. Remarkably they still succeed in reaching the FA Cup Final (losing to Bolton 2-0) and win the home leg of the European Cup semi-final 2-1 against AC Milan.*

LEFT: *Dennis and Wilf McGuinness feed the birds in Rome 1958 before heading to Milan for the European Cup semi-final.*

Two men who kept the Red flag flying
Dennis with Jimmy Murphy, United's chief coach and manager of Wales who missed the fateful trip to Munich. Murphy guided United to the 1958 FA Cup Final in Busby's absence - here they prepare for the 1958 season with a spot of training in Blackpool

to the secretary Walter Crickmer so it could be sent to the consul for the visa required. He was ecstatic! "I hardly ever made journeys like that in those days, it was like a wonderful adventure for me and they were a great bunch of lads. I really was very excited." However, on the Sunday his happiness turned to anger and frustration. He found out that Roger Byrne had taken a knock against Arsenal and was doubtful for the Red Star game so Geoff Bent would go in his place to Belgrade.

Ronnie was seething and told Jimmy Murphy that he was going to speak to Matt Busby when the team returned to Manchester. "I'm going to ask for a transfer! He [Matt Busby] never had any intention of taking me," he told Busby's assistant. "Can you imagine how I felt when a few weeks later I got my passport back and saw the visa giving me permission to enter Belgrade stamped on it."

It was a cold, damp and depressing Monday morning when the United team and officials boarded the coach for Manchester Airport. Jimmy Murphy wasn't going with them but had wished the party all the best. Jimmy was the manager of Wales, who were playing a World Cup qualifier at home against Israel. Bert Whalley took Jimmy's place alongside Matt Busby. The players were having a laugh and a joke and knew they were in for a long, tiring and boring journey to Belgrade. Mark Jones was late and apologised to Busby and afterwards took unmerciful stick from the rest of the players. The party was happy discussing the various newspaper reports of the Arsenal game. Manchester, like other industrial cities in those days, always seemed to be cloaked in thick fog caused by the thousands of factories belching out clouds of smoke from their tall chimneys. So it came as little surprise to find it foggy at Ringway and discover that their flight was delayed by over an hour. The journey itself would take six hours with a stop at Munich for re-fuelling.

After their last visit to Europe against Dukla Prague, United hit the obstacle they had feared - returning home in time to fulfil a league fixture on the following Saturday, which was in reality less than twenty-four hours later. After the Dukla game United had, as usual, arranged to fly back to Manchester on the Thursday morning. However England was fog bound and BEA's scheduled flight was grounded. Walter Crickmer, United's secretary, hurriedly phoned to make alternative arrangements and managed to get seats on a Dutch Airlines flight going to Amsterdam, the nearest point clear of the fog, from where they could travel back to England. The press, unfortunately, couldn't be accommodated and had to stay behind until the following day. They got back to Manchester via Zurich and Birmingham, a journey which took them over sixteen hours. This kind of journey would have done United's players no good whatsoever, so it had been decided that in future the club would charter their own plane.

The aircraft they chartered was an old Elizabethan, piloted by Captain Thain and Captain Rayment, Radio Officer Rodgers and three cabin staff, William Cable, Margaret Bellis and Rosemary Cheverton. There were 38 passengers including the players, club officials, press and a few others. After refuelling at Munich the plane carried on to Belgrade, but the weather conditions were terrible, with poor visibility. United's plane was in fact the only aircraft to land in Belgrade that day due to the atrocious conditions, a fact that didn't do the players' state of mind much good.

Once they had landed and disembarked, a coach took the team to the Hotel Metropole. On the journey the United party were amazed to see so many armed soldiers wandering the streets, even in the hotel there was an armed presence on every floor.

The hotel was clean but had little of the comforts familiar to an English hotel. The only good thing as far as the United party were concerned was the beautiful view of the River Danube. When the players went for a stroll they were amazed to find many locals walking about without shoes despite the inclement weather - those lucky enough wore makeshift footwear fashioned out of old car tyres. There appeared to be queues everywhere and the shops had hardly anything in them but still people queued.

"We were still suffering in Manchester from the aftermath of the war, and rationing had only just finished," said Dennis, "but this place was bad, really bad. We felt so sorry for the people especially the older ones and the children. If this was how communism was then they could keep it." There were a few lighter moments though when Tommy Taylor and Jackie Blanchflower decided to take a twirl on a frozen lake but soon stopped their capers when they were told Matt Busby was just around the corner.

Although it was cold and frozen and doubts were expressed about the playing conditions the squad were told that the game would definitely take place. The night before the game the team went to a cinema. The film was in English and as the players made their way inside, armed guards were moving paying customers from the first couple of rows and telling them to sit elsewhere. It was amusing to notice that hardly anybody apart from United's party could understand what the film stars were saying.

A few hours before the game, the hotel lobby and lounge were full of people seeking photographs and autographs. On their way to the stadium the team saw thousands of fans walking to the game, they were all smiling and chanting "Red Devils" and "Busby Babes", much to the delight of the English press. The game had certainly stirred their imagination and 52,000 spectators, including hundreds of soldiers, were inside for the kick-off.

By kick-off most of the snow was melting and the sun was out. The pitch was frozen solid in parts and like a swamp in others. Roger Byrne was a doubt up to an hour or so before kick-off, and his loyal understudy Geoff Bent was ready to take over, but after a fitness test Roger was declared fit.

United knew they had their work cut out to hold on to their slender 2-1 lead and Red Star knew they had to attack the Manchester team in non-stop fashion. But the Yugoslavs' plans floundered within the opening seconds when Dennis had the ball in the back of the Red Star net. Taylor made a run from his own half, holding off several challenges. As he entered the Red Star penalty area everyone expected him to shoot but instead Tommy passed to his striking partner who rammed the ball home. United were soon two up following a Bobby Charlton effort that almost lifted the net rigging out - it was a Charlton special, struck with power and precision. Soon afterwards Bobby had scored another - United were 3-0 up, 5-1 on aggregate.

Shocked by this start, Red Star, roared on by the home crowd, launched an offensive. Tackles were becoming niggly and tempers frayed. United kept their heads trying not to rise to the provocation. The fouls continued - Kenny Morgans was deliberately kicked on his knee and had his right thigh ripped open by a defender but no action was taken by the Austrian referee. The Belgrade team lost their poise and their forwards were appealing for fouls and free kicks as the United defenders thwarted their attempts. At last Red Star scored through Cosco, two minutes after half-time. Then, after a scramble of bodies in the penalty area, Tasic lost his balance and fell over, pulling Foulkes over as he did so. The referee gave a penalty, much to United's dismay and Tasic scored.

The crowd were now uncontrollable and in a frenzy

of excitement. Then Red Star got a free kick just outside the area. Kostic took it and, according to Dennis Viollet, the ball struck his head sending Gregg the wrong way - the ball trickling into the goal. 3-3. Red Star were just a goal behind on aggregate and there were only three minutes left. Red Star desperately wanted a replay but United's defence stood firm and the team celebrated as the final whistle blew - United were through to the semi-finals for the second successive year.

Immediately, Bert Whalley and first team trainer Tom Curry rushed onto the field and ordered the team back into the dressing room. There, along with the reserves, the press and the aircrew, they celebrated with bottles of beer brought over by Bert and Tom for such an occasion. Tommy Taylor and Eddie Colman draped towels around their waists and did a Latin American rumba, much to the delight of everyone. The newspaper reporters were acting as a backing outfit along with the pilots, Thain and Rayment. The stewardesses waited outside the dressing room until the lads had showered and changed.

Matt Busby had been into the Red Star dressing room to shake hands, being the diplomat that he was, to thank them for a good game. As he made his way to United's dressing room he saw the stewardesses waiting to enter and Matt told them he would check if it was all clear for them to go inside. Tommy Taylor was still dancing and, not realising, his manager was entering the room shouted out: "Bring those girls in here!" A few warning coughs from the players and Tommy turned round to see Busby inform Tommy: "The ladies will remain outside, thank you, until you're all decent." Matt winked at Captain Rayment as Tommy hurriedly dressed, much to the amusement of Dennis and the other players.

Back in the hotel everyone was busy getting ready for

the official post-match banquet in the British Embassy that night for both clubs. The players didn't like these affairs and would sooner have found their own enjoyment, however Matt Busby had insisted they attend. Each player received a tea set and a bottle of gin. Despite the game being extremely physical, there was a strong bond between the two sets of players because they appreciated each other's ability. Although the adrenaline was high, sleep was the last thing on their minds. With all the pressure and tension gone, the players were in a happy and contented frame of mind.

After the speeches, the three Yorkshire lads Tommy Taylor, David Pegg and Mark Jones, broke into their native anthem, Ilkla Moor Bah Tat with the rest of the team joining in the chorus. Roger Byrne had scribbled a note requesting permission for the players to be excused while they went for a drink together and Busby agreed. The players quickly filed out of reception and headed for various places. Dennis, Bobby Charlton and big Frank Swift, the former Manchester City and England goalkeeper who was now a journalist, went for a drink with some British Embassy officials. It was quite a mild night in comparison to their arrival in Belgrade.

The following morning the Manchester party packed their belongings and said their farewells to the hotel staff and various other officials. Dennis was still smiling to himself about a little prank that Tommy Taylor and Eddie Colman had got up to but nearly got caught out. They were going around the different rooms switching shoes that had been left outside room doors to be cleaned and they almost got caught out by Matt Busby. Tom Curry reminded the players that it was exactly twelve months to the day that United had achieved one of their greatest ever victories when they beat Bilbao, and like now, progressed to the semi-finals of the European Cup.

The coach took the party to Zenum airport for the return

flight back to Manchester. It was the same plane they had arrived on, a twin engine BEA Elizabethan, the RMA Lord Burleigh. The players didn't like flying but they were moving into the future and this was the quickest way to travel. They had a fair journey to Munich where they stopped to re-fuel - it was bitterly cold and the thick snow made it feel even colder. As the aircraft made its descent into Munich it came through dense cloud. Everyone got off the aircraft and went for refreshments while the journalists phoned their newspaper offices. When the announcement came for everyone to board the plane the passengers were laughing and joking. The two pilots checked the wings for snow and seemed satisfied that they did not need cleaning. An hour later everyone was back on the plane. The first take-off was aborted when the two pilots detected an uneven engine sound.

Captain Rayment pulled the throttle back and taxied back to prepare for a second attempt. Both pilots agreed to open the throttle more slowly this time. Forty seconds later, the same thing happened as the plane attempted to take off again and came to a halt halfway down the runway.

Captain Rayment told the passengers over the intercom not to worry as it was only a technical fault. The party disembarked and went into the lounge. They sat down and a great deal of small talk and nervous banter was going on, with Frank Swift the main instigator. It looked likely to be quite a few hours before they could leave, when to the surprise of everyone the call came for them to board the aircraft again.

As they boarded, Frank Taylor, a journalist, told Albert Scanlon: "In the RAF, if you didn't take off at the first attempt, the flight was cancelled!" Albert never replied. Dennis said that there never was a seating plan - Albert Scanlon sat at the front of the aircraft playing cards with Bill

Foulkes, where Dennis and Bobby Charlton joined them. They had been asked to swap places by Tommy Taylor and David Pegg. "Tthey thought it would be safer at the back," said Albert.

As the plane taxied and was cleared for take-off, Captain Rayment radioed the control tower telling them he was ready for take off. The last message from the aircraft to the control tower was made by Radio Officer Rodgers who informed the tower that the aircraft was rolling. Shortly afterwards came a howling and whistling sound. Albert watched a steward come running out from the cockpit and quickly strap himself into a seat, which wasn't reassuring.

BANG!

Passengers and luggage were scattered all over the plane, it was like being in the middle of a whirlpool. The aircraft seemed out of control and went round in circles. There was another explosion and the tail end of the plane broke off and burst into flames. The rest is history.

The aircraft was torn in half and several passengers had been thrown clear and landed in the snow. Rescuers were soon on the scene and along with Captain Thain, Peter Howard and Harry Gregg they searched the remains of the aircraft for anyone they could help. As they searched there was a worrying dripping, the smell of petrol and pall of dense smoke - they thought it would blow up at any second.

Still they searched the wreckage. The stewardesses Margaret Bellis and Rosemary Cheverton and Radio Officer Rogers worked tirelessly in an effort to help the injured. Harry Gregg rushed back into the burning aeroplane ignoring the order to "run for it" and he came out clutching what appeared to be a handful of rags. It was a baby, the twenty-two-month-old daughter of Vera Lukic, whose husband was the Yugoslav air attachÈ. United had agreed to give her a lift to England. The baby's face was bruised but she was still alive. Gregg handed the child to one of the stewardesses and rushed back into the plane. This time he came out of the burning aircraft with the baby's mother. This was bravery of the highest order!

Bill Foulkes tried to help Matt Busby, who was still in his seat on the ground. He was freezing cold. Billy rubbed his hands and body to bring some feeling back into Matt's body. Incidentally, he was the only one to survive of those who were facing forward on the plane. It was carnage! Bobby Charlton and Dennis had been thrown clear of the smoking aeroplane still strapped into their seats. "Everything was unnaturally quiet," said Bobby Charlton recalling the crash. "Then I saw Dennis next to me, and he had a nasty gash and his head was resting on a metal hub. The only thing wrong with me was a long scratch down one cheek."

When the wreckage had been checked, seven players were found dead: Roger Byrne, Geoff Bent, Eddie Colman, Mark Jones, David Pegg, Billy Whelan and Tommy Taylor. They were priceless, the backbone of Manchester United. Brilliant footballers and genuine characters who fitted into a team pattern that became the envy of every other team in the British Isles. Two weeks later Duncan Edwards lost his battle for life and passed away.

Three United officials also perished. Among them was Walter Crickmer, one of the finest administrators any football club could wish for. Walter had been associated with Manchester United for 38 years, becoming club secretary in 1926. In 1938, Walter had instigated the now-famous United youth policy and with Louis Rocca, took charge of United's first team for the 1931-32 season between the reigns of Herbert Bamlett and Scott Duncan.

Another of the dead, Bert Whalley, had joined United from Stalybridge Celtic in 1934 and made his debut in 1935. It was during the war years that dear old Bert gave United his best years as a player, appearing in nearly 200 games. After the war he appeared briefly for the first team before receiving a very bad eye injury while coaching schoolboys in Stockport. On the way to play in a reserve game at Newcastle, Bert mentioned he was having problems with his vision and was taken to Newcastle Infirmary where they wanted to admit him. Bert insisted he wanted to return to Manchester.

On Christmas Eve 1947 Bert was in hospital facing grave doubts about the sight of his eye and, worse than this, he knew that his career as a player was finished. He was understandably depressed about his future. That night, feeling as low as any family man could feel in the circumstances, Bert was visited by Jimmy Murphy. Jimmy knew that Bert's playing days were finished and mentioned his plight to Matt Busby.

On one of Bert's worst nights, where he was really upset, Matt Busby walked to his bedside. After the usual pleasantries, Matt could feel the depression, he put his hand on Bert's arm and told him to stop worrying. "Don't get upset Bert," said the United manager in a calm, reassuring tone. "Whatever happens there will be a job for you at Old Trafford." Bert never tired of telling everyone afterwards that Matt Busby's visit was the finest Christmas present he could have hoped for. He died in the seat next to Matt Busby. Tom Curry, the first-team trainer, also perished - a lovely warm-hearted man who always had a kind word for everyone.

Eight newspaper reporters also died in the crash, brilliant writers on this wonderful game. Many's the time that United fans didn't agree with what they wrote about their red-shirted heroes, especially the controversial Henry Rose. However they were all fondly respected and missed dearly. Alf Clarke, *Manchester Evening Chronicle*, Don Davies,

Manchester Guardian, George Follows, *Daily Herald*, Tom Jackson, *Manchester Evening News*, Archie Ledbrooke, *Daily Mirror*, Henry Rose, *Daily Express*, Eric Thompson, *Daily Mail* and the legendary England goalkeeper, Frank Swift, who wrote for the *News of the World*.

"These reporters were the cream of writers," Dennis once remarked. "They wrote vivid descriptions about the matches they watched so their readers felt as if they had actually been at the game themselves. There was very little muck-raking, that came later in the 1960s, although I must mention dear old Henry Rose. He loved mixing it in his articles. I recall him being very unkind and unfair to Tommy Taylor on a few occasions. Tommy had scored five goals in two England matches and Henry had a right go at Tommy. All the lads were extremely annoyed with Mr Rose and I remember Matt Busby and Jimmy Murphy having words with him. For all that he liked a bit of fun. Players might not have always agreed with what they wrote but on the whole we all got along with each other. They had a job to do and so did we, we respected each other. Great reporters and genuine fellows."

Matt Busby, Johnny Berry, Jackie Blanchflower, Dennis Viollet, Bobby Charlton, Albert Scanlon, Kenny Morgans and Ray Wood, along with Harry Gregg and Bill Foulkes ended up in hospital. Frank Taylor, another prominent journalist, was also very badly injured. Peter Howard, a *Daily Mail* photographer and Ted Ellyard, his colleague, received minor injuries. Pilot Ken Rayment was fatally injured, Mr Miklos died and his wife was so badly injured that she never walked again.

The surgeons, doctors and nurses at Munich's Rechts der Isar Hospital worked tirelessly in tending to the sick and injured from the crash. When news of the disaster was relayed to Manchester, people just couldn't believe it. When it finally sunk in people were openly crying and grey clouded the city once again. The only way to describe the atmosphere was a chill hysteria, a dark cloud fell over the people as they struggled to come to terms with loss of the team they loved.

Dennis was in hospital in Munich for a few weeks with severe head injuries. He and Bobby Charlton had been at the front of the aircraft near Bill Foulkes, Harry Gregg and journalist Frank Taylor. Dennis later said that even after the first two failed attempts he didn't think that anyone was particularly worried that the plane wouldn't eventually take off at the next attempt. He expressed the view that had David Pegg stayed where was, with him and Bobby Charlton instead of moving further down the plane to sit with his best friend Eddie Colman, he would probably have survived.

"The aeroplane was an old Elizabethan which had wings on top of the fuselage," Dennis recalled. "Looking out through the snow- flecked window I could see the wheels. I watched them on the final attempt to take off and felt a terrific surge and then a loss of power. Even then, I don't think anyone was too worried, it was just a question of waiting for the plane to leave the ground. The first I knew things were not right was that we had come off the end of the runway and were ploughing through a fence and across a road. I turned to Bob [Charlton] and told him to relax, he too had seen what was happening. The next thing, I heard a terrible grinding, tearing noise and looking in horror through the window I saw the wing of the plane being torn away. There was an almighty bang and the side of the plane had a huge hole in it. I felt myself fallingfalling- falling into pitch darkness. Then, in what seemed a matter of seconds it was all over.

"Bob and I, still in our seats, were 70 yards away from the plane. I had no socks or shoes on my feet, I was freezing cold, and my head was aching. It was then that I saw the full horror of what had happened, the twisted wreckage of the aircraft with steam or smoke rising from the tangle of metal. My head was split wide open and I was covered in blood but Bob seemed to have received only a slight knock to the back of his head. It's strange what people do in certain circumstances. Bob just got up and walked away. I was not really conscious and didn't know what had happened. I remember walking back to the plane and Bob was there with Bill Foulkes and Harry Gregg. Bob put his arm round me and I asked him a stupid question: "Have we crashed Bob?" It was then I understood what had happened for I could see the carnage all around me. It was an absolute nightmare, a scene of utter destruction, with mangled wreckage and bodies lying in the snow. I felt terribly angry at what had happened. I just wanted to dash into that wrecked plane, find the pilot and attack him."

Dennis said that he often had flashbacks of the disaster. He remembered people arriving on the scene after what seemed an eternity as he and the other survivors staggered around in the freezing snow. He heard voices in English and German and they were trying to calm him down. Then he recalls being put into the back of a Volkswagen van. Bill Foulkes was also in the van looking after Matt Busby who was making a groaning noise and had dreadful injuries and a Yugoslavian lady who was also badly hurt. Bobby Charlton had also climbed into the van, Bill Foulkes was asking them if they felt alright, but Dennis said he felt that he was going to be sick and Bobby said he felt the same.

The van set off and Dennis fell unconscious but was suddenly wideawake again as the van began swerving at top speed in the snow. "I thought we were going to crash. As I looked up I saw Bill Foulkes with his hands around the driver's neck trying to strangle him. The van was swerving all over the place. The driver was obviously anxious to get us to the hospital and going a bit too fast. Bill felt he had to stop him going that fast. Everything worked out fine and a second crash was avoided."

As they went into the hospital, Dennis spotted Frank Swift lying dead on a stretcher and he passed out again. The next thing he remembered was waking up in a ward with four or five other patients, all Germans who couldn't speak a word of English. In all the confusion the hospital officials must have put him in the first vacant ward they could find. It wasn't until the following day that Dennis could think clearly. His ankles and feet were causing him a great deal of pain. It appeared that he somehow lost his shoes and socks in the crash and hurt his feet walking about in the slush and snow afterwards.

"I was very pleased to see my feet were still there," said Dennis. "I suddenly started remembering things that happened. I saw many of the lads on the ground among the debris of the plane. I tried to dismiss these things from my mind because I felt sure it just wasn't true, or at worst, like me, they had merely been unconscious for a while. I was relieved when Bill Foulkes came to visit me and I asked him how Eddie Colman was? It was then that I realised that the pictures flashing through my mind were in fact real and not just a nightmare. It had actually happened. I saw some of the other lads when the nurses put me into a ward with Kenny Morgans, Bobby Charlton, Jackie Blanchflower and Johnny Berry. Johnny was critically ill and was moved to another room. Jackie asked a nurse if she would get him a Carlsberg. That sounds just like Jackie, I thought, I asked if she would bring me one as well."

Dennis was kept in bed for over two weeks and was not allowed to take a bath or a shower. He wasn't allowed to go upstairs to visit any of the other casualties. Matt Busby,

Johnny Berry, Duncan Edwards, Kenny Morgans, Ray Wood, and Bobby Charlton were all on the same ward. When Dennis was allowed out of bed and given permission to walk upstairs to see the other injured people the first person he met was Matt Busby. Matt was so ill that he had not been told the full extent of the crash. "How are the rest of the boys?" he whispered to Dennis. Dennis, not knowing himself who had died, didn't know what to say to his manager.

"I never saw Duncan again," said Dennis. "He had been put on a life support machine and his incredible will and strength had kept him alive for so long, I wasn't allowed out of bed when he eventually died. I used to play cards every day with Jackie Blanchflower, then one day they released me from hospital providing I returned every day for treatment. I readily agreed and after treatment I would sit with Jackie and the other lads. The *Daily Express* very kindly relayed a telephone commentary to us in the hospital of the game against Sheffield Wednesday and they did the same for the game against Nottingham Forest a few days later. After listening to these matches I wanted to get back home quickly. I was thinking about everyone back in Manchester and how my family must be feeling."

Ray Wood, the Manchester United goalkeeper who, like Dennis, was a survivor of the crash recalls being in the Rechts der Isar Hospital along with the other injured. Earlier in their careers they lived near each other, Ray in Flixton and Dennis in Urmston. They would catch the same number six bus to Old Trafford and sit upstairs smoking. Ray and Dennis always had a laugh together.

Once he was discharged, Ray came back to Manchester but he was still injured and in terrible pain. His jaw and teeth were badly damaged in the crash and he still needed an operation. United arranged for him to go into St Joseph's

Hospital in Whalley Range, a private hospital run by an order of nuns. The day after the operation in which Ray was to have all his teeth taken out and surgery to his jaw, he was obviously feeling very sore and uncomfortable.

Dennis entered Ray's private room, walked over to his bedside and with a beaming smile on his face asked: "How you feeling today Woodie?" Ray told him that he was in pain and added that his jaw felt as if it had been punched by Floyd Patterson, the world heavyweight champion. "I've brought this for you, Ray," said Dennis, and presented him with a very large, very hard, green baking apple.

Matt Busby's wife Jean and their daughter Sheena were staying in the same hotel as Dennis. Jean and Sheena would visit the hospital every day and night, visiting all the beds, talking and listening to the sick and injured. Both displayed remarkable courage and fortitude. Even though her husband had been given the last rites from a Catholic priest and was gravely ill, Jean and her daughter still went around the hospital speaking to everyone and attempting to cheer them up. Dennis recalled one night while in the hotel bar: "We were both upset and we started drinking brandy and we relaxed a little. After a few more drinks we decided to dance a polka, and ended up dancing around the bar. The hotel staff were annoyed and asked them to stop dancing. Jean was told that if she did not stop dancing she would have to leave the hotel."

A few years later, after Matt Busby had been knighted, Dennis said: "I remembered the incident in the German hotel when Jean was told to behave or she would be asked to leave. I bet that was the only time Lady Busby had been threatened with eviction."

It was March 4th before Dennis was allowed to return to England. He was overjoyed. He rushed to the hospital in Munich, thanked the doctors and nurses profusely, said his goodbyes to his friends, Matt Busby and Frank Taylor, packed his sparse belongings and set off for Manchester. He refused point-blank to fly back! He went by train to the Hook of Holland and then took a ferry to Harwich. It was a long and laborious journey but Dennis felt better for it.

"I was still suffering from violent headaches, but managed to eventually fall off to sleep." On the morning that the ferry berthed in England there was a knock on his cabin door, a steward brought him a cup of tea and some biscuits and excitedly shouted: "You've won, you've won!" He then gave him the news that United had beaten West Bromwich Albion in a sixth-round replay, in front of over 60,000 people at Old Trafford the previous night. Dennis was delighted to hear that Colin Webster had scored the solitary goal and Bobby Charlton made it with a brilliant run. "This was a lovely welcome home for me," said a smiling Dennis.

Once back home with his wife and children, Dennis was suddenly struck by the impact the crash in Munich had had on everybody. He was touched by ordinary people stopping him and expressing their concern for his health. Many told him how sorry they were about the people who had perished in the crash, but despite the kindness shown him, he still felt empty and lost.

"I remember going back to Old Trafford for the first time since Munich. There was a strange feeling about the place for me," he said. "When I walked into the dressing room and then out onto the pitch, there was a strange silence, I cannot really describe the strange feeling that came over me. I knew at that moment that for me, and I suspect other people as well, Old Trafford would never be the same again. But I realised that life had to go on and I desperately wanted to get back training and helping the club."

In later years, when discussing events after he came home from Munich, Dennis gave the opinion that though

Manchester United had enjoyed a great deal of success since the Munich disaster, he didn't believe that the teams that followed were anywhere near as good as the team that perished. "There was something special about the Manchester United team before the crash. That side possessed some extraordinary players and characters. Their ability was tremendous and they were all getting better and better because of the experience we were gaining. The Busby Babes, a name by the way that neither the team nor Matt particularly cared for, had a unique bond of togetherness and an unquenchable, unbreakable spirit. Most of us had grown up together in the Manchester United youth teams, I had been at the club since leaving school, playing with Roger Byrne, Eddie Colman, Duncan Edwards and David Pegg. Though some had not grown up in Manchester, they were only of school age when they joined and we all grew up as teenagers together and we were genuine friends. Seriously, we would have gone through a brick wall for United. We had a camaraderie the like of which you would find hard to get at any other club, it had gone never to return. I noticed this as the years moved on."

The Busby Babes

The famous Busby Babes, or the Red Devils, as they had affectionately become known, were a truly wonderful team - perhaps the greatest club side the British Isles have ever produced. The famous line-up usually read: Wood; Foulkes, Byrne; Colman, Jones, Edwards; Berry, Whelan, Taylor, Viollet, Pegg. Below is a brief appreciation of them:

RAY WOOD: GOALKEEPER.

Tall and lean, Ray was one of the few players for whom Matt Busby paid a transfer fee. Ray was bought from Darlington and played three times for England. A steady and reliable keeper with no frills, Ray was a great professional with a laid-back attitude. He gave United sterling service until being replaced by Harry Gregg.

BILL FOULKES: RIGHT FULL-BACK.

Affectionately known as 'Cowboy' because of his bandy legs, Bill eventually played over 650 matches for United, receiving just one England cap. A teak-tough, straightfaced and uncomplicated player, he later switched to centre-half, and won two more Championship medals, an FA Cup medal and, fittingly, a European Cup medal in 1968, having scored a vital goal against Real Madrid along the way.

ROGER BYRNE: LEFT FULL-BACK AND CAPTAIN.

A class player, Roger played 33 consecutive games for England up to Munich and must surely rate among the best left full-backs ever to play for England. With the speed of a former left-winger, he was tough and could be cantankerous at times. He had played in the 1952 championship side. Roger was an intelligent person who was studying to become a physiotherapist in preparation for when his playing days were over. Well respected by management and players, Roger was a captain who led by example.

EDDIE COLMAN: RIGHT-HALF.

A Salford lad through and through, Eddie was the cheeky chappie of the team, always ready for a laugh and a joke, he loved playing pranks on his team-mates and training staff at Old Trafford. Eddie was also known as the player with the Marilyn Monroe wiggle when he played and was potentially one of the greatest right-halves in British football. Immensely liked by all his team-mates, his death cost not only Manchester United, but England a star.

MARK JONES: CENTRE-HALF.

Mark was a giant of a man, standing 6 feet 1 inch and tipping the scales at 14 stones. He was one of three

161

Yorkshire lads in the team. He and Jackie Blanchflower were in constant competition for the centre-half spot in the team. Mark was a big, powerful stopper who feared nothing or nobody on the field. Off the field he was a quiet pipe-smoker and budgie-breeder. He was unlucky that Billy Wright was captain of England and regarded as an institution, which prevented big Mark from becoming an England regular.

DUNCAN EDWARDS: LEFT-HALF.

There are quite genuinely no words to describe this colossus. Over the years various wing-halves have been compared to 'Big Dunc'. Terry Venables, as a youngster, was one and Kevin Beattie of Ipswich was another, but in all honesty this was, and is, totally unfair to the players mentioned. In life there comes but one legend, one special sportsman that everyone can identify with and Duncan Edwards was such a person. He really could do the lot and play in any position. Pass, shoot, tackle, head, run, Duncan was exceptional at everything. He had already played for England 18 times and was only 21 when he perished, having sustained fatal injuries in the Munich tragedy.

JOHNNY BERRY: OUTSIDE-RIGHT.

Johnny was the oldest member of the team and the smallest at 5 feet 5 inches. He joined United from Birmingham City for £15,000 in the 1951-52 season. A speedy, tricky right-winger, Johnny played four times for England and was unlucky that in his position was also that of both Stanley Matthews and Tom Finney. Johnny was as brave as they come and survived the Munich air crash, only to discover that his injuries were too bad to continue playing football.

BILLY WHELAN: INSIDE-RIGHT.

Billy was a beautifully cultured player with lovely ball control and a deadly eye for goal. This young man's future was destined for greatness. Billy played four times for Eire and made nearly 100 appearances for United, scoring over 50 goals. He was a devout Catholic, whose religion gave him strength at Munich.

TOMMY TAYLOR: CENTRE-FORWARD.

Big Tommy was one of the most popular players in the Busby Babes team. Signed from Barnsley in 1953 for £29,999, he became a Manchester United legend. Known as the 'Smiling Executioner' Tommy was a prolific scorer, playing 46 games and netting 28 goals for Barnsley and then 189 appearances, scoring 128 goals for United. He played 19 games for England, scoring 16 goals while in 'B' internationals he played twice and scored four times. More than this, Tommy was a wholehearted player who never knew when he was beaten. He was often criticised by the press, particularly while playing for England, even after scoring two hat-tricks for his country.

DAVID PEGG: OUTSIDE-LEFT.

David was a handsome fellow who used to have the girls swooning after him. He was an excellent left winger as well and would most certainly have been one of super stars of the 1960s era when top players were treated like pop stars. He made his first team debut in December 1952, less than three months after his 17th birthday. He played only once for England but many more caps seemed assured for this talented player.

Keep The Red Flag Flying High!

After the shocking events of Munich, life at Manchester United had to carry on. The Football authorities helped re-arrange the games for the remainder of the season but United were still involved on all fronts: the FA Cup, European Cup and in the hunt for the First Division. Just forty-eight hours after the disaster, United were due to play their fierce Midland rivals Wolves - a game which inevitably was cancelled.

The club was in turmoil. Interestingly, Dennis is featured on the cover of the rare programme that had already been printed for the visit of Wolves. This programme was supposed to have been incinerated, but quite a few escaped and have since become very expensive collectable items. Coincidentally, Dennis made his return to United's first team after Munich in the re-arranged game against Wolves later in the season.

Jimmy Murphy kept Manchester United going throughout this terrible ordeal. Almost single-handedly he hauled the club from the ashes and watched, as like a Phoenix, it rose again. Jimmy had been over in Munich visiting the sick and injured, getting everybody laughing again. Once out of view, he would break down and sob like a baby. People often forget that Manchester United could have gone under, had Jimmy not pulled them together just as Matt Busby had asked him on his sick bed. "Keep the flag flying, Jimmy," Matt had commanded. Murphy did more than that, much more.

After visiting Munich he was back at Old Trafford working night and day, both in the office and on the training field, trying to organise a team to fulfil the club's engagements in all three competitions. Many a time staff would see him with his head in his hands, crying, wondering how he was going to field a team. One morning shortly after the air crash, the phone rang in Murphy's office. It was Mr Mitchell, the Luton Town chairman. After enquiring if there was any help Luton could give to United, Jimmy Murphy said: "Well actually there is Mr Chairman, I would like Jack Crompton back here, helping us out."

Of course, Jack Crompton had been Manchester United's goalkeeper for many years until his retirement in 1956 to take up a coaching job with Luton. Mr Mitchell agreed to his return. Les Olive, another club stalwart who once worked closely with Walter Crickmer, now found himself shouldering the administrative duties of the club. Meanwhile, the FA broke with tradition by allowing cup-tied players to turn out for United in that season's competition. But Murphy learned the hard way that, though sympathetic, only Liverpool and Nottingham Forest actually offered any practical help in the way of players.

Jimmy was desperate. He was spending 18 hours a day at Old Trafford and working himself to a standstill. Eventually he signed Ernie Taylor from Blackpool. Ernie was a fantastic inside-forward and Stanley Matthews was always praising him. The press claimed that Murphy was going to sign some big names, but initial offers of help from rival clubs often turned to nothing and many proposed signings failed to materialise. But two hours before United played Sheffield Wednesday, Jimmy signed Stan Crowther, a robust winghalf, from Aston Villa.

"United Will Go On", proclaimed the bold headlines on the front of the United Review for the FA Cup fifth round tie against Sheffield Wednesday - a mere 13 days after Munich. The sombre programme paid a poignant tribute to all those who had perished or were injured in the tragedy. United's sense of loss and bewilderment was solemnly reflected in the programme line-up which showed eleven blank spaces opposite the eleven Sheffield Wednesday names.

Murphy had to select a team from the players remaining in United's heavily depleted squad. He also had Munich survivors Harry Gregg and Bill Foulkes in his team. In reality neither Gregg nor Foulkes should have played so soon after their horrendous ordeal, but they wanted to help Murphy and United out of the crisis. The teams lined up as follows:

United: Gregg; Foulkes, Greaves; Goodwin, Cope, Crowther; Webster, Taylor (E), Dawson, Pearson, Brennan.

Sheffield Wednesday: Ryalls; Martin, Johnson; Kay, Swan, O'Donnell; Wilkinson, Quixall, Shiner, Froggatt, Finney.

Their manager was Eric Taylor. Sheffield Wednesday captain Albert Quixall recalls that emotional evening: "The draw had already been made before the air crash and I was devastated by the disaster. I remember being at home listening to the radio when a newsflash broke into the programme and said the plane carrying the Manchester United team and officials had crashed. Immediately my first thoughts were what the hell was going to happen to our game against them the following week, little realising the gravity of the terrible situation. Naturally, when the grim news came through about the players, it left me very sad indeed.

"You see these were great pals of mine, from international, Army and schoolboy days, players such as Roger Byrne, Tommy Taylor, Duncan Edwards, David Pegg and Mark Jones. When the match finally came round nearly two weeks later there was no way Sheffield Wednesday could have won, the whole country was behind United and I suspect so were the rest of my side. I led my team down the tunnel after United, never could the emotion of that evening have hit anybody harder. Two of the United side, Mark Pearson and Shay Brennan were actually making their debuts in the first team and incredibly it was this pair, out on the left wing, who caused all the problems. Shay scored the first goal straight from a corner at the Manchester end and I was sure the crowd blew it in! Brennan also got United's second, before Mark Pearson, who was a Sheffield lad incidentally, opened us up for Alex Dawson to make it three. The actual game was a blur, United somehow managed to play some football, despite the emotion and deservedly knocked us out 3-0."

The first league game after Munich, a 1-1 draw against Nottingham Forest, drew over 66,000 spectators - a record attendance for a league match at the time. Three meetings with West Brom in a week, twice in the FA Cup and a home league match, showed that football was really back on Manchester United's agenda, although the devastating news of Duncan Edwards' death left a numb feeling throughout the football world.

The first game at the Hawthorns ended 2-2, Ernie Taylor scoring and making a goal for Alex Dawson, before West Brom scored with a last-minute equaliser. The replay on the following Wednesday night was another emotion filled night to Old Trafford.

Future snooker star John Virgo was at this game. John was a fanatical United supporter in his younger days and this match remains particularly vivid to him. "Manchester United meant a great deal to me, and my neighbours in Salford. It was only a short walk down Trafford Road past the Docks and over the swing bridge to Old Trafford. It was a release to go to watch United, particularly when you could watch players of the calibre of big Duncan Edwards, Eddie Colman, Tommy Taylor and of course, Dennis Viollet. When the air crash destroyed that side I was probably too young to know what was really happening."

John was among the thousands who witnessed the

incredible scenes at Old Trafford during March and April 1958, as a makeshift side kept Manchester United ticking over. One game which really sticks in John Virgo's mind was the sixth round FA Cup replay against West Bromwich Albion in March 1958. "It was shortly after Munich and the crowds Manchester United were attracting were incredible in those days, for this cup-tie I had to be in the ground before 6pm to have any chance of watching the game."

West Bromwich Albion had a fine side, including future England manager Bobby Robson, future Arsenal coach and classy England full-back Don Howe, Ray Barlow, Ronnie Allen, Derek Kevan and Brian Whitehouse, who later joined Manchester United's coaching staff. United knew they had their work cut out to get any kind of a result. It was a close game at Old Trafford, Harry Gregg was outstanding in United's goal and extra time seemed inevitable, when something happened that very few present will ever forget.

Bobby Charlton, not long back from the injuries he sustained in the crash, moved out onto the right wing and seemed to beat half a dozen defenders before squaring the ball to Colin Webster who had moved into the middle and Colin coolly slotted the ball past Sanders in the West Brom goal. With the crowd emotional and the noise stupendous, the referee blew the final whistle. A miracle had occurred, United were through to the semi-final after an unforgettable end to an unforgettable game of football. The ground opened up to the United team, people were openly sobbing hysterically and the Reds were on their way to Wembley. Three days later they met again at Old Trafford in a league game, United going down 4-0. The Cup game had drained the players so much that the result was not unexpected.

News came through at this time that the European

authorities had allowed United to travel overland to play their semi-final against either Dortmund or AC Milan, allowing them time to get back to England to fulfil their league commitments. Because of promotion into the first team other youngsters were appearing in the Central League team: Nobby Stiles, the teenage Collyhurst kid and Johnny Giles, the Dublin-born inside forward among them.

United's league form was in truth, abysmal. In fact, the only victory United achieved in the league after Munich was a 2-1 Easter Monday away win over Sunderland. Meanwhile three top-class amateur players from the famous Bishop Auckland team came to United's rescue": Bob Hardisty, Derek Lewin and Warren Bradley. These three played mostly in the reserves but Bradley, a fast-raiding right-winger, later turned professional and went on to play for England. Two home draws followed, against Sunderland and Preston North End.

But the lure of Wembley remained the prime goal. In the semifinal at Villa Park, against Second Division Fulham, United drew 2-2. Bobby Charlton scored two blockbusters to give United a replay at Highbury. Although Fulham were a Second Division team, they had some wonderfully talented players. Tony Macedo was tipped to become a truly great goalkeeper, George Cohen went on to play at right-back for England in 1966, while Roy Bentley and Johnny Haynes were established England internationals.

The replay the following Thursday afternoon made a national pastime of absenteeism as the game was televised live and record viewing figures were broken. United annihilated the team music hall comedian Tommy Trinder kept in the headlines. Alex Dawson got a hat-trick, the first player to get three goals in an FA Cup semifinal since the 1948 semi-final when Dennis Viollet's idol, Stan Pearson, did the trick. Alex remains the youngest post-war player to score a hat-trick in the FA Cup. Shay Brennan and Bobby Charlton added a goal each to give the Reds an emphatic 5-3 victory and, just as the late Roger Byrne had prophesied following the 1957 defeat, return the club to Wembley.

The depleted United team had achieved wonders - Jimmy Murphy had worked non-stop to make sure they upheld United's famous fighting spirit. Dennis, meanwhile, had not kicked a ball in anger since the crash. Through training he was making a steady improvement and there was speculation about a fairy tale return in time for Wembley.

On April 21st, United played their postponed game against league leaders Wolverhampton Wanderers at Old Trafford. This game was just one of United's nine fixtures in April that year. Jimmy Murphy was pondering the situation very carefully. Should he risk Dennis Viollet or rely on Mark Pearson, the 18-year-old youngster who had given valiant service to the club in this crisis? On the down side was the fact that Dennis had been warned by doctors that any further bangs to his head could have severe repercussions for him, but he was desperate to play.

"I really wanted to play again," said Dennis, "I couldn't stand waiting around any longer and I went to talk to Jimmy Murphy. He understood how I felt and said as long as I got permission from the doctor I could play. After the FA Cup semi-final I persuaded him that I was fit enough and they finally allowed me to test myself in a competitive game. Jimmy selected me for a reserve game, it was a wonderful, wonderful moment when I finally ran out onto a pitch again, even if it was only in the reserves. Later, Jimmy selected me to play in the first team against Wolves. They were topping the league table and were a very hard and robust side."

It was a beautiful spring evening with a bright sun in the sky and Dennis was selected to play. Wolves were in no mood to ease his way back into first team action however and the championselect hammered United 4-0 but though there was no disputing Wolves' easy victory, Dennis stood out like a sore thumb. He was brilliant! Taking on the Wolves defence single-handedly, he dribbled past man after man, shot when he saw an opportunity and was without doubt United's Man-of-the-Match. Murphy was delighted. A fit, strong Dennis Viollet was a bonus for him and the team. A further match against Chelsea, a 2-1 defeat, kept Dennis in the picture. The onus was on Jimmy Murphy. Would he go for experience and choose Dennis for Wembley or revert to the 18- year-old Pearson.

After a great deal of soul searching Jimmy Murphy told Dennis he would indeed be playing against Bolton Wanderers at Wembley. The year before he had failed a late fitness test and missed playing in the final against Aston Villa. His name was in the match programme as down to play, but he was not selected. This time the roles had been reversed: no name on the official programme, but he was in the team. This was amazing after just two weeks back in competitive football and three months following Munich.

The unlucky players were Kenny Morgans and Mark Pearson. "Jimmy called me to one side," said Dennis when recalling his selection for the Cup final. "He told me I would be playing at Wembley. I was over the moon with joy!" Despite feeling on top of the world at his good news, Dennis was soon brought back down to earth when the Manchester United FA Cup team was officially announced. He received several letters telling him he had no right to be playing at Wembley because he had not featured in any of the cup matches since before Munich. He treated the letters with disdain. Dennis mentioned the correspondence to a few friends and word got around. Jimmy Murphy got to know and pulled Dennis to one side. "Forget them. Let's get on with winning that final, you're in the team and that is that."

Murphy had decided to switch Alex Dawson to outside-right and play Dennis in his favoured inside-forward position. Morgans had made a few appearances in the first team since coming back from his injuries at Munich. He had played mostly on the left wing but had played a couple on the right wing as well. Murphy decided Kenny had not regained the confidence he showed before Munich. Many considered that Mark Pearson, known as 'Pancho' because of his long sideburns, could consider himself more than a little unlucky in missing out. However he had not played in the last three league games for the first team. Murphy had toyed with the idea of playing him but realised that when a player as good and experienced as Dennis Viollet was available, there was no choice. So Dennis played!

It was Dennis's brilliant hat-trick that had begun the Cup run and on Cup final day, May 3rd 1958, Wembley's 100,000 capacity crowd was bathed in sunshine. Emotions were running very high as Matt Busby, walking with the aid of sticks, and looking pale and ill, sat with the United officials near the pitch. Busby had made a miraculous recovery from the many injuries he had sustained at Munich.

Unfortunately United received the blow they didn't need when Bolton scored after just three minutes. Nat Lofthouse, the 'Lion of Vienna', was the scorer. Nat was an old-fashioned type of English centre forward, very much respected not only by his own teammates, but by the opposition as well. "It was a real sickener to be a goal down after only three minutes," conceded Dennis. "The Wembley turf was beautiful but very spongy and we knew that we now needed two goals if we were to lift the trophy."

Dennis had a couple of opportunities, and before the

crash he would most probably have put at least one of them away. However, it wasn't meant to be. He tried, but nothing came off for him in this game. The enthusiasm, fervour and passion that had been so significant in United's recent run-up to the final seemed to have diminished completely. Bobby Charlton drove a cannonball shot against the post with Eddie Hopkinson, the Bolton goalkeeper beaten and amazingly the ball bounced back into the arms of the grateful keeper. The United fans groaned and looked up to the heavens.

Then in the 55th minute Lofthouse scored a very controversial second goal. A high crossed ball was easily caught by Harry Gregg. Nat Lofthouse, moving forward like a tank, charged Gregg and the ball over the line. Gregg was flat out in the net, hurt and needing attention. Surely this was a foul? However, the United players were shook rigid when the referee, Mr Sherlock of Sheffield, had no hesitation in awarding a goal. The United fans vented their anger. The same thing had happened the year previous when Peter McParland had charged Ray Wood. But the players, although annoyed with the referee, showed no sign of petulance and got on with the game, after Harry Gregg received treatment from Jack Crompton. In the end Bolton were worthy winners, Nat Lofthouse was one of England's greatest ever centre-forwards and deserved his winners' medal. In later years, Nat praised the Busby Babes and especially Tommy Taylor who took his place in the England team.

Later that night, at the club's official reception in the Savoy Hotel, nobody was downhearted. A few of the doctors and nurses who had looked after the injured in the Munich hospital were among the guests. Dennis and the other survivors spent time chatting to them, however, when he sat down to speak to the doctor who had warned him of the dangers of playing football again, she kissed him and, laughing, scolded him. Dennis knew United were beaten comprehensively, but he enjoyed the occasion nevertheless. "The families of some of the lads who died in the crash were at the banquet," said Dennis. "I felt sad and guilty. Here I was supposedly enjoying myself, while their sons or brothers were no longer with us."

United had to put the disappointment of their low-key performance at Wembley to the back of their minds because the following week, European Cup action returned to Old Trafford. The league games had finished, with United ninth in the table.

Dennis, though obviously upset at Wembley performance, got down to the task of facing AC Milan in the first leg of the semifinal of the European Cup. There were 44,880 in Old Trafford as the teams ran out onto the pitch. Milan were a tough skillful team with Uruguayan centre-forward Schiaffino, one of their world-class stars. It was this player who put AC Milan into a first-half lead which threatened to blow United apart. Dennis had other plans however. Five minutes from half-time, he spotted centre-half Cesare Maldini's misdirected backpass to his goalkeeper. Dennis nipped in smartly and in typical poacher's manner, put the ball into the Italian goal to make it 1-1.

As the second half began it became obvious that Maldini and Viollet were the principal players and with less than eleven minutes of the game remaining, Dennis hared down the wing with the ball seemingly glued to his boots. Centre-half Maldini raced across to tackle him, Dennis quickly cut inside, the two men were shoulder to shoulder. They collided and down went Dennis and the Danish referee pointed straight away to the penalty spot. Bedlam broke out immediately, the Milanese moaning and gesturing, even their officials got in on the act. When order was restored, little Ernie Taylor placed the ball on the spot, stepped back and hammered it via the underside of the bar into the net. Old Trafford erupted, United had won 2-1. Could they reach a second Cup final?

Dennis was delighted with this result over a tough, classy Italian team. However, he knew that it was going to be an uphill struggle when they visited Milan for the return leg for the right to face Champions Real Madrid in the final.

"I'm glad we got a result tonight," remarked Dennis. "Jimmy has done magnificently in getting a team together and taking us to Wembley and, after the disappointment of losing on Saturday, getting a win tonight. Some of the younger lads, like Mark Pearson, are potentially very good players but I feel sorry that they are having to be pushed into the first team because of our circumstances."

The San Siro Stadium, Milan was a hotbed for the return. A crowd of over 100,000 fevered Italians created a cauldron of sheer hostility and hatred. Before United had set foot in Italy their press had stirred up a frightening hatred of Milan's opponents. The British press was astounded at the bile coming from their Italian opposite numbers, fanning the fury of the Milanese - clearly United's patched-up side were in for a very tough game. This attitude seemed strange. Let's face it, United in their current condition position posed no real threat to Milan and there certainly appeared to be no need for this kind of hysteria from the Italians.

Milan won as expected, 4-0 in a game full of niggly fouls. German referee Albert Deutsch allowed far too many infringements to go unpunished. United tried hard with young Mark Pearson getting stuck in and Colin Webster, Ronnie Cope, Kenny Morgans and Freddie Goodwin the pick of United's players. Just before half-time, the referee blew his whistle and stopped the game. It was amazing really, but everyone stood for a minute's silence with the United players and English press thinking the silence was for Munich. However, they later learned that it was for an Italian FA official who had died. Mark Pearson was warned three times by the referee for aggressive play when all he was doing was giving back a little of the treatment he was receiving. Colin Webster was nearly lynched by Milan players and officials after clashing with Fontana. But in the final, Milan lost to Real Madrid, after extra time.

Jimmy Murphy was relieved when the game was over. He rushed his team back to the dressing room as quickly as possible. Dennis had not had a great game by any stretch of the imagination however he had only been back in training for three weeks and he wasn't yet his usual sharp self. Murphy knew the close season was just the tonic United needed to relieve the turmoil of Munich.

When asked by newspapermen what he thought of the game, Murphy smiled and said he had no excuses, but thought the referee was much too biased. Ernie Taylor shouted that this was the worst game he had played during his seventeen-year career. Dennis sat in the dressing room looking deflated and dejected. His mind seemed a million miles away. The following day the English press were scathing in their reports. Terrence Elliot, writing in the *Daily Express* seemed to speak for everybody when he declared it: "The Dirtiest Game I've Seen." Bobby Charlton had missed both games because he had been selected to play for England.

Despite Munich and his injuries, Dennis finished the season with 23 goals from 31 first-team appearances over the three competitions. What he needed more than ever was a good long break from the rigours of football and the psychological aftermath of the events of Munich. The whole club needed to come to terms with the loss of close friends and team-mates. The close season would give the United management time to evaluate the future for the club. The playing staff would be scrutinised and a list of possible signings drawn up.

*

During the close season Dennis rested and enjoyed the company of his family. One day he was in a reflective mood and started talking about his career at Old Trafford and some of his earlier team mates. He mentioned the Busby Babes tag: "We have had many other names from the wags on the terraces, but the Busby Babes tag has lasted," he said smiling. He went on to say that at first he and other United players were not keen on this moniker, but bit by bit they all grew to accept it.

"It became more than a tag. It became like a medal, the badge, almost, of a secret society of youngsters being groomed, we hoped for stardom. Notice I said 'hoped'. That was as far as we dare go. Big heads was the last thing we dare be with the Boss and Jimmy around." Dennis said that it was explained to him by Busby, Murphy and Bert Whalley, that there were no short cuts to guaranteed success, no assurance that they would make the grade, no endless conveyor belt that could provide young footballers to order from some sort of HG Wells factory.

Puffing on his cigarette, Dennis continued: "One of the popular ideas from my early days at Old Trafford was that kids like myself, Roger Byrne, Jeff Whitefoot, Mark Jones, Brian Birch, Don Gibson and the rest were almost like mechanical youngsters. Rigorously drilled to set moves and reactions, like chess pieces moved around to a pattern by mastermind manager Matt Busby. In fact the opposite was the case. No youngsters at any other club ever had more fun or freedom than we had, or were encouraged to play football to their own style. We remained individuals. We didn't, of course, just play as we liked. There were the pre-match talks when Matt would outline the strengths and weaknesses of our opponents. His knowledge of players all over the country was incredible.

"Matt Busby would hardly ever hold an inquest immediately after a game, he would wait until Monday morning and sit the team down and calmly and rationally discuss the week-end game. He would never, ever criticise an individual but would instead generalise and when he got the player on his own would discuss his particular contribution."

Dennis talked about the myth of the lack of two-footed footballers at United. "A lot of nonsense is talked about two-footed players and some boys being sent out with a tennis shoe on one foot and a football boot on the other in an effort to make them two-footed. Hour after hour, we hear, they slog away boring themselves to death and getting nowhere. We Busby Babes were lucky to have the old brigade around. Not enough credit has been given to those great fellows: Allenby Chilton, Stan Pearson, Henry Cockburn and the rest but we had to learn patience. It didn't follow that just because you were an inside-right you would play in that position, or even play at all. I waited three years for my first outing with the seniors, and that was at Newcastle at outside-right after being a wing-half and inside-forward for the 'A' team and the Central League side. That was a sign of the times at the club, we had very good players waiting to fill every position."

From the Shadows

Before Manchester United were able to contemplate rebuilding their position as the top club team in the country, England showed what an awesome task it was going to be during the 1958 World Cup finals in Sweden. England had lost three regulars in Roger Byrne, Duncan Edwards and Tommy Taylor and although the England selectors could find experienced replacements from other league clubs, Manchester United were not afforded that luxury.

They had lost eight first team players - a frightening proposition. Only one Manchester United player, Bobby Charlton, was selected by England to go to Sweden as part of their World Cup squad. But had Bobby completely recovered from the horror of Munich? Dennis certainly hadn't but he knew he had little chance of selection although he was shortlisted along with 39 others for the initial squad. He was disappointed, but not surprised, when he failed to make the final selection.

Bobby Charlton had made his England debut at Hampden Park against Scotland a couple of months after the Munich disaster. It was April 1958 and he scored a magnificent goal in England's 4-0 victory, but otherwise he failed to sparkle and by his own admission didn't have a great game. Bobby's trip to Sweden was disappointing because he sat on the sidelines for the whole tournament, watching England's elimination after a play-off against Russia at the group stage.

However, three other members of the United staff left Sweden with happier memories. Harry Gregg was voted best goalkeeper in the competition, helping Northern Ireland to reach the quarterfinal stage where they lost to 4-0 to France. Ireland had lost Jackie Blanchflower's services due to injuries sustained at Munich although his brother Danny captained the Irish team to their marvellous achievement in reaching the last eight. Wales were managed by Jimmy Murphy while Colin Webster was in the team. They gallantly reached the quarter-finals only to go down 1-0 to Brazil, the 17-year-old Pele scoring the only goal.

During the close season Matt Busby went to Switzerland to recuperate from his injuries. There were a few sceptics who claimed that Matt would retire from management because, while the physical injuries might plague him for years, the mental scars would be even harder to overcome. The heroic Jimmy Murphy also took a break.

After his summer convalescence Busby returned to the club he loved. Meanwhile, in July 1958 UEFA invited United to compete in the 1958-59 European Cup, as a tribute to the club's services to football and also for being the first English side to take part. United readily accepted the invite and were drawn against Young Boys of Berne.

Champions Wolverhampton Wanderers were also in the draw and the Football League refused United permission to take part because they were not champions. UEFA officials pointed out that the rules were their concern and had been relaxed to allow other non-champions to play in their competition. United appealed and were successful, but the matter wasn't over. The joint Football Association and Football League committee met and decided that Manchester United could not, after all, enter the European Cup that season. United were forced to agree with this decision but it caused a lot of bitterness.

Instead, United went on a pre-season tour to West Germany. The visit to Munich was more of a 'thank you' to the people of the city for their kindness after the disaster.

They had trained hard and were looking forward to a more settled team. Many of the players who had been involved in the air crash told Matt Busby that they did not want to fly, not yet anyway. So the journey to Germany was a long and tiring one. Overnight sleeper from Ostend to Munich followed by a ten-hour train journey from Munich to Hamburg. More importantly, these matches gave Busby and Murphy a fair idea of what to expect of the coming season.

While the team was in Munich, Matt Busby, Dennis, Ray Wood, Kenny Morgans and Albert Scanlon visited the Rechts der Isar Hospital, armed with huge bunches of flowers for the nuns and nurses who had looked after them so splendidly during their stay after the crash. Unfortunately, Professor Maurer, the miracle worker at the time of the crash, was away on holiday in Italy.

United turned their attention to the tour games against a combined Bayern Munich 1860 team and Hamburg. Both games ended in defeat, 4-3 in Munich and 2-0 in Hamburg. Dennis recalled the Hamburg match: "I was walking with Matt Busby in Hamburg's huge deserted stadium and as we walked I was feeling a little sad, I couldn't help thinking that things would never be the same again for the club. But, as if he was reading my thoughts, Matt turned and looked at me with piercing eyes and said quietly but very firmly, 'Dennis, I have had the best and I'm telling you, that I will have the best again' before he walked away."

During these friendly games Albert Scanlon was eased back into the team. "It was quite an ordeal to be actually playing once again," admitted Albert. "I had hurt my leg in training and many thought it was the leg I injured during the crash, but it wasn't. The run out did me a power of good."

On Saturday August 23rd 1958, the new United played their first league game against Chelsea at Old Trafford. The team: Gregg; Foulkes, Greaves; Goodwin, Cope,

McGuinness; Dawson, Taylor (E), Viollet, Charlton, Scanlon. 52,382 fans were inside the ground as United hammered the Londoners. Billy Foulkes was the official club captain, a great honour but not a job Bill relished. Bobby Charlton, who seemed to mature very quickly after Munich, was in top form and scored a blistering hat-trick with each goal hitting the back of the Chelsea net with power and precision. Alex Dawson weighed in with two goals in a convincing 5-2 win. That ace goalscorer Jimmy Greaves replied for Chelsea. Dennis had been asked by Matt Busby to play centre-forward. Obviously Dennis wasn't the big, bustling type of centre-forward, he was more the withdrawn kind of scheming striker, feeding his colleagues and snatching goals whenever possible. He did what his manager asked and as time would tell, he became quite proficient in this role.

Bill Fryer, a well-respected journalist for the *Daily Express*, wrote: "Dennis Viollet and Ernie Taylor didn't manage to score any goals but both these players provided the gallop-stopping genius that Chelsea lacked up front. And I make the astonishing assertion that United being badgered right and left to sign a centre-forward have the best in the business already in that complete footballer Viollet. Not that numbers meant so much on the United shirts. Bobby Charlton was as central as Viollet and England could do so much worse than use this devastating twosome in the same way."

A midweek game against Nottingham Forest followed, and once again United were in top form, thrashing the Midland side 3-0, with rocket-booted Charlton netting two more goals while Albert Scanlon got the other. The football United were playing was superb to watch and the forward line was lethal. Although Dennis had not got on the score sheet yet, he was providing the openings and playing well. Matt Busby was delighted at the way his team was playing and the steady improvement they were making. "It wasn't so much the score the team won these first two matches by but the manner in which they played," said Matt. He singled out Bobby Charlton, Albert Scanlon and Dennis for a special mention. Meanwhile, Johnny Berry and Jackie Blanchflower, the only two survivors who hadn't yet returned to playing football, were going to Old Trafford regularly and hoping to even start light training, although it must be said that Blanchflower's progress was much slower. He was still walking with a limp and suffering with his right arm. Sadly, the two players were broken-hearted when they were later told by surgeons that they would never play football again.

Bobby Charlton was becoming a real drawcard for the Reds. Both he and Harry Gregg were often besieged by autograph hunters wherever they played. Harry was regarded as the best goalkeeper in the world while Bobby was a controversial and exciting star.

Dennis found himself on the scoresheet, his first of the new season, as United lost 2-1 at Blackpool - a game in which Bobby Charlton missed a penalty. "It will be my first and last," he told his team-mates.

Dennis was on tenterhooks all week, however, as his wife Barbara was due to give birth. On the Friday, the day before United were to play Nottingham Forest, Dennis became a father for the third time as Barbara presented him with another beautiful baby daughter, who they later christened Deborah. The following day, a 1-1 draw in the return with Nottingham Forest with Bobby again on the scoresheet, was followed three days later by a 6-1 rampage against Blackburn, Dennis celebrating the birth of his daughter by scoring twice.

In any list of Manchester United's greatest players, the name of Johnny Carey will inevitably appear. 'Gentleman' Johnny captained the club from the war to the early 1950s before turning to management at Blackburn Rovers. In later years, while recalling his first managerial job, he said: "I had some very enjoyable days at Ewood Park, lovely people, and some excellent players like Bryan Douglas, who I rated very highly indeed. Ronnie Clayton, Roy Vernon, Peter Dobing and Ally McLeod all helped me tremendously, so much so that we were sitting proudly on top of the league table. We were undefeated when we went to play United in our first season back in Division One. Everyone was so kind to me talking about the old days, the only trouble was we lost 6-1."

Having not played each other for 27 years, West Ham and Manchester United now played each other twice in a week. United lost at Upton Park 3-2, a game in which Bobby Moore made his West Ham debut. The Hammers deserved to win but their victory was eased by the loss of Wilf McGuinness to injury. Wilf moved out to the right wing and Dennis was switched to the half-back line. McGuinness made a goal for Colin Webster and with a few minutes of the game remaining rammed home a goal himself that had West Ham fans howling for the final whistle. Dennis gave a fine display as an attacking wing-half. United didn't have to wait long to for revenge, as they trounced West Ham 4-0 in the return - Albert Scanlon getting his first hat-trick for United, Colin Webster scoring the other.

Quix the Word!

This was a rebuilding time for United and there would be a great deal of comings and goings at the club. On the coaching side, John Aston senior took up a coaching position with the club. Meanwhile Matt Busby needed another inside-forward as a replacement. In September he bought the blond-haired Albert Quixall from Sheffield Wednesday for a British record £45,000. Quixall was one of the new stars emerging in football in this period. Modern in outlook, he always had immaculate hair and wore the shortest of shorts, long before they became fashionable.

Albert had played for the Yorkshire club for ten years, making his debut at 17 and winning his first England cap at 20. He was a beautifully balanced player, full of creativity and a lovely passer of the ball. He was not a prolific goalscorer, getting only 63 in 243 games for Sheffield but had been capped five times for England before joining United.

Albert became an overnight celebrity when he moved to United. "Harry Catterick [the Wednesday manager] called me into his office to meet Matt Busby. I signed virtually straight away without knowing the fee and went off to play a round of golf. Soon all hell broke loose with hordes of reporters and photographers chasing me from hole to hole!

"Later that evening I went over to Manchester and appeared on the Tonight programme with Cliff Mitchelmore, that was when the record fee really hit me. It seemed for a while as if the whole world was on fire."

Quixall made his debut in the 2-2 drawn home game with Tottenham which Dennis missed through injury. Albert recalls: "Running out of the tunnel brought back memories of that emotional FA Cup tie seven months earlier, while thinking that Roger, Duncan and Tommy should have been there as well."

Straight after the Tottenham match, United left for their overland journey to Switzerland for the first leg of their friendly match against Young Boys of Berne FC It was a disappointing trip because the Swiss side won comfortably 2-0. Busby continued to believe that his team needed these types of games against continental opposition so that his players could gain the experience required to beat the best on the continent. More importantly, these games brought in extra revenue for the club, a requirement following Busby's recent acquisition of Quixall.

A 1-1 draw with rivals Manchester City at Maine Road was followed by the return game with Young Boys of Berne at Old Trafford. United cruised to a 3-0 victory, with Dennis on the scoresheet. Then in an experimental first Saturday night league game, against Wolverhampton Wanderers at Molineux under floodlights, United were hammered 4-0. Ray Wood was in goal because Gregg was on international duty with Northern Ireland. Bobby Charlton and Wilf McGuinness were also missing, on duty with England, while Ronnie Cope was injured. The early season promise seemed to have disappeared, the team would win the odd game but draw and lose more than Busby envisaged, but nevertheless, the crowds still flocked to Old Trafford.

United's form was a puzzle to supporters. Frank Taylor of the News Chronicle-Dispatch was the only journalist to survive the Munich air crash. He spent twenty-one weeks in the German hospital. Writing about United's problems, he suggested a traditional English centre-forward was Busby's answer. He suggested Derek Kevan, the powerful West Bromwich Albion front man or Nat Lofthouse were of the type required. But these kind of players didn't grow on trees. Besides, United had young Alex Dawson! While it was true that the United quartet of Quixall, Viollet, Charlton and the soon-to-depart Ernie Taylor were all lightweights, they could most certainly play a bit.

Matt Busby and Jimmy Murphy were in a quandary. The new squad of youngsters coming through the United system were much too young to play regular first team football for long periods. But no other club in the country could boast inside forwards of the calibre and potential of Quixall-Viollet-Charlton or their replacements, Giles-Dawson-Pearson. Their eventual solution was to leave things as they were - time would put things right eventually.

Dennis was playing at outside-right for the first team because this had become a problem position for Busby. Dennis didn't argue when he was asked to play in other positions, he knew the club were struggling and would do anything to help, as all the other players would willingly have done. Busby knew Dennis was in good form and also realised that he needed Dennis and Bobby Charlton firing in the goals if United were to challenge for honours. In reality Dennis was wasted out on the wing, but it didn't stop Busby telling the press: "I forecast that Dennis Viollet will develop into a really great outside right within the next few months."

In the 3-2 defeat at Everton, Dennis was moved back to winghalf when centre-half Ronnie Cope pulled a muscle and was forced out on the right. Ronnie still managed two goals though. A 2-1 away victory over Leeds was United's first for seven games and brought a huge sigh of relief from fans and management. The morale of the United players had not faltered but after seven games it had become depressing for players and supporters. It was the first defeat Leeds had suffered at home that season. However a week later at Old Trafford it was back to the doldrums, Burnley triumphing 3-1. The only positive aspect of the game being Albert Quixall's first United goal, a header.

Although the first team were blowing hot and cold, the Central League team were performing well under the circumstances. This team had been hardest hit by the Munich disaster and the rebuilding efforts. By the end of November 1958 they lay fourth in the Central League table with 22 points from 18 games. Players such as Bobby Harrop, Roy Holand, Joe Carolan, Tommy Spratt, and Harold Bratt might not mean a lot to present-day United followers, but these players kept the United system going. Of course the likes of Mark Pearson and Shay Brennan were playing brilliantly and waiting their opportunity to get back into the first team. There was also little Warren Bradley - who would soon gain a spot in the first team while Johnny Giles, Nobby Lawton, and Nobby Stiles were also improving leaps and bounds.

For the away game at Bolton, Busby decided that he would settle on a forward line and leave them together for as long as possible. However with Dennis still injured, Warren Bradley was promoted from the reserves where he had been having a great season. In the event United were hammered 6-3, with Alex Dawson scoring twice and Charlton getting the other. The fog was so thick that Bill Foulkes had to run back and tell Harry Gregg that it was half-time. There was nothing to boast about the scoreline though. This defeat saw United's dismal form continue although there were a number of redeeming features displayed by the team. Warren Bradley, up against the tough-as-nails England international Tommy Banks, had a tremendous game on the right wing. Toward the end of the match Banks switched places with Roy Hartle in an effort to subdue little Bradley.

Matt Busby took the team to Blackpool following the Bolton debacle where Dennis got himself fit once more. Speaking before he made his comeback against Luton the following Saturday, Dennis said: "Warren Bradley has been a revelation in our forward line, his speed and first time passing, without even pausing to control the ball, is so accurate - I thrive on this kind of service."

The break seemed to be a turning point in United's fortunes as they embarked on a 12 match unbeaten run. It began in low-key fashion with a 2-1 home victory over Luton at Old Trafford in front of 42,428 spectators. More importantly Dennis was back on the scoresheet and the Old Trafford faithful saw the old Dennis the Menace again, razor-sharp and as quick as lightning.

A 4-3 away win at Preston, with Dennis, Bradley, Charlton and Scanlon scoring, was followed by a 3-2 win at Stamford Bridge. United were now playing neat football, their passing was a delight to watch. United had sold Stan Crowther to Chelsea a week before and it was he that gashed Bobby Charlton's leg so severely that Bobby had to go off for treatment, never to return. United were even more determined with ten men - Goodwin and McGuinness covered acres of ground in the hectic second half as the London club piled on the pressure. Harry Gregg almost got on the score sheet in this game, kicking the ball from the edge of his area as far as the Chelsea penalty spot where Dennis challenged the Chelsea centre-half Scott, who promptly headed the ball over his own goalkeeper.

Over the Christmas holiday period, United played Aston Villa home and away. They won both games. The first match, at Old Trafford on Boxing Day, saw the Reds prevail 2-1 in front of another bumper 63,098 crowd. Quixall and Dennis scored the goals. A tribute was paid to Ernie Taylor in the programme of this game following his transfer to Sunderland. Ernie had played just 34 games for the first team but the bare statistics do not reveal the wonderful service and much-needed experience he gave United at a critical time. He not only organised the team on the field but was also instrumental in helping the younger players on the training pitch. A lovely man, and a big-hearted player, Ernie was a gentleman.

The away match at Villa Park saw United make four changes. Ian Greaves replaced Joe Carolan, Albert Scanlon moved over to the right wing in place of Bradley, while Mark 'Pancho' Pearson stood in for the injured Charlton and Reg Hunter made his debut on the left wing. The pitch was like a cow patch and Villa, using Wolves tactics, made life particularly difficult. Fortunately United's defenders soon came to grips with their tactics and the atrocious playing surface, running out 2-0 winners - Dennis and Mark Pearson getting a goal apiece.

Pearson's effort was particularly spectacular. Standing in the centre circle he beat Jimmy Dugdale, the experienced Villa centrehalf, and with a clever back-heel beat Aldis for speed before nonchalantly slipping the ball past Sims in the Villa goal. Dennis was the first to congratulate him on a beautifully executed goal. Dennis's strike was a typical piece of opportunism - Scanlon drove a fierce shot at the Villa goal, Sims only half-gathered the ball and before he could blink Dennis had it in the back of the net.

The Reds' form continued with a 3-1 Old Trafford victory over Blackpool. This was the game in which the great Stanley Matthews was booed unmercifully by United supporters. Joe Carolan tackled the great man and Stan took a tumble in the penalty area - although to be truthful the great dribbler dived like the proverbial dying swan. He got a penalty and the Old Trafford fans didn't like it one bit, especially after Ewan Fenton scored from the spot kick. Matthews was booed throughout the game and this was unusual for the time as United supporters didn't tend to do such things and were noted for their fair-mindedness.

The press reports preferred to ignore the boos and concentrate on the positives: "There wasn't a forward on the pitch to touch the standards of Dennis Viollet," wrote Tony Stevens in the Empire News. "Bobby Charlton won't get a sniff at the next England team as an inside-forward if Dennis Viollet is about," he concluded. Dennis was embarrassed by these comments, he didn't like his team-mates being criticised in any form. However in this match Dennis's reading of the game and movement on and off the ball inspired United to play some great football. Bobby Charlton, incidentally, scored two crackers with

Dennis notching one.

Over the years the FA Cup has been littered with giantkilling exploits but Manchester United had managed to escape relatively unscathed. However on January 10th 1959 all that changed with an ill-starred visit to Third Division Norwich City. What made the result all the more surprising was United's excellent form. They had won eight successive games before their Carrow Road nightmare. The pitch was bone hard, the weather perishing and the sky a battleship grey. United played well below par and were hammered 3-0. Stunned supporters travelling home were of the opinion that Busby should have fielded his Central League forward line in this game because the fans believed the hard conditions would have suited them.

To fill in the blank fourth round date, United played a friendly at Swansea. Colin Webster had been allowed to leave Old Trafford in October 1958 to join his hometown club. It turned out to be a cracker of a game - the final score 6-4 to United. Webster scored against his old club while Johnny Giles made his first team debut and showed some great touches. Three times the Welsh team took the lead. Dennis scored after twelve minutes, then Mel Charles, brother of John, put them in front again only for Bobby Charlton to equalise. Charles again put Swansea ahead only for Scanlon to level the scores once again. Quixall and Charlton scored in quick succession before Reg Davies got another for the Welsh side and Bobby Charlton completed his hat-trick. It was the kind of game to bring spectators through the turnstiles. Dennis and Colin Webster had a drink and a chat about old times afterwards. Colin told him how much he missed Manchester and how the Swansea manager Trevor Morris had been using him as a utility forward.

On the last day of January 1959, United played Newcastle at Old Trafford in one of the most exciting matches for many years. This was football at its best with thrills, skills, and goals. United let slip a 4-1 lead, allowing the Geordies to make the final score 4-4. Dennis was outstanding in this game, delivering exquisite service to both United wings who ran riot. The first half was all United - Scanlon was fouled and Charlton scored from the spot, Quixall got on the scoresheet before Albert Scanlon scored himself. Dennis scored after taking a beautifully flighted ball from Bradley and picking his spot. Newcastle, with an inside forward trio of brilliant ball-playing forwards in Ivor Allchurch, Len White and George Eastham, then responded and with the Reds looking as if they were strolling to victory, the Magpies pulled level. Jimmy Scoular roughed Bobby Charlton up something shocking and was loudly booed. It was the only occasion that Bobby was actually seen to be very upset and annoyed with an opposing player's tactics. It must be stressed that the teak-tough Newcastle player was extremely ruthless, nevertheless, it was a brilliant attacking game of football!

On January 11th United played another European side, Wiener Sport Club of Austria. Wiener were national champions and European Cup quarter-finalists. Matt Busby had seen them beat Juventus 7-0 and they had beaten Dukla Prague on aggregate to confirm their undoubted pedigree. The Reds, back to full strength, won 1-0 with Dennis notching the only goal of the game after 14 minutes - 37,834 paying spectators enjoying a thrilling game.

It was a special week for Dennis because he was also appointed club captain. Following the Newcastle game Bill Foulkes, who had been captain since Munich, was rested. Bill had not missed a game for two seasons so it was understandable that he would run out of form at some time. He had taken over the captaincy from Roger Byrne during the most difficult period in the club's history and needed a break from the responsibility. Billy himself believed that concentration on his own game would see him back in the first team in the near future.

But United's impressive league form continued. After a 3-1 win at Tottenham, Matt Busby, who very rarely singled out an individual for praise, made an exception. "Dennis Viollet was exceptionally good today. He is playing like Hughie Gallacher," he told the assembled press. That was some praise from Busby, a big fan of the Scottish international. Busby continued by telling the press that England manager Walter Winterbottom had told him privately that the pattern of centre-forward play he wanted for England was the Dennis Viollet style, and Dennis had been playing at outside-right at the time.

United beat rivals Manchester City 4-1 at Old Trafford in front of over 60,000. Bobby Johnstone scored for City after just ten minutes but after that it was all United, with the Quixall-Viollet- Charlton forward line playing magnificent football. However, as good as the inside-forward trio performed, Albert Scanlon was just as big a menace for the City rearguard. His powerful running and thunderous shooting brought gasps from the large crowd. Freddie Goodwin opened the scoring for the Reds following a superb pass from Dennis. Bradley got the second, a rebound after a Scanlon blockbuster nearly broke the crossbar. Albert got the third and Bradley the fourth. All four of United's goals came in a 20-minute spell. City were completely shell-shocked. Wilf McGuinness was playing his defensive role to perfection and no cause seemed lost while Wilf was around. After the Derby clash it was off to the seaside again, staying once more at the Norbrek Hydro Hotel in Blackpool in readiness for the much-anticipated crunch match with bitter rivals Wolverhampton Wanderers at Old Trafford.

Peter Slingsby, a journalist on the *Manchester Evening News*, said that he put Manchester United's brilliant displays down to playing a 4-2-4 system. "When Dennis Viollet is fit he has a marked effect on the whole side. He has no peer when it comes to scheming, he has not lost his 'bite' in the target area and has such high ability he can inspire the players around him to touch the heights of greatness. Dennis is a vastly underrated player."

In a vintage game, United defeated Wolves 2-1 with a last minute goal from Bobby Charlton following a superb pass from Dennis, after Dennis himself had scored the first. These were the kind of games where the value of Dennis Viollet was really seen to its full effect. His darting runs, the easy way he slid passes through the tight, well-drilled Wolves defence was a thing of beauty, his shooting and footballing brain could not be equalled by any other player on the pitch. That he could perform like this against the top teams was vital to a forward.

United were now level with Wolves at the top of the league table and there were really only three teams in the title race: United, Wolves and Arsenal. Dennis and his team-mates just wanted to savour the victory over their nearest rivals rather than think about what might be. There were calls for all five Manchester United forwards to be selected for England - surely Dennis deserved his first England cap. United's form was majestic, a remarkable achievement so soon after Munich. But could they go on to win the championship? The next game would go someway towards answering that question.

67,162 fans, including England manager Walter Winterbottom, packed Highbury for Arsenal's game against Manchester United. A hostile reception greeted the Reds and sadly, once the referee blew his whistle to start the game, there was only one team in it - Arsenal!

The United forward line was unrecognisable from the previous week - they hardly functioned at all. The defence attempted to stem the tide of home attacks but under heavy bombardment, they inevitably caved in. The Reds were three down in half an hour. Tommy Docherty and his wing-half partner Dave Bowen ran the game, tackling like terriers, snuffing out United's talented spearhead and supplying their rampant forwards with the ball at every opportunity. Dennis and Warren Bradley scored to make it a respectable 3-2 at the final whistle, but in fairness the score did not do the Gunners justice. They had whipped United fair and square.

Dennis was very disappointed with the way the team had played, especially in front of the England manager. Dennis was hoping he might still have a chance of selection for the forthcoming international match against Scotland and for England's South American tour at the end of the season. Otherwise he'd blown his chance once more.

What a difference a few days make. For their next game, the following Monday at Ewood Park, United looked like a completely different outfit to that which had seemed so clueless against Arsenal. Rovers scored after three minutes and looked good until United's half-back line put the shutters up and Dennis got his forwards moving sweetly. Warren Bradley scored two good goals and his opposite wing partner 'Our Albert' Scanlon got the third in an impressive 3-1 away victory. Bradley and Scanlon were now enjoying the softer pitches and thriving on the service Quixall, Viollet and Charlton were giving them. Everton were beaten 2-1 at Old Trafford on Saturday, Freddie Goodwin and Scanlon scoring.

United were entering the title run-in and the following match against West Bromwich at the Hawthorns was bound to be a tense affair. Albion were fifth in the league so this would be another proving ground in United's bid for the championship. Dennis got his team off to a great start by scoring after just a minute's play - it was a brilliant, well-schemed and well-taken goal. McGuinness moved the ball to Quixall who delivered a lovely ball to Charlton who put Dennis through to score. Those two rampaging wingers, Bradley and Scanlon, also scored to give United a 3-1 win. Mind you, United didn't come out of this game unscathed. Maurice Setters, the tough-tackling West Brom right-half, clattered into Quixall, damaging his ribs while Bradley, Goodwin and Cope were also injured.

England Honours?

Before United's next game there were a pair of important representative fixtures. Bobby Charlton, Wilf McGuinness and Albert Scanlon were selected for the England Under-23 team, while Dennis was picked in a Football League XI. United's staff were pleased that Dennis seemed to be getting nominated at long last for representative matches, having waited a long time for recognition. In fairness, Dennis should have been capped before Munich, after all he was playing as well, if not better than any other inside-forward in the league at that time.

In the *Manchester Evening News* of March 9th, David Meek congratulated Dennis on his selection for the Football League to play the League of Ireland. "He is the most underrated, overlooked forward in football," he wrote. "Dennis Viollet of Manchester United is deceptively quiet and his unassuming displays have finally been recognised for what they really are - shrewd and brilliant." He went on to say what United supporters were saying: that if Dennis played as he did for United, the next stop would be a full cap for England against Scotland at Wembley on April 11th, followed by a place on England's summer tour to

South America.

England manager Walter Winterbottom had watched Dennis regularly and marvelled at the way he knitted the United forward line together. Winterbottom thought Dennis was a superb schemer, but as well as scheming, Dennis had scored ten goals in 15 games. In three England internationals and two Inter-League games this season, four players had been tried in the number nine jersey: Brian Clough, Bobby Charlton, Nat Lofthouse and Len White. It seemed incredible that Dennis had not been given an opportunity much earlier.

Matt Busby and Jimmy Murphy were among those who believed that Dennis Viollet should have been capped several times before the Munich disaster. His pedigree was first class, as a schoolboy he was the pride of Manchester: Captain of Manchester Boys, Captain of Lancashire Boys and Captain of England Boys, he had gone through the Manchester United youth system and made his debut at 19 while doing his National Service. Tommy Taylor rightly caught the eye as United's spearhead and, although on the fringe of international selection for two or three years, Dennis was somehow overlooked. He was now 25 and playing better than ever.

There was a great deal of concern about the health of Matt Busby during this period. Rumours were flying around that Matt might retire from football. He had not been well for quite some time, the injuries sustained at Munich were still troubling him. He had been advised by a hospital specialist to get away from football completely and take a long holiday. Matt put all his own worries behind him to wish Dennis all the best for the game in Ireland. "Just play your normal game and you will be fine," Matt told his captain.

The match between the Football League and the League of Ireland was on Tuesday 18th March 1959, at Dalymount

Park, Dublin. It turned out to be a terrible football match in more ways than one and poor Dennis seemed to be scapegoated for it. It was a goalless game and the entire 90 minutes seemed completely devoid of any kind of skill or excitement. The Irish fans were not slow to show the English players their frustration and disappointment.

The Football League team was, on paper, quite a good selection. McDonald (Burnley); Howe (West Brom), Shaw (Sheffield United); Clayton (Blackburn Rovers), Gratrix (Blackpool), Flowers (Wolves); Wilkinson (Sheffield Wednesday), Broadbent (Wolves), Viollet (Manchester United), Haynes (Fulham), Holden (Bolton).

The following day's newspapers criticised the English players unmercifully for not trying and said that the majority of the team looked as if they had turned out only because they had to and not because they wanted to impress the selectors. Even the Irish League officials had a verbal blast at the English lads. Worse still, 16 minutes from the final whistle, Colin McDonald, the Burnley goalkeeper, was carried off with a broken shin sustained while saving a shot which would have given the part-timers of Ireland their first victory over a Football League team.

Bob Pennington, writing in the *Daily Express* said: "I write off, on this fumbling form, new boys Derek Wilkinson and Doug Holden as England wingers, and I report sadly that Dennis Viollet flopped at centre-forward in an inside trio that rarely coordinated. "

But David Jack, writing in the Empire News said: "I am told that Dennis Viollet is likely to be made the scapegoat for Ireland's St Patrick's Day footballing frolics, but if that happens you can be quite sure the wrong man has been condemned. It was a deplorable game in Dublin. In my opinion England should drop Johnny Haynes and Peter Broadbent and play Quixall, Viollet and Charlton."

Dennis was obviously upset and bitterly disappointed at the way things had turned out in Dublin. No player goes out on the field not wanting to win a game or try his best. But turning on the style is not always possible. Although he played in the middle between Peter Broadbent and Johnny Haynes, two exceptionally good players and full internationals, they didn't gel together as a trio all night. The press campaign to get Dennis selected for a representative game had worked but it seemed half the reporters had dismissed his efforts as quickly as they had backed him before. A few others claimed Dennis should play alongside United colleagues Quixall and Charlton because they knew each other's style of play so well. This seemed more sensible if only because the United trio were playing magical football and making and scoring plenty of goals.

When Dennis arrived back at Old Trafford, Jimmy Murphy could tell Dennis was a little upset and down-hearted. He put his arm around his shoulder and reminded him about the stick his mate Tommy Taylor had to endure every time he played for England. Even then journalists would write that Taylor should have his striking partner [Dennis] playing with him for England. "Don't you worry son," said Murphy. "We here know how good you are. Keep playing like you are and you will get selected for the England team." Dennis felt much happier after Murphy's words of encouragement. Then later, Matt Busby pulled him to one side and told him not to let the criticism affect him. "Go out against Leeds and show them how good you really are."

This Was The Real Viollet

When Manchester United played Leeds United at Old Trafford, there was an air of expectancy amongst the spectators. Leeds had recently lost their manager and it was rumoured that Don Revie was about take the job. Still, they came to Old Trafford to get both points and with Bobby Charlton's big brother Jack playing at centre-half and Don Revie himself at right-half, they were wellequipped to spoil United's title chances.

Dennis still felt a little down in the dumps after Dublin. He had not performed anywhere near his usual standards and desperately wanted to show the selectors his true form. Well, as it turned out at Old Trafford, Dennis might not have covered himself in glory in his game for the Football League, but he gave a 24-carat display against Leeds. He scored a spectacular hat-trick: his shrewd football brain and nimble footwork a wonder to watch.

Dennis, the pale ghost of a leader, hit three beauties as United kept their championship challenge alive. This was not the Viollet of Dublin, a fumbling flop as the Football League centre-forward. No, this was the Old Trafford Viollet - dealing a fatal blow to Leeds' hopes. He was thoughtful and probing, deep and striking, and so masterly in control. The difference between the Irish game and the Leeds match was that Dennis was playing with familiar colleagues. After 14 minutes he received the ball, with his back to goal, just inside the box. The Leeds defenders expected him to pass but he swivelled and belted the ball into the net past Ted Burgin and into the net. On the hour Dennis moved on to a through pass, steadied himself and thudded the ball into the goal off the far post, while in the 85th minute Bobby Charlton sent him away with a beautifully-timed through ball which split the Leeds defence wide open. Dennis moved like lightning, feigned to shoot, pushed the ball nearer the goal and before Burgin could advance, whipped it under the bewildered keeper's diving body. That was Den's answer to the critics - a show-stopping hat-trick.

That result left United and Wolves head to head in the race

for the First Division Championship and by coincidence the two clubs were due to meet in the prestigious FA Youth Cup. United had won this trophy for the five years of its existence when, on March 16th 1959, United Youths travelled to Molineux for the quarter final of the FA Youth Cup. Stan Cullis, Wolves' hard-line manager, had been seething for the past few years because United had held a monopoly over the trophy and he had been singing the praises of his youngsters for years - this was the showdown he had waited for. Cullis believed that now was the time his youngsters would do the business especially as, after Munich, United would not have a youth system to match that before the tragedy. Unfortunately, he underestimated Jimmy Murphy's powers of motivation. He had fired his lads up with a burning desire to wipe the floor with Wolves. The team lined up as follows: Gaskell; Smith, Ackerley; Stiles, Haydock, Nicholson; Moir, Giles, Chisnall, Spratt and Elms.

Matt Busby, two directors, a significant number of first team players and the entire United coaching and training staff travelled to cheer on the new Babes and watched Murphy's mob win 3-0, Chisnall, Elms and Spratt the goalscorers. Cullis was ill and so missed this drubbing by Busby's youngsters. The show of unity by the club was particularly significant, it underpinned United's continued belief in their youth system.

Indeed, so well had United's youngsters performed that many newspaper reporters were of the opinion that the entire Old Trafford star-making system was back to pre-Munich standards. This was utter nonsense of course. Of the team that played at Molineux that day only Nobby Stiles and Johnny Giles became household names. Collyhurst-born Stiles went on to gain League, European Cup and World Cup winners medals while Dubliner Giles would become one of the greatest inside-forwards of the sixties, winning a hatful of honours with Leeds United.

Of the rest, Phil Chisnall played in the first team before being transferred to Liverpool, David Gaskell became United's first team goalkeeper after Harry Gregg and won an FA Cup winners medal in 1963, while Frank Haydock played six times for the first team. Jimmy Nicholson became an Irish international at 17 and was unfairly compared to the great Duncan Edwards, but made only 58 appearances for the first team. Ian Moir, on the other hand, was heralded as a revelation but after 46 first team games faded out of the picture before moving to Blackpool.

The devastating effects Munich had on United's youth operation was underlined by their loss of dominance in the competition. Their exit in 1959 to Blackburn Rovers 4-1 on aggregate in the semi-final emphasised this. The club next won the Youth Cup in 1964 when the likes of George Best had arrived. In this way the youth set-up suffered more than any other part of the club because, despite the best efforts of Murphy and his staff, United were forced to promote many youngsters too soon which had a negative effect not only on the level of experience of United's first team but on the length of the careers of the players involved.

Another home game was next against Portsmouth, which saw the one millionth spectator of the season rattle through Old Trafford's turnstiles. Pompey, despite their lowly position, were bound to be tough opposition. They had enjoyed 32 years in the First Division but in front of 52,004 fans the Reds hammered them 6-1. Bobby Charlton and Dennis got a brace each, Bradley got one with Hayward scoring an own goal.

The two points took United a step closer to the title. Since defeat to Arsenal, United had won five games in a row, scoring 17 goals and conceding only 4. However the odds still favoured title favourites Wolves - one point ahead with a game in hand. In fairness it must be said that the Midlands club had the better balanced team while United, despite their brilliant attacking forward line, were unreliable in defence. A point emphasised by their scoring 83 goals but conceding 58 to this point of the season. Still, United were showing remarkable signs of resilience and few could believe that they could triumph so soon after Munich.

Sadly, as if to emphasise their defensive frailties, United were thrashed 4-2 at Burnley, a result that surely ended United's hopes. They gave away two early goals and from there on in it proved an uphill struggle despite goals from Dennis and Freddie Goodwin.

Two days later came the return match with Portsmouth at Fratton Park. Former club captain Bill Foulkes was back in the team after an eleven-match absence while England team manager Walter Winterbottom was present once more to check on Dennis's form. However, after Bobby Charlton opened the scoring, Pompey fought like tigers and gave United a few frights, Peter Harris scoring Portsmouth's equaliser. But Bobby again and Warren Bradley added goals to give the Reds a comfortable 3-1 victory.

A lovely volleyed effort from Dennis in a 3-0 home victory over Bolton preceded a scoreless draw with Luton. The Luton match was definitely an opportunity lost as they were due to take on Nottingham Forest in the FA Cup Final in a matter of weeks and were just going through the motions. The game was a huge disappointment for all concerned, especially as with only two games of the season remaining, United now had 53 points from 40 games, while Wolves had 55 points from 39 and the odds were firmly stacked in Wolves' favour.

However, as United got ready for their final home game at Old Trafford against Birmingham City, Matt Busby said that the club and supporters should look back over the season and feel satisfied at the progress the team had made so soon after Munich. "The players will learn from this experience," prophesied the manager. However all the newspaper talk concerned Bobby Charlton and his quest to beat Jack Rowley's club record 30 goals in a season. Bobby needed two more to beat Gunner's record.

As it turned, Albert Quixall scored the only goal of the game to give United a 1-0 win, while the last game of the season at Filbert Street, saw a 2-1 defeat - Warren Bradley getting United's consolation goal. So Bobby didn't beat Rowley's goalscoring record but his tally of 29 league goals made him the club's leading scorer.

This was most certainly not the end to the season the team had wanted. But they did beat Manchester City 4-0 in the Manchester Senior Cup, Bobby Charlton scoring two sensational goals, while Dennis lifted his first trophy as captain. Taking everything into consideration, United had done better than many imagined in their first full season after Munich. Indeed it could be said that they shook the world of football by finishing runners up to a strong outfit like Wolves and, if the truth be known, they also surprised themselves by doing so well after the tragic events of the previous season.

Record Breaker

Following the emotional season of 1958-59, with the return of Matt Busby, the rebuilding after the air disaster and the accomplishment of finishing runners-up, success was always going to be difficult to sustain.

But another hurdle had been overcome in the close season. The team had flown for the first time since Munich when they travelled to Germany for pre-season games in Munich and Hamburg. Bayern provided the first opposition, in what turned out to be an explosive start to the season. Albert Quixall remembered the game clearly. "In the first half I noticed their goalkeeper liked to wander off his line. So at half-time I told Dennis to pass the ball to me straight from the kick-off and I duly lobbed the ball over the keeper from the centre circle! It was timed at four seconds. However, late on in the game I stupidly slapped a Bayern player across the face, after he had been kicking me throughout the game, and I was promptly sent off. This probably took my goal away from people's minds, with most of the stories concentrating on my dismissal." Joe Carolan followed Albert into an early bath as United, down to nine men, won 2-1 with another goal from Dennis. The new club captain was raring to go and was anxious for the season proper to get started. He knew deep down though, that despite all the praise being lavished upon the team after the magnificent season they had enjoyed things would get decidedly tougher.

To add to this uneasy feeling within the club was the growing discontent among professional footballers across the country. The system of virtual serfdom that had existed in football since the start of the professional game was coming under attack and many prominent players demanded changes to their contracts. Fulham's Jimmy Hill was instrumental in the negotiations as the Players' Union representative. Their main aim was to abolish the maximum wage, which stood at £20 a week for all professional players regardless of division. On top of this basic wage players received bonuses of £4 for a win and £2 for a draw in the League and bonuses of between £5 and £25 for winning the various rounds of the FA Cup. Clearly Dennis, as captain of one of the biggest clubs in the land, would have a great deal of input into the negotiations which would unfold throughout the 1959/60 season.

United's first league game was away at West Bromwich Albion on August 22nd - a red hot day. Dennis put United in front after 18 minutes of what would prove to be a momentous season. David Burnside equalised and Bill Foulkes unluckily headed into his own net. Dennis came to the rescue once again with the equaliser in the 72nd minute only for Burnside to grab a late winner for a 3-2 victory for the Albion. United then played Chelsea the following Wednesday at Old Trafford and this ended in another defeat (1-0), Jimmy Greaves the scorer.

The next match was again at Old Trafford, and saw United get their first win of the new season by beating Newcastle 3-2. Dennis scored twice and Bobby Charlton hit the other, all United's goals coming in the first 35 minutes. Four goals from three games was not a bad start for Dennis.

United's next game was at Stamford Bridge and the lure of United was becoming a fact of life in football. They had become a big draw wherever they played so it was hardly surprising that 66,579 spectators squeezed into Stamford Bridge with thousands of others locked out. As ever, United reserved one of their best displays of attacking

Top: The depleted United line-up 1958-9.
Perhaps this was United's most remarkable ever season, the year after Munich they finished second only to Wolves. The key to United's success was the inside-forward trio of Albert Quixall, Dennis Viollet and Bobby Charlton *- here pictured with a recovered Matt Busby. Many pressmen claimed they should have appeared together for England.*

ABOVE: *Dennis runs out at Highbury 1960, United mascot Jack Irons greets him.*

LEFT: *Dennis receives the Evening Chronicle Player of the Year award 1959*

AND THE WINNER IS!
Mrs Dorothy Green is presented as Miss Manchester United 1959 - Dennis, Bobby Charlton and Wilf McGuinness preside.

Dennis, Jimmy Shields, Shay Brennan and Albert Quixall at a Jack Coggan reception.

Dennis with Barbara and friends at Jack's place

WELL DONE DENNIS!

By creating a new club scoring record Dennis Viollet has eclipsed the figure of thirty goals set up by Jack Rowley in 1952. When we congratulated him on his fine achievement United's skipper was quick to praise his team mates and remind us that team work is essential if goals are to be scored.

Dennis has been with the club since 1949 when he joined as a Manchester Schools player and Captain of England Schoolboys. This is his eleventh season with the club during which time he has hit 141 goals.

THIS PAGE

ABOVE: *United enjoy a taste of pre-season European travel in Germany.*

RIGHT: *Dennis and Wilf McGuinness receive advice from the local dole office in the event of a players' strike*

OPPOSITE

LEFT: *Dennis sets the mark by which all future United strikers are judged - 32 league goals in 36 games in 1959-60*

BOTTOM: *Dennis relaxes at home in between goals against Blackburn* (TOP) *and Burnley* (BOTTOM).

LEFT: FRONT ROW: (left to right) Tony Allen, Laurie Leslie, John Ritchie, Peter Dobing, Dennis, Bill Asprey, and Jimmy Robertson at pre-season training.

OPPOSITE PAGE
CLOCKWISE FROM TOP
LEFT: *Dennis meets legend Stan Matthews in the Stoke dressing room; Albert Quixall nearly signs for Stoke; Dennis looks unusually tense in the dressing room; Dennis in more relaxed mode meeting goalkeeping legend Gordon Banks.*

TOP: *Dennis runs out alongside goalkeeper Laurie Lesley in his first game for Stoke at Bristol Rovers 20th January 1962.*
MIDDLE: *Dennis celebrates an English league goal for the last time in his final match for Stoke at home against Leicester City 1967.*
BOTTOM: *A champagne finish as Dennis, Don Sutcliffe* (LEFT) *and Eric Skeels* (MIDDLE) *celebrate the end of a great career.*

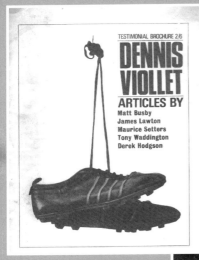

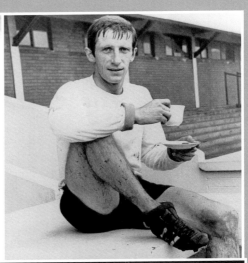

CLOCKWISE FROM TOP LEFT: *Dennis's testimonial programme complete with hung-up boots; Dennis relaxing with a brew after training, 1966; receiving a momento following his testimonial in 1967 from legendary Stoke fan Peter Bailey; and making last minute pre-match preparations*

football for the capital. The Quixall-Viollet-Charlton spearhead rediscovered its form: Albert Scanlon was the flying winger of old and Warren Bradley was back to the form he had displayed all last season, having fully recovered following England's South American tour. The half-back line played with poise and Shay Brennan and Wilf McGuinness fed the forwards a diet of wonderfully placed passes. The Chelsea defence was tied in knots as the United team attacked them constantly as England manager Walter Winterbottom witnessed United run out 6-3 winners - Dennis getting two of the goals along with a brace from Bradley and one each from Charlton and Quixall.

There was plenty of discussion regarding Albert Quixall around this time. He had been at Old Trafford for almost a year but several supporters and journalists had not been over impressed with his form. However Dennis jumped to his team-mate's defence and said if there was a better inside-forward in England than Albert Quixall he certainly hadn't seen him. "As a forager and schemer I think he would be at the top of any list. When he first played for us, we played ten matches and won only one. I know this worried Albert a great deal, he was also worried about the price of his transfer and thought he had put a jinx on us. But really it was a battle Albert had to fight alone. People told me they knew Albert was a great player, but they thought he didn't work as hard as he should! Well this season he has worked like a Trojan."

Dennis was delighted with the victory at Chelsea saying: "This was United's greatest game, at least in my time. What a wonderful experience! I rate our victory over Chelsea the finest exhibition of football by a Manchester United team in which I have ever played. I always considered the 10-0 licking of Anderlecht in the European Cup three seasons ago as our best display, but I've changed my mind because that Anderlecht match was too one-sided to be a real test. Chelsea played well, but we played better, and we touched the highspots in a way I have never experienced before. I feel proud to be captain of a team that played such excellent football."

Following a 1-1 draw with Birmingham City at St Andrews, United took on Leeds at home and thrashed them 6-0. Warren Bradley and Bobby Charlton grabbed two apiece with Dennis and Albert Scanlon scoring the others. However, three days later, again at Old Trafford, Tottenham panned the Reds 5-1, Dennis scoring United's only goal. That home defeat was deflating, nevertheless Spurs were a top-class team in every respect and were building a side that would later claim the League and Cup double.

United's mixed fortunes continued with a 2-2 draw at Leeds followed by a disappointing 3-0 defeat to rivals City at Maine Road and a 4-0 hammering at Preston North End. For the Preston game Dennis was moved to right-half and acquitted himself well while Alex Dawson led the forward line. The team was struggling and Matt Busby was trying desperately to sign new players and had made enquiries at several English and Scottish clubs before United's friendly with European Cup holders Real Madrid.

Matt Busby knew in his heart that the re-building of Manchester United was going to be a huge job, perhaps the hardest job he'd had as a manager. In the past he had shunned the transfer market believing, and rightly so, that home reared players brought carefully through the United system were more committed and easier to fit into his own system. However following Munich, every one of United's teams was disrupted. Players had to move through the system far quicker than was planned and quite a lot of promising youngsters fell by the wayside. Indeed the aftermath of the crash had a knock on effect far bigger than Busby and

Murphy had anticipated and so to keep United's name in the newspapers Matt decided to bring the best European teams to Old Trafford for prestigious friendly games.

The United manager enjoyed a good relationship with Don Santiago Bernabeu, the Real Madrid President. In 1959, Matt flew to Madrid and asked Mr Bernabeu to bring Real to Manchester. At this time the Spaniards had won the European Cup four times since its inception and would make it five later that season. They were travelling to different parts of the world playing friendlies and receiving fantastic sums of money for their appearances. It was estimated that it would cost any other English club £12,000 before Real Madrid would even consider playing.

In his meeting with the Real boss, Busby explained that the Munich disaster had almost made United bankrupt and it would be wonderful for everybody concerned if they could consider helping United in their plight. Mr Bernabeu smiled at Matt, turned to Real Madrid's business manager and told him to make all the arrangements for Busby's request, adding: "For half our normal fee, and a return game." So on October 1st 1959 Real Madrid played United at Old Trafford.

United were 16th in the league when these two magnificent clubs faced each other. Real played all their stars: Gento, the flying winger; Puskas who had wanted to join United; di Stefano the great Argentine striker; Didi the classy Brazilian - they were all there. Real won 6-1, di Stefano and Puskas scored twice with one each for Gento and Pipillo. Warren Bradley scored United's consolation.

As expected Real gave a masterful exhibition of wonderful football far removed from the hustle and bustle of our English league. This was football of the highest order. Individual skills, players ghosting into positions while losing their defenders, shooting with the accuracy of missiles, intelligent football, dribbling, showmanship. It was everything the crowd of 63,500 had hoped and wished for. Madrid's magic was on display and the fans stood clapping and cheering both teams off the pitch. Obviously everybody connected with United were disappointed with the result but the players didn't really expect anything else. This was a steep learning curve for United's youngsters and in their next match three days later against Leicester City at Old Trafford, it seemed a little bit of the Madrid magic had rubbed off on the Reds because they dazzled Leicester 4-1. Bobby Charlton scored after five minutes, Dennis after 17, then Albert Quixall got a goal with Dennis getting the fourth.

Meanwhile, Busby had been up to Scotland to speak to Scottish full-back Eric Caldow of Glasgow Rangers. They agreed terms for the player to join United. Unfortunately Caldow had to leave almost immediately because he was due in Ireland for an international match.

Busby told supporters that with only eight points from the first ten games, neither he nor the players were happy. He added that he wasn't making any excuses but they had not had that vital bit of luck in certain games, which every team needs at some point in the season. He also assured the fans that the club would not just wait for results to change, and that he would search for new players. But Eric Caldow, the player Matt thought he had agreed terms with, changed his mind and eventually declined his offer.

Against Arsenal at Old Trafford, United cruised through winning 4-2. Dennis was once more on the scoresheet along with Quixall, Charlton and an own goal. Playing centre-forward for Arsenal that day was Dennis's schoolboy chum David Herd, who scored one of Arsenal's goals. Matt Busby had wanted to sign Herd for quite some time and phoned the Gunners on several occasions enquiring if they would part with him. As yet they hadn't agreed. Nevertheless, Busby would not give up his ideas and Dennis's chum remained top of Matt's shopping list.

The bit of luck mentioned by Matt deserted United again as they were unlucky in defeat to champions Wolves 3-2 at Molineux, Dennis on the scoresheet once more. Wolves were going for their third successive League championship, but the Reds gave them a torrid time. United were without Charlton, missing on international duty and Albert Quixall who was injured. Mark Pearson and Johnny Giles took their places and performed excellently. Wolves took a disputed lead through Murray, the United defence claiming it was way offside. But within minutes they had increased the lead through Peter Broadbent. Dennis forced Stuart to head into his own net, Murray scored another disputed goal before Dennis ripped one into the net with the type of ferocious right-footed drive that fans expected from Bobby Charlton. Still it wasn't enough and United were condemned to another defeat.

On the positive side however, Dennis's goalscoring was now being discussed at length in the newspapers. He was getting goals at an amazing rate yet he was also the 'brains' behind the build-up play. Not only did he score but he interchanged with his wingers and dropped deep to help in defence. He was so calm and assured that his presence gave his less experienced team-mates confidence.

United's next game against Sheffield Wednesday at Old Trafford brought a winning smile back to supporters' faces as the Reds triumphed 3-1. Warren Bradley was on the scoresheet again and Dennis, making his 200th League appearance, celebrated with a brace. Those two goals saw his total to 14 for the season, making him top First Division marksman. Walter Winterbottom witnessed Dennis's storming performance.

Three days later Dennis played centre-forward for the Football League against the League of Ireland at Ewood Park, Blackburn. The newspapers were claiming that Dennis's selection for the Football League was his big chance. Eric Thornton, writing in the *Manchester Evening News*, told readers: "Dennis has only himself to blame if he fails to shine in this game. He has never had it so good. He will have a Lancashire crowd cheering him on and a Lancashire flavoured forward line to help him." Dennis would be joined by John Connelly (Burnley right-winger), Peter Dobing (Blackburn inside-right) and Ray Parry (Bolton inside-left) in the forward line.

Schemer-Striker Dennis Has The Kopa Style!

Bobby Charlton was one of the first to congratulate Dennis when he heard the news that his captain had been chosen to play for the Football League against the Irish. Bobby was well aware that Dennis had played in the same fixture the season before and had not had a good game and consequently went out of the international reckoning.

"Surely this will lead to a full England cap for Dennis at last, an honour which no one deserves more," said Bobby. He continued by saying that for a long time Dennis had been one of the most under-rated players in the game. "He has been the guiding light in the revival of United and no one can deny his greatness. Is his best position inside-forward, centre-forward or outside-right? I suppose a player of such constructive ability is a little wasted out there [on the right-wing] and should be in the middle of the field. The great thing about Dennis is his speed. Everything he does is carried out so swiftly that opponents have no time to recover.

"No player has quite the same ability to draw a cluster of defenders around him, hold them off with feints and changes of balance, and then, in a flash, burst past them and throw the game wide open with one pass. As a blend of schemer and striker I don't think he has an equal. The only parallel to his current style of centre-forward play is Raymond Kopa, the brilliant French international who played for Real Madrid. Dennis and Kopa are very much alike in the way they play. Kopa, too, is a fine outsideright - who can ever forget him playing in that position for Real Madrid at Old Trafford? Kopa has the talent to mould his style to any role he is asked to fill."

Albert Quixall concurred with Bobby's assessment: "Inte rnational honours have always been just around the corner as far as Dennis is concerned." Albert had been advocating for years that Dennis should receive England recognition.

In the event the Football League team beat the part-timers of the Irish League 2-0. However, it was not a good game by any stretch of the imagination. Dennis started well, scoring after just four minutes but as the game progressed Dennis faded badly and though on the winning side he knew he had not impressed England manager Walter Winterbottom. The following day, looking forlorn and pensive, Dennis said: "They talk about the Spanish blighting your life, but as far as I'm concerned it's the Irish! I played last year against the Irish League and this week I played against them again. Although our 2-0 victory this time was certainly a big improvement on our 0-0 draw last year, I know only too well that I did not play well. We won but played badly. We were simply not together as a team." On a brighter note for Dennis, his nephew David Goodwin, who had been a ballboy for United, signed amateur forms and made his debut in United's 'B' team that weekend.

United drew their next league game against Fulham at Old Trafford 3-3 - Charlton, Scanlon and Dennis on the mark. Fortyeight hours later, United flew to Madrid for the return match against Spanish masters Real Madrid in the glorious Santiago Bernabeu Stadium. Real Madrid were, as always, perfect hosts as they made the United players and officials very welcome. Their hospitality was out of this world, they couldn't do enough for the Manchester party. The match ended with Real Madrid winning but not by the easy margin widely predicted. The game ended 6-5 (yes 6-5!) to Madrid. United would have beaten their hosts but for two diabolical penalties awarded by the biased French referee. The sporting Spanish crowd cheered United off the pitch at the end of a wonderfully exciting and entertaining game. A big banquet was attended for the players and officials of both teams. Senor Santiago Bernabeu stood up, took the microphone and told those assembled: "Mr Busby is the greatest man I have ever met in football!"

After their trip to Spain, it was back to the mundane task of improving league position. Another 1-1 draw, this time against Bolton Wanderers at Burnden Park, Dennis making a late goal for Alex Dawson, was followed by a 4-1 demolition of Luton Town at Old Trafford - Dennis again on the mark with two goals, while Goodwin and Quixall got one each. Against Everton at Goodison, United were determined to break a poor run of away form that had seen them win just once in September against Chelsea. They got off to a good start and played some delightful football and, after a couple of minutes, Dennis put them in front. The pitch was like treacle and the stronger Everton players got stuck into the Reds to such a degree that by half-time they had scored twice through Thomas and a penalty from Collins - United ended up on the losing side again 2-1.

Johnny Berry was slowly recovering from the injuries

he sustained at Munich. He had been told by doctors that he would never be able to play football again. Johnny travelled to the Everton game on the coach with the United team. He was now working as a clerk but remained depressed about his career ending so dramatically. Dennis sat down beside him and tried to cheer Johnny up but there was little he could do to make him feel better about the loss of his career.

There was better news for Kenny Morgans, another Munich survivor. He had been able to play again but could not get back into United's first team. He trained diligently and hard enough, but there was something missing from his game. He was nowhere near the player he had been before the crash. Kenny had played for Wales Under-23s against Scotland at Wrexham. Jimmy Murphy was there as the manager of Wales while Matt Busby went along to watch Kenny play. His performance had improved, he used both feet and seemed to have regained much of his confidence. United wanted him back challenging for a position in the first team again.

Dennis in Hot Water

In November 1959 Dennis found himself shrouded in controversy. He had inflamed the Football League and the FA, Wolverhampton Wanderers, their players, officials and fans, by writing an article in the *Manchester Evening News* supposedly attacking Wolves after they had reached the quarter-finals of the European Cup.

Dennis said he didn't believe Wolves were the best ambassadors for British football because they were not typical exponents of the English game. "I know their style of play gets results but I would hate to see many matches between teams like Wolves. The trainers would be working overtime." Dennis said that whenever Wolves were criticised because of their powerhouse play, they replied by saying their forward line was one of the smallest in the game. "The strength and power of Wolves lies in their defence. You don't need power in attack when you have the Wolves defenders behind you."

When discussing their involvement in the European Cup, Dennis said he didn't think Wolves would win the coveted trophy. "Their power-football may get them through another round but I cannot see it taking them to the final. Even if they do bring this fabulous trophy to England for the first time, I wonder whether their style would enhance our reputation in the arts and graces of the game." He went on to claim that Wolves reigned supreme in the First Division because they were a powerhouse team, in the same vein as Bolton.

Everybody who watched football knew that what he said was fair comment, because both clubs were supremely fit and did have big, strong, powerful players. True, they also possessed a great deal of skill, but usually they ground down their opponents with strength rather than class and panache.

Andy Kerr, Manchester City's Scottish international, said he was right behind Dennis in his article about Wolves, "But only up to a point," said Kerr. "Dennis is entitled to his say like anybody else, but I don't agree that Wolves are poor soccer ambassadors."

Suddenly Dennis faced the threat of a severe reprimand, a possible suspension or heavy fine for his remarks. The League intended to bring in a new rule to prevent players making statements in the newspapers or magazines about other clubs. The League management committee had been trying to gag players for a couple of years and one of their officials told the press: "We are going to stop these attacks one way or another."

In turn, Wolves' manager Stan Cullis replied to Dennis's criticism saying: "Viollet is entitled to his opinion. It is not part of my policy to comment on the players of another club. I prefer to let the public judge matters for themselves." It was a storm in a teacup really, over-hyped sensationalism designed to sell papers.

Nevertheless Stan Cullis was annoyed and his club eventually sent a letter of complaint to the League. He was a blunt, outspoken man who believed that players should be seen and not heard. One morning while Dennis was in Matt Busby's office, the phone rang. Matt's secretary answered the call and, putting her hand over the mouthpiece, told him it was Stan Cullis on the phone and that he was extremely angry. Matt turned to Dennis and said: "I know what he wants, it's about your newspaper article, now you answer the phone and speak to him." Matt left his office smiling at Dennis's uncomfortable conversation with the Wolves manager.

In the event Dennis was proved right about one thing: Wolves, having beaten Red Star Belgrade 4-1 on aggregate in round two, were hammered 9-2 by Barcelona over two legs in the quarter-finals in what remains their last appearance in the European Cup.

Hat-Trick

For Manchester United's home match against Blackpool on December 5th 1959, Matt Busby rocked the soccer world when he dropped four regular first-team stars: Harry Gregg, Warren Bradley, Wilf McGuinness and Bobby Charlton. All four were internationals. David Gaskell took Gregg's place in goal, Alex Dawson took Bradley's right-wing spot (though he and Dennis would be interchanging throughout the game), Mark Pearson replaced Charlton at inside-left and Shay Brennan took McGuinness's place in the half-back line. Albert Quixall, when asked by reporters about the changes, said that he felt certain that his four team-mates would not be looking for transfers to other clubs. Albert said that unlike other clubs United didn't refer to the reserves as the 'stiffs.' "There is no first or second team at Old Trafford, we are all as one unit," he said.

After Wilf McGuinness played for Manchester United reserves against Aston Villa at Villa Park, he was pleasantly surprised at the standard in United's Central League team. Speaking a couple of days later to Dennis Viollet he said: "Tell the lads not to ease up, or they will be joining me in the reserves!" Dennis smiled and told Wilf to keep plugging away and he would soon get his place back. Wilf then told waiting reporters: "I can warn my former teammates that there are more challengers knocking on the first team door than the four who have already moved in. It is no wonder our reserves are top of the Central League."

Dennis was sympathetic to Wilf's position, after all no player likes to be dropped from the first team. However, Wilf told his captain that if he was totally honest he shouldn't grumble about being dropped and knew that it had been on the cards. Wilf, being the loyal club man he was, had even told Matt Busby a few weeks before that he was worried about his form. Quite rightly, Busby told Wilf that he would decide who plays when and where in Manchester United's team. There the matter ended! Some newspapers had suggested that Wilf would ask for a transfer. "I haven't the slightest thought about asking for a transfer," Wilf told Dennis. "I know when I am well off and that is with Manchester United, even if that involves playing for the 'A' team!" McGuinness went on to say that he had met quite a number of former United players who had left the club and later regretted it. One player who left Old Trafford for another First Division club told Wilf that if he had the chance he would go back to United, even if it meant sweeping the stands.

The Football League management committee and the Professional Players' Union held a meeting in London to discuss the article written by Dennis in the *Manchester Evening News* in November. Dennis had been told to contact Alan Hardaker, the Football League secretary, for a private chat with him about the article. Dennis explained to Mr Hardaker that his views were not meant to be in any way offensive to the Wolves players or officials and that "no malice was intended. The article was a genuine attempt to compare two contrasting styles of football."

He continued that he had been asked to base his article on a frank analysis of Wolves' style of play and how he thought they would fare in the later rounds of the European Cup. Dennis gave his honest views on a question that he had been asked to discuss in an article. There was talk that the Football League were going to insist on controlling players' comments in these type of articles, but Cliff Lloyd of the Players' Union said he would fight any new effort to gag the players and stressed that they were backing Dennis to the hilt. "We believe in the freedom of the players to express their personal views, even though sometimes some of us may not agree with them." Mr Lloyd then made the point that some of the players found it necessary to write these articles because their wages were insignificant and that this was the reason the Players' Union were trying to negotiate new contracts for their members.

Indeed it had recently been revealed that the entire Manchester United playing staff were drawing maximum wages for their age. It appeared there was no such thing as a sliding scale at Old Trafford and that as soon as a player reached the age of 20 he went on to £20 a week even if he was only in the third team. The first team win bonus was £4 but only £2 playing for the reserves. At this time United's Central League team were in such winning form that they frequently picked up £22 a man against the £20 of club captain Dennis Viollet.

After the meeting in London, Dennis was told that neither the Football League nor the FA would press any charges against him. Cliff Lloyd wrote to Wolves in answer to their claim that Dennis had "attacked" them in print. It was all quickly forgotten.

Afterwards, Dennis said he felt as if his whole world had been turned upside down. "It's been quite a week," he said. "There were quite a few familiar faces missing when Matt Busby selected United's team to play Blackpool. Yes, it's quite a team shuffle, but the moral is quite clear - we have all got to fight for our first team places at Old Trafford and I'm not forgetting myself either. It is just like the days when we had seven or eight internationals in the reserves. I don't think there will be any moaning from the dropped players - even though they are all internationals."

Dennis was thankful for a return to action as he scored twice in an easy 3-1 victory over Blackpool. The re-shaped team played quite well with Dennis continually switching with Alex Dawson, then dropping deep and coming through to join the United forwards.

For the next game, away at FA Cup holders Nottingham Forest, United played possibly their best football of the season. Forest were not a free scoring side but their defensive capabilities were first class. United were unchanged from the Blackpool game and Dennis needed just one more goal to equal his best-ever tally of 21 in a season.

Initially, United looked likely to be overwhelmed. Forest attacked relentlessly and the Red rearguard came under such intense pressure that Pearson was forced to drop back to help out. Gathering the ball Pancho slipped up and

Wilson, the Forest centre-forward, nipped in and shot hard and low past Gaskell. Young Pearson held his head in his hands but Dennis told him to forget it and get on with the game.

Minutes later Pearson and Dennis combined to set up Dawson. Alex ran on to a lovely short through ball and planted it into the net. From then on it was all United: Pearson hit the bar just before half-time; Quixall had the Forest defence going all ways as he slipped the ball through for Dennis, who drew Forest keeper Thomson, before slotting it home.

In the second half United played vintage football - Scanlon and Viollet the most prominent players. Albert went on a fast, powerful, streaking run and banged in a terrific goal. Afterwards he made two chances for Dennis which he converted with aplomb.

After the match Busby declared: "I am delighted with our lads today. The whole team touched peak form and have now set themselves a standard they are anxious to maintain. Dennis Viollet's hat trick was brilliantly taken." The Club Captain told reporters: "This 5-1 victory was a team triumph, every player excelled. The four promoted lads and the 'old' boys as well.'

As *Manchester Evening Chronicle* reporter Peter Slingsby was making his way into the car park after the game, John Doherty stopped him and told him: "We were great today, Peter. I hope we can keep up this kind of form." Doherty was one of the original Busby Babes and was quite friendly with Dennis, who had been a guest at John's wedding. After winning a championship medal in 1955-56 and playing in 26 first team games, he had been transferred to Leicester City. John eventually received a very bad knee injury that forced his eventual retirement from football but he followed United at every home and most away games.

"Dennis was brilliant," John enthused. "You could play him in any position and he would excel. He was one of those players who could scheme, act as a link-man, play as an attacking midfielder and, more importantly from a team point of view, he could score goals, and I do mean score goals. Bobby became famous for his cannonball shots and spectacular long-distance shooting and rightly so because he could certainly blast them. But I've seen Dennis score like that but he was also fantastic at getting those little tap-ins. He could dribble his way through the tightest of defences and score, volley them in, walk the ball into the goal.

"When he was just put in the team to get goals he became a goal-poacher supreme. There were so many roles he could play for United. He was only slightly built but for all this he was hard to knock off the ball, his balance was unbelievable. He could play on bone hard grounds and also mud heaps, and he always looked in control of the situation.

"Mind you, he was at his best when he played with big Tommy Taylor. Those two were great for each other. Many a time Tommy would go up for a high ball and Dennis would anticipate where he was going to nod it and it would be in the back of the net before you could blink your eye. They seemed to have a telepathic understanding. On other occasions Dennis would have the ball and run towards the opposition goal and it would be Tommy who would seem to know where Dennis was going to deliver the ball and he would make his run, and nine times out of ten he'd be in the right spot, and another goal was scored for United.

"Both of them made goals for each other and should have been picked for England together. Perhaps Dennis never got the headlines because what he did on the pitch was appreciated more by his team-mates than the newspaper reporters. The United fans loved him. He was a quiet, courteous man on the field, never one to shout and bawl.

Dennis was always available to help out his colleagues by being in a position to receive the ball."

Going back to Manchester on the team coach Dennis was telling the younger players that he and the Nottingham Forest wing-half Jeff Whitefoot joined Manchester United together as kids. "We were two of the original Busby Babes," Dennis told them. He went on to say that one of the things they both wished was that the FA Youth Cup had started when they first went to Old Trafford. "We were just a year or so too old, I often think back and wonder how a team including Mark Jones, Jackie Blanchflower, Bill Foulkes, Freddie Goodwin, Ronnie Cope and myself would have made out. We certainly missed something in not having a Youth Cup to sharpen us up and introduce us into the big time atmosphere."

Everyone seemed in a happy frame of mind but the day's success was spoiled when news came through that poor Wilf McGuinness had broken his leg playing against Stoke City reserves. When Dennis arrived back in Manchester he immediately enquired about his pal and was told that Wilf had had the bad luck to have broken two bones in his right leg - it was a bad break. Wilf, being the cheerful character he was, told Dennis and other visitors that he expected to be back playing first team football before the end of the current season. He was the first United senior player to break a leg since the Second World War. Sadly, after several attempts to get over his injury and return to fitness, the leg was damaged beyond repair and Wilf's playing career was over.

After reaching the heights against Forest, Manchester United's next two games, both at Old Trafford, saw them plumb the depths as a week before Christmas they lost at home to West Brom (3-2) and lost to Burnley (2-1) on Boxing Day.

There was plenty of newspaper speculation regarding

the robust, tough-tackling West Brom wing-half Maurice Setters joining United. For the return game against Burnley at Turf Moor, Matt Busby dropped Mark Pearson and brought back Bobby Charlton. Bobby had played three reserve games and had not really excelled, however Busby said he was giving Pearson a rest in readiness for the FA Cup tie with Derby County in the New Year.

What a day it turned out to be for Matt Busby. First he became a grandfather and then he saw his team snap into their best form against Burnley. The two games with Burnley highlighted United's unreliable form. Beaten comprehensively by the Clarets at Old Trafford, two days later the same teams met at Turf Moor and this time United gave an exhilarating display. Dennis scored two fabulous goals, while Albert Scanlon also netted twice. United played superbly and should have scored more. This kind of fluctuating form left United mid-table at the end of the year. It was an obvious disappointment following their runners-up spot the year before.

Alex Dawson was one of the most exciting forwards to emerge from Old Trafford's assembly line of stars. After Munich he played in a number of highly emotional games although he was only a teenager. In 93 first team appearances he scored 54 goals which bears comparison with any other United striker. He scored on his League debut and still holds the record as the youngest post-war player, at 18, to score a hat-trick in an FA Cup semi-final (against Fulham in 1958). He moved to Preston North End in 1961 and was a prolific scorer for them. At Old Trafford he was referred to as the 'Black Prince.' Alex was liked by everyone at the club. A quiet, unassuming lad, he rarely socialised with the senior professionals like Dennis, Bill Foulkes, Bobby Charlton, Harry Gregg or Albert Scanlon. He could usually be found in the company of Mark Pearson, Nobby Lawton and Reg Hunter: lads who had joined United at the same time as him.

However, on the afternoon after the Burnley game, Alex was approached by Dennis who told him: "We're going to the Queens Hotel and you're joining us." Alex smiled and politely declined the invitation, saying he had to meet his girlfriend but Dennis told him to forget his girlfriend for a few hours and join them. Alex reluctantly agreed and off they went to the Queens Hotel.

The lads had a meal and wine was ordered. Dennis told the waiter to put it on United's bill. Alex looked on horrified when he heard this but saw that Dennis and the other players were thoroughly enjoying themselves, having a laugh and a joke. Things got more serious when Dennis ordered more wine. Alex, being younger than the others, was concerned that Matt Busby might find out. Dennis told him to relax and stop worrying himself.

The next morning at training, Jack Crompton told Dennis that Busby wanted to see him in his office. "I thought we were all in trouble," Alex recalls. "Dennis never batted an eyelid as he walked up the stairs to Matt's office. We all waited with baited breath for him to come back down. Suddenly he walked back and as one we all shouted. 'How did you go on Dennis?' He replied: 'Oh don't worry, we don't have to pay.' We couldn't believe it. 'How did you get out of that Tricky?' asked Harry Gregg. Dennis grinned and said he hadn't told us but the boss had become a grandfather for the first time, so when the boss asked what we were celebrating in the Queens and why the drinks had been charged to the club's account, Dennis told Matt: 'We were celebrating you becoming a grandad.' Matt smiled and said it was ever so nice of us all and not to worry, the club would pay the bill!"

By New Year's Eve 1959, football supporters and writers

were choosing their particular player of the year. Dennis himself had been suggested in quite a few newspapers and soccer publications. However Tom Finney, the brilliant Preston forward, and Jimmy McIlroy, the classy Burnley forward, seemed to be the overwhelming choices.

But Dennis's choice of Player of the Year involved none of the above: "My choice is a player whose performances are so quiet and unspectacular that he rarely gets the acclaim he deserves. Yet he is playing so well that if I were the England manager, he would be in my team without a moment's hesitation. I'm talking about Bill Foulkes."

Dennis went on to say that although his team-mate was not the best distributor of the ball, he was most certainly the best defender by a long shot. "In my humble opinion, Bill is playing as well now as he was when he was capped for England against Ireland in 1954."

A New Dawn

It was out with the old and in with the new - as the decade that would eventually herald new freedoms began. In an era when new ideas would challenge the accepted way of doing things in all walks of life, football was, unusually, at the vanguard both on and off the pitch.

The 1960s would herald a new kind of glory for Manchester United. Matt Busby and Jimmy Murphy's rebuilt team would eventually bring honour and glory to the club as the Reds went from strength to strength. And even at this early stage the club's hopes were high with the Central League team topping their division and the Youth team going like an express train in the FA Youth Cup, things certainly looked up for the club.

More importantly, preconceptions were being challenged in football as the Players' Union continued their fight to have the maximum wage abolished. As yet the football

Record Breaker

authorities had resisted the players' demands but by the end of the decade players would go from virtual slaves to superstars.

Unfortunately United's first match in the Swinging Sixties saw a 7-3 humiliation at Newcastle. This was the first time under Busby that his team had conceded as many as seven goals in a competitive game. And almost immediately the manager went hunting for defenders. Jimmy Murphy and Johnny Aston senior checked on Ollie Burton, a big centre-half who played for Newport County. Len Choules and Glyn Evans, two defenders from Crystal Palace, had also been checked but nothing came of it. United were also very keen on Welsh international Mel Nurse from Swansea City. However their manager, Trevor Morris, said he was not for sale to anyone.

In the end an answer to United's centre-half problem proved to be right on their own doorstep. John McGrath, the Bury centrehalf, went on to play for Newcastle and Southampton with great distinction.

Attempting to forget last year's humiliation at Norwich City, United travelled to the Baseball Ground to take on Derby County and beat them after a tense struggle. United cruised into a 4-0 lead, before their defensive frailties resurfaced and allowed Derby back into the game. However they finished on the winning side, 4-2.

Meanwhile Busby had ended all speculation by signing 23-yearold Maurice Setters who would also be available for the fourth round tie against Liverpool. There was also plenty of newspaper speculation that Albert Scanlon would be capped for England. Reporters were in raptures about Albert's left-wing performance at Derby.

Later that week, Scanlon made his 100th league appearance against Birmingham City at Old Trafford in a match United won 2-1. Dennis scored again, along with

Albert Quixall. After losing at Tottenham (2-1) the Reds beat Liverpool 3-1 at Anfield in the fourth round of the FA Cup - Bobby Charlton scoring two beauties, Bradley grabbing the third. The Old Trafford Derby quickly followed but the game ended in an exciting yet scoreless draw.

Next, Preston North End visited Old Trafford as United were held once more, this time 1-1. Dennis scored United's goal, a rare, majestic headed goal. As Dennis headed the ball downwards, Dunn, who had jumped with him, was beaten and the ball ricocheted into the net. This was Dennis's 27th strike of the season, just three short of the club record held by Jack 'Gunner' Rowley. This game was a sharpener for United's fifth round FA Cup tie against Sheffield Wednesday at Old Trafford, or so the newspapers claimed. The game ended up with the Reds losing 1-0, Wednesday scoring from the spot.

The FA Cup exit was swiftly followed by a 3-1 trouncing at Leicester. Nevertheless, Dennis showed his versatility at Filbert Street, appearing at outside-right. The night was wet and depressing, but Dennis shone like a beacon: here, there, everywhere. United tried out their new formation with Dennis on the wing and young Alex Dawson up front but to no avail, Leicester won on merit.

Their next game, at Bloomfield Road, Blackpool once more emphasised the Reds' topsy-turvy form. United ran out easy winners (6-0). Until this match Bobby Charlton had gone eleven games without a goal but against the Seasiders he got his timing back and lashed in a hat-trick. Dennis added two more to take him a step nearer the club record, while Albert Scanlon was the other scorer. But after the elation of the victory over Blackpool, it was down in the dumps again as United lost 2-0 at home to Wolves.

The following week United played neighbours Manchester City in a 'friendly' at Maine Road. The only drama to come from this grim match was the promise of the Reds' re-arranged attack. Young Johnny Giles gave a delicate display on the right wing, inside-left Mark Pearson emphasised his close control and beautiful skills, while Dennis, who moved back to lead the attack for this game, showed all his cunning and brilliance. After half an hour City got a penalty. As their normal penalty-taker Ken Barnes was not playing, up stepped stand-in captain, big Bill Leivers. He fluffed his chance. Dennis then became the first United forward to beat Bert Trautmann this season when he hit a low drive into the City net after 44 minutes. United's leader notched up another goal in the 64th minute after taking a square ball from Bobby Charlton and placing it into the goal. Colin Barlow pulled a goal back for the Blues but Charlton rammed home the third to give the Reds victory. Tommy Heron and Frank Haydock, two youngsters from the Central League side, also played in this game.

For the home match against Nottingham Forest, Dennis played at inside-right in place of Albert Quixall, Johnny Giles was switched to the right wing and Alex Dawson led the attack once again. The crowd were urging Dennis to beat the club record but it was thunderbolt Bobby Charlton who got onto the scoresheet twice with Dawson netting the third.

Dennis was able to relax a little from his goal-scoring chase by refereeing a Showbiz charity match at Fallowfield. Among those playing in the match were famous ex-footballers Len Shackelton, George Hardwick, Wally Barnes and Billy Wright, along with celebrities of 1960, Ronnie Carroll and Dave King. This little break obviously did the trick for Dennis when in his next game for Manchester United he would make history. After the Showbiz match Dennis was invited for a drink with the celebrities. He enjoyed himself immensely, always a smiling affable person he proved quite a hit with the entertainment crowd.

Congratulations Dennis!

March 26th 1960 proved a memorable day in the life of Dennis Sydney Viollet. United were playing Fulham at Craven Cottage and Dennis created a new club goalscoring record. United beat the London club 5-0 but Dennis stole the show, scoring twice and eclipsing the record of 30 goals set by Jack Rowley in 1952. Dennis now had 31. The promoted Central League trio of Giles-Dawson- Pearson also scored. United demoralised Fulham so much so that their supporters gave their team the slow hand-clap. This was unfair, because the Londoners could do very little about the agility and class of United's fluent forward line playing bewitching soccer.

Dennis scored the first two goals in the first half, setting up his team-mates for a win bonus and a taste of champagne. When the game ended, the team congratulated their captain. This was a remarkable achievement for Dennis because he had scored his 31 goals in just 34 games - a record that still stands to this day, fortyone years on. The record was all the more remarkable for a player who had distinguished himself in five different positions this season.

Back in the dressing room Matt Busby shook his captain's hand and told him how pleased he was for him. They had both been through a traumatic experience at Munich and this was indeed a special occasion for both of them to savour.

On the train journey back to Manchester Matt Busby broke open the champagne and toasted Dennis. "This is a truly unique and historic achievement, Dennis," said the manager, adding when the clapping had subsided, "Everyone at Manchester United is extremely proud of you and we wish you every success in the coming seasons." Dennis, a big smile on his face was touched and embarrassed.

He declined to make a speech, but he later told reporters that he could never have beaten the record had it not been for the help of the other players in the team. He did say later that he would never have scored so many without the help of Albert Quixall's fabulous skills. "He really is the most unselfish player I have ever played with," concluded Dennis. Modest and sincere, that was darting Dennis.

Having played 239 times in the Cup and League since making his debut against Newcastle United in April 1953, Dennis's overall goals tally had now reached 141 - a truly phenomenal record considering that he was used in so many different roles. A quiet, unassuming person, he must go down as one of the most loyal and devoted club men Manchester United have ever had.

After the brilliance of Fulham, the Reds went to Hillsborough and lost 4-2 to Sheffield Wednesday. Dennis scored again, as did Bobby Charlton. This was the last goal Dennis would score in this, his record breaking season as later in the game Dennis picked up a knee injury and played only once more game against West Ham United, where he injured his knee again and missed the last two matches.

But for the injury and missing six of the last seven games, who knows just how many goals Dennis would have scored? The Reds won five and lost two of the remaining seven games of the season. So United had finished a disappointing but respectable seventh in the league table and had scored an amazing 102 goals but conceded an even more amazing 80.

The most satisfying feature of the season for United was the winning of the Central League Championship by six clear points scoring 114 goals in the process - the club's future looked safe. Many of the Central League players were another season older and challenging for first team places. It was no secret that this was what Matt Busby wanted, playing strength just like it used to be before Munich, where every first team position was covered and the second team players were posing questions for the regular first teamers.

While the United players and officials readied themselves for their tour of Canada and America, Bobby Charlton and Dennis trained at the Cliff before joining up with the England team. Both had been selected to go on a short European tour with their country. This was, of course, wonderful recognition for Dennis, although he wasn't getting his hopes up too high that he would get a game. Nonetheless, it was just reward for his record-breaking exploits during the season.

At last! England Cap Viollet

So exclaimed the headlines in the *Daily Mail* of Thursday May 20th 1960. Yes, Dennis had been told by England manager Walter Winterbottom that he would be making his England debut on the following Sunday in a game against Hungary in Budapest.

"Yes, he's in the team-and he deserves it," Walter Winterbottom told enquiring reporters. It appears that Johnny Haynes had requested that Dennis be included in the team. At a team discussion a couple of days before the game, the England manager turned to Haynes and asked if he would prefer to play in his club position, inside-left? Haynes replied "No," pointing out that Dennis would prefer to play in his natural position, as he would partner his team-mate, Bobby Charlton.

The England team line-up: Springett (Sheffield Wednesday); Armfield (Blackpool), Wilson (Huddersfield); Robson (West Brom), Swan (Sheffield Wednesday) Flowers (Wolves); Douglas (Blackburn), Haynes (Fulham), Baker (Hibs), Viollet (Manchester United), Charlton (Manchester United).

Dennis couldn't have picked a harder match to make his debut, he was certainly jumping in at the deep end. Journalists dubbed him Manchester United's 'Mr Brains'. Spurned by his country a year ago when he was probably England's finest forward, he was going to play against a rejuvenated Hungarian side in front of over 80,000 partisan spectators in the Nep Stadium. If that were not tough enough, he would be opposing the vastly experienced Magyar right-half, and their greatest player, Dosidor Bundszat. A baptism of fire by anybody's reckoning!

England started the match adventurously. In the first half Dennis made a lot of penetrating runs and was playing with confidence. England fought well but were reduced to scrambling defensively and Dennis, like a few others, faded. It was no surprise when Hungary's 19-year-old 'wonder boy' Florian Albert scored twice to give Hungary a 2-0 victory. However the home fans cheered England off the pitch for their fighting qualities. The Hungarian manager Louis Bartti admitted: "England shook me. Their best player was Charlton." Walter Winterbottom concurred. "This was our best match of the season, but the Hungarians deserved to win."

Both Bobby Charlton and Johnny Haynes are of the opinion that Dennis had been extremely unfortunate to get his first cap against such tough opposition. "I felt sorry for Dennis," remarked Johnny Haynes. "We were up against it and it was so hot, almost unbearable. Dennis was facing Bundszat, one of the top European players, and that was a tough task indeed. He deserved to be selected again but he had to wait over a year to get another chance."

Bobby, who went on to play over a hundred games for England said: "Dennis should have been a regular in the England team during the middle fifties. He and Tommy Taylor were a truly awesome striking combination. There were a lot of gifted insideforwards during that period, however. Dennis was a brilliant player and like I say, he should have been capped then. When his chance did come against Hungary we had had a hard season although Dennis had broken the club scoring record, something he still holds to this day."

After the England tour, Dennis and Bobby jetted over to America to join up with their Manchester United club mates who were in St Louis preparing to play a Catholic Youth XI. Dennis played and scored in a 4-0 win, Alex Dawson and Albert Quixall scored the other goals. This was Dennis's first taste of soccer stateside and he scored further goals against Pacific Coast and New England All-Stars before finishing up with a hat-trick in Philadelphia against the Ukrainian National team.

Dennis Viollet's career seemed to come to life at the wrong time. Not only had he broken Jack Rowley's record but he was also finally recognised by his country and picked for England. And, though his International debut didn't have the dream ending he had hoped for, it at least went some way toward the recognition he deserved. Now, following a remarkable season of success, Dennis Viollet of Manchester United and England could take a wellearned break.

A Season of Frustration

Although finishing seventh in 1959-60, and despite Dennis's personal achievements, there was no mistaking the decline in Manchester United's fortunes. The youngsters were not coming through as they had previously, the huge crowds had started to drift away while for Dennis it signalled the end of an era. Nevertheless, the first full season of the Sixties promised to be interesting. There were complaints that First Division admission prices had risen to 2s 6d (12.5p) while there was an open threat of a players' strike.

As has already been mentioned, the maximum wage any player could earn from his club was £20 per week. There were a few fringe benefits of course. Players of the standing of Dennis, Bobby Charlton and Albert Quixall often wrote weekly or fortnightly columns for local newspapers for which they received a few pounds. But as a rule neither they nor other players could receive more than £20.

They were in reality slaves - the best players in the First Division earned the same wage as a Fourth Division player, while a club had to graciously grant a player's leave from a club. It was during this period that John Charles and Jimmy Greaves were lured to Italy where they could earn huge sums of money because there was no maximum wage. Later, Denis Law, Joe Baker and Gerry Hitchins joined them. The danger that English football would lose all its top stars was obvious but the football authorities and chairman remained defiant.

Dennis and Bill Foulkes were now among the club's longest serving players and the youngsters respected them enormously, seeking them out for advice and encouragement. Bill would start the new season in the right full-back spot, but would eventually take over from Ronnie Cope at centre-half where he would remain until his retirement. Bobby Charlton was maturing rapidly, but would be used mainly as a left-winger after Albert Scanlon moved to Newcastle. Shay Brennan would eventually make the right fullback position his own during the coming season, while a young Irish lad, Jimmy Nicholson, would play most of the season at lefthalf and a little terrier of a footballer from Collyhurst, Nobby Stiles, would make his first team debut and gain valuable experience for greater feats with United and England. Irish international left-back Noel Cantwell joined the club later from West Ham while Wilf McGuinness had handed back his walking sticks and begun light training.

Dennis played in seventeen of United's opening eighteen games and scored ten goals. He alternated between leading the attack and his favoured inside-left position. But United won only two of their opening ten games, losing six and drawing two. This was certainly not good enough if the club were hoping to challenge for honours.

After losing the first two games, United went to Maine Road for the third game. This was not the sort of fixture needed at this particular time, but in adversity, the team put on a battling performance. The weather conditions were awful, the rain pelted down non-stop and the wind made pretty football impossible. The pitch was terrible with lakes appearing all over the ground. Despite all this, both sets of supporters enjoyed the game until referee Arthur Ellis abandoned the match after 59 minutes. However, while it lasted it was a thrilling end-to-end Derby with thrills and spills a-plenty. United had Quixall and Charlton on the wings while City had a new star in their ranks, a young, skinny-looking Scotsman by the name of Denis Law.

It was Law who put City ahead after five minutes, then Dennis scored before Alex Dawson soared to the skies to nod the Reds in front. Joe Hayes equalised before the match was called off. It really was a thrilling encounter despite the shocking weather conditions.

Matt Busby was trying different formations, hence Bobby Charlton on the left and Albert Quixall on the right. In the two games they won, the team looked championship material. Everton were thrashed 4-0 at Old Trafford with Alex Dawson (2), Charlton and Jimmy Nicholson getting the other goals. Their second victory, again at Old Trafford, saw West Ham hammered 6-1. Dennis and Bobby Charlton each scored a brace, Scanlon got one and, after Dennis had been tripped, Quixall scored from the penalty spot.

On Wednesday October 13th 1960, United played another friendly against Spanish giants and World Champions Real Madrid. It was a pity the Reds were playing Real, having made their worst start in the League competition since the war. For experience United fielded two 17-year-old wing-halves, Nobby Stiles and Jimmy Nicholson. Nobby had made his first team debut a few days before at Bolton. Both were outstanding for the Reds and after a very exciting game, United eventually lost 3-2 to Real Madrid, Mark Pearson and Jimmy Nicholson scoring United's goals.

Many critics said that because of the friendship that existed between the two clubs, Madrid took it easy on United. This was nonsense. Anybody in the vicinity of the Madrid dressing room at the interval they would have heard Alfredo di Stefano laying down the law to his team-mates. The Spanish players were also on a £60 win bonus so we can be certain there was no easing up.

On October 15th the Reds visited Turf Moor to play First Division champions Burnley and were obliterated.

Tony Dunne, who cost the club £5,000 from Shelbourne the previous April, made his league debut, the first of 415 league appearances for United. In a game of non-stop entertainment, that had the Lancashire crowd howling with delight, Burnley played like true champions. Ray Pointer gave Burnley the lead, but Dennis quickly equalised. Connelly and Joyce made it 3-1 and once again Dennis cut back the deficit, making it 3-2 at half-time. John Connelly, who would later join United, scored again but Dennis pulled it back to 4-3 to complete his hat-trick. Finally the elegant Jimmy McIlroy settled the breathless game 5-3. This was the prelude to an amazing four matches in seven days, two of which were in a new competition, the Football League Cup.

Wilf McGuinness was still battling his way back to fitness after a broken leg a few months before. While doing a spot of training on his own, he told Dennis he would be back in the first team in no time. Dennis knew that Wilf's determination was frightening at times, he smiled and encouraged his team-mate. A short while later, Wilf was told he would have to go back into hospital for a bone-grafting operation. He was gutted, but though it meant months more treatment, Wilf showed the grit and determination that had made him a Busby Babe.

After the debacle at Burnley, United beat Newcastle 3-2 at Old Trafford. Dawson, Setters and Nobby Stiles scoring the goals. There was a great deal of murmuring amongst the Old Trafford faithful, they wanted to see their beloved United challenging for the games top honours not struggling for respectability. What many didn't seem to realise was the time and patience it took to build the kind of squad United had before Munich. In fact the pre- Munich team of the Busby Babes, were unique in football. A club would be extremely fortunate to find itself with one such team, to find a second could prove impossible.

But that great team of the mid 50s wasn't only about exciting players and technical skill - that could probably return. Rather it was the spirit fostered within the club in that period that could never be bought. As Dennis Viollet himself said: "Manchester United will never be the same again. Before the crash only Johnny Berry, Tommy Taylor and Harry Gregg cost a fee, the rest of us grew up together. All the teams were developed by United and the spirit was fantastic, it was one for all and all for one." However, it took years to build that kind of empire and during this period Busby knew he couldn't wait years for the club to get back to pre-Munich strength. He had to buy top quality players and soon.

The United faithful were down to the bare bones in this period. The rush of sympathy caused by Munich had seen attendances rise to an average of 53,258 in 1958/9 but just two seasons later the average had dropped to less than 40,000. For instance, the Old Trafford gate for the visit of Nottingham Forest was a mere 23,628, the Reds' lowest since before the air crash and the advent of floodlights. Despite this, United gained another victory (2-0) - Dennis on the mark again with two goals.

A couple of days later, United played Fourth Division side Exeter City in a League Cup replay - having drawn 1-1 in Devon. Dennis missed this tie which United won 4-1: Quixall (2), Dawson and Pearson the scorers. Sadly, the game drew just 15,662 fans and United went out in the next round when they played Bradford City. It was a Wednesday afternoon match and a post-war low crowd for United of just 4,670 witnessed a shock 2-1 defeat. The pitch was wet and muddy but still this was a humiliation for the Reds who even took the lead, via Dennis, in the 25th minute. Harold Bratt made his one and only appearance having joined United straight from school.

United's dismal run continued. A defeat (2-1) at Arsenal where they played with plenty of spirit could be considered unlucky. But back at Old Trafford, the Reds could only draw 0-0 with Sheffield Wednesday and followed this with a 3-1 defeat to Birmingham City at St Andrews. As if to make matters worse, Johnny Giles was stretchered off with a broken leg after 23 minutes. Back at Old Trafford the Reds snapped the losing habit by beating West Bromwich Albion 3-0. Dennis scored along with Dawson and Quixall. Then on Monday evening, November 21st, the Reds faced Bayern Munich in another of the kind of international fixtures that Matt Busby and Jimmy Murphy enjoyed. United rose to the occasion and won convincingly 3-1. Noel Cantwell, the West Ham United left full-back, had signed for United only hours before making his debut in this game. Alex Dawson scored a hat-trick and proved the star of the game.

Noel had cost United £29,500, a record fee for a full-back at the time. A clever, cultured player, the Irishman's time at West Ham had given him a great deal of experience while his strapping six-foot presence made him a must in a United team that had yet to find its defensive feet after Munich. Added to this Cantwell could play in several positions. He went on to make 144 first team appearances while captaining the team in the 1963 FA Cup final victory against Leicester City. He left in 1967 to become manager of Coventry City. The Irish international liked a good time and found a soul mate in Dennis, so much so that they remained close friends for years after their respective careers ended.

"I first saw Dennis play in the fabulous Busby Babes team against Charlton Athletic when Bobby Charlton made his first team debut and scored two cracking goals," Noel recalls. "What a team they were, so fluent and majestic. Dennis Viollet made that team run like clockwork. When

I signed for United, Dennis was Club Captain and he very kindly let me stay at his home for a few months. In those times when a player arrived on a transfer from another club, he went into digs, not in top class hotels like they do today. We went training together and Lord he was fast of foot and quick thinking and a great goalscorer - the records prove that. But there was so much more to his game. As a defender it was great when you know you can knock a ball to a teammate and you know where to find him, and what he would do with the ball once he had it!

"I remember as if it was only yesterday sitting with Denis Law and Matt Busby in a restaurant, Dennis had moved to Stoke and we were discussing the merits of certain great players to have graced Old Trafford and Matt turned to us and said: 'I would have Dennis Viollet in my best team that has ever played for Manchester United!' That was some tribute wasn't it? Matt loved Dennis, thought the world of him. I agreed with him because he was so easy to play with. He wasn't an individualist like Bobby. Although Bobby was a brilliant, world-class player, he would drop his shoulder and go off on one of those surging electrifying runs beating man after man, but you never knew what he was likely to do, but you knew what Dennis would do. Which was a great advantage when you're playing."

On November 26th United played Cardiff City at Ninian Park. The Reds were desperate to score their first away victory of the season. In the 18th minute, Dennis crashed into the Cardiff goalkeeper Graham Vearncombe and went down as if shot by a high-powered rifle. He had broken his collarbone. United seemed right out of luck because this blow came just weeks after Johnny Giles had suffered a broken leg. Not surprisingly, United went down 3-0 and it would be four months before Dennis returned to first team action. While Dennis was laid up with his injury,

Matt Busby made enquiries about several players he wanted to bring to Manchester United. Maurice Setters took over the captaincy while Dennis was out of the team.

The next seven league games produced four home victories, two away wins and a draw. That United achieved this success without Dennis proved a surprise. They also beat Middlesbrough in the FA Cup 3-0 at Old Trafford. The Teessiders were captained by the volatile Brian Clough, but Bill Foulkes had him handcuffed for the entire match. It was not as if the Reds had an easy programme of games, indeed far from it, as amongst their scalps were Chelsea (home and away), Manchester City (5-1) and an amazing 2-0 victory over the runaway leaders of the First Division, Tottenham Hotspur.

Alex Dawson led the way goalwise, hitting hat-tricks against Chelsea and City. Alex was also the central figure in an unforgettable match against Tottenham which should have been played on the Saturday at Old Trafford, but because of dense fog was re-arranged for the following Monday night. The Spurs team would go on to win the Double that season and was packed with world-class players. They deserved all the accolades they received. However, on this Monday night, United outplayed, outgunned and outshone them to win 2-0. Nobby Stiles put United in front then Harry Gregg dislocated his shoulder and had to leave the field for treatment. Alex Dawson took over in goal as there were still no substitutes allowed at that time. Gregg came back with his arm in a sling, he obviously could not go back in goal but instead took Dawson's place at centre-forward, and it was he who backheeled the ball for Pancho Pearson to score United's second goal to spark scenes of jubilation.

It proved a costly victory for the Reds because Ronnie Briggs, United's 17-year-old third team goalkeeper, was thrown into first team action against Leicester City in United's next game and saw six goals fly past him. On the same day Dennis made his longawaited return to action with a run-out in a reserve match against Barnsley at Old Trafford. Ironically, Dennis saw United's reserve goalkeeper Eddie Lowery get injured and carried off on a stretcher, while a short time later in the same match they lost the services of Michael Lorimer, a left full-back, leaving the reserves with only nine fit players. They lost 1-0. However Dennis scored the following week against Bolton's reserves and Busby decided to play Dennis against Sheffield Wednesday in the fourth round of the FA Cup at Hillsborough. He wasn't really match fit, but he helped United secure a 1-1 draw thanks to a Noel Cantwell penalty that he hit so hard it nearly sent the Sheffield goalkeeper into orbit.

Dennis was probably pleased he missed the replay at Old Trafford as United were thrashed 7-2 with poor Ronnie Briggs in goal. He had now conceded 14 in three first team games and Matt Busby was a very worried manager. His goalkeeping problem had reached crisis proportions and with both Harry Gregg and David Gaskell out of action, he signed Mike Pinner, an amateur English international, on loan. It was back to the reserves for young Briggs and also for Dennis, who played another Central League game against Manchester City but picked up another injury so was sidelined again. It was a couple of weeks later when Dennis appeared in action again. He played in a Central League game at Old Trafford against West Brom, and scored in a 4-1 defeat. But after the brilliant victory over Tottenham, United went into decline, winning only one of their eleven League and Cup games.

On January 8th 1961, after a great deal of soul-searching, Dennis decided to resign as club captain of United. It wasn't a decision he took lightly. He was still out of action with a broken collarbone and decided that it was only right that Maurice Setters should be installed as the permanent skipper of the club. Dennis had been captain for almost two years. What swayed his decision more than anything was the improved form of the team when Maurice had taken over earlier in the season - the team had won seven and drawn one from eight games. "It is obviously the best thing for the club," Dennis explained. "The team has done wonderfully well since Maurice took over as skipper and in my view it would be wrong for me to step back now." Setters, the former Young England captain, had proved himself to be a natural born leader - forceful, sometimes almost military in his enthusiasm, he had inspired the side.

Meanwhile the threat of a Players' strike loomed closer. Players from every League club were talking about striking for the abolition of the maximum wage. Wilf McGuinness, although only 21, was United's union representative. Wilf needed help and advice because if the strike went ahead, as looked likely, the players would receive no wages from their employers and would have to sign on at the Unemployment Office.

Wilf explains: "Dennis was injured like me, so I asked him if he would come to the unemployment office while we found out our rights so I could inform the United players. He readily agreed. After Munich, Dennis Viollet became a great leader as well as a wonderful captain and all the United lads went to him with our problems and grievances and he always had time to help and give sensible advice. It was funny really seeing me with my walking sticks and Dennis with his arm in a sling traipsing through the dole office. Can you believe it, Manchester United players going into an unemployment office. It caused some leg-pulling from fans and certain reporters, I can assure you. Jimmy Murphy and Matt Busby had been players themselves so they agreed with what we were doing. Thankfully, the union won the day and everything went back to normal. I couldn't thank Dennis enough. Dennis is part of United's history, he will never be forgotten. I have heard it said that he was never the same player after Munich? Well none of us were! Dennis was a great footballer, a legend and a man I am proud to say was my friend."

Matt Busby had gone into hospital for an operation on his back and was due to go away to recuperate after his hospital stay. Meanwhile things were certainly not going the way United would have liked. Apart from their in-and-out form, the FA Youth Cup team failed to reach at least the semi-final stage of the competition for the first time since its inception. After losing their last two games, and hearing that Dennis had scored twice against Blackpool reserves on Good Friday, Jimmy Murphy, in charge of first team affairs while Matt Busby was convalescing, decided to recall Dennis to the first team for the home game against Fulham.

On April Fools Day, 1961, United played Fulham at Old Trafford and Dennis returned to first team duty, having missed 17 league games and a couple of FA Cup matches. Johnny Giles also returned after his broken leg and young Jimmy Nicholson made his first team comeback after injury. Their return brought better fortunes for the first team. It was great to see Dennis playing first team football again, his presence seemed to rejuvenate the whole team and United played some beautiful soccer. He was sweeping inch-perfect passes out to both wings and making lightning fast runs through the bewildered Fulham defence. United won 3-1, Dennis scoring along with Bobby Charlton and Albert Quixall. It was clear that United needed Dennis Viollet and they went unbeaten with him in the team until the end of the season.

Two days after beating Fulham, the Reds beat Blackpool 2-

0 at Old Trafford, and drew 1-1 with West Brom at the Hawthorns. Then, in a game Dennis had been itching to play since October, United played Burnley at Old Trafford. Remember, Burnley had beaten the Reds 5-3 at Turf Moor, and Dennis had scored a hat-trick but ended on the losing side. He desperately wanted to play in this game. Albert Quixall scored his first hat-trick since arriving at Old Trafford and Dennis scored his second hattrick of the season against Burnley as United beat the League Champions 6-0.

Birmingham City received a football lesson and were thrashed 4-1 in another Old Trafford thriller. Mark Pearson scored two cracking goals and was unlucky not to get his hat-trick, while Dennis found the net again and Quixall scored from the penalty spot after Mark Pearson was brought down following a mesmerising run past four defenders. Pearson had made his first team break earlier in the season. He was a maker, rather than a taker, of goals, although he had a terrific shot with either foot. Mark was one of those highly talented players who just lacked that vital bit of luck that all youngsters need to reach the highest pinnacle of the game. It remains a mystery to United followers why he never achieved true greatness. Anyhow, this season had seen him blossom.

Continuing their end of season romp, Preston were hammered 4-2 at Deepdale with Bobby Charlton and Maurice Setters scoring two apiece, a result that sent Proud Preston into the Second Division. The last game of the season saw a 3-3 draw with Cardiff at Old Trafford. Bobby Charlton again bagged a brace with Maurice Setters netting the third.

Indeed, such had been their end of season form that United finished in exactly the same position as they had the season before, in seventh place. Bobby Charlton finished as the club's leading goal scorer with 21 goals from 39 games.

In spite of being out of action for four months, Dennis scored 15 in 24 matches, Alex Dawson got 16 from 28 games and Albert Quixall scored 13 from 38 games. Despite an injury-plagued season that had seen him resign the club captaincy, Dennis was able to go off on the postseason tour of Malta and Italy with high hopes that his troubles were behind him.

Farewell United

Dennis Viollet had been a Manchester United footballer since 1949. He had won two First Division championship medals, played in an FA Cup Final, two European Cup semi-finals, become an England international and record goalscorer for the club. Now in his thirteenth season at Old Trafford and aged 28, He appeared to still have a good five seasons left in football at the highest level.

Over the years he had watched the wonderful 1948 Cupwinning team of Rowley, Pearson, Carey, Chilton, Mitten and Aston go on to win the 1952 First Division Championship. He had learned from their experience and eventually replaced them in the never-to-be-forgotten Busby Babes team. He had been involved in an air crash that almost cost him his life, a crash in which he saw several of his close friends perish while others had their careers ended because of the injuries sustained. He had returned to the post-Munich United team and helped rebuild a club devastated by the crash. As recently as two seasons before he had set a club record (that still stands today) for League goals in a season and entertained the Old Trafford faithful for a decade.

Nevertheless United's pre-season tour in the summer of 1961 would be Dennis's last with the club. United beat FC Bayern 2-0 and drew 1-1 against First Vienna, both games being good tests for the new season. In July, David Herd had signed from Arsenal, and made his debut against FC Bayern, when he was named 'Man of the Match' and scored an excellent goal. Herd led the attack while Dennis played inside-right in both games, and scored United's goal in the 1-1 draw.

A Scottish international, David Herd had first played football in Manchester. His father Alex was one of Manchester City's finest players in an era when Matt Busby played for the 'Sky Blues'. David used to watch his father a lot in those days and later played in the same forward line as him when both were players with Stockport County. Busby had had Herd in mind for some time, however his signature didn't necessarily signal the beginning of the end for his schoolpal Dennis Viollet's career at United. Indeed Dennis welcomed David with open arms - he had been looking forward to playing alongside his friend for some time.

When the season proper commenced, United travelled to West Ham and drew 1-1 and their first home game of the new season saw Chelsea in opposition. The United line-up read: Gregg; Brennan, Cantwell; Stiles, Foulkes, Setters; Quixall, Viollet, Herd, Pearson, and Charlton. Maurice Setters was retained as captain. The Reds won 3-2 Dennis, Herd and Pearson scoring the goals. Chelsea had sold Jimmy Greaves to an Italian club to join Denis Law, Joe Baker and Gerry Hitchens in the land of the Lire.

Dennis's form remained good. He played the opening nine games of the season, scoring four goals. Of those nine games, the Reds won six, drew two with just one defeat. In one of these games United beat the all-conquering Double winners Tottenham Hotspur 1-0 at Old Trafford. Dennis was playing superbly at insideright. After beating Manchester City 3-2 at Old Trafford when Dennis scored along with Nobby Stiles and a Dave Ewing owngoal, Dennis received an unexpected honour.

On the same day Fulham beat Ipswich Town 4-2 at Portman Road, Ipswich. Immediately after the game

Johnny Haynes, the captain of England, telephoned Walter Winterbottom, the England manager to tell him he had picked up a slight knock.

Meanwhile, in Manchester, Dennis was relaxing at home ahead of United's midweek fixture against Aston Villa, when he received an SOS from the Football Association telling him to report immediately to England headquarters. He was absolutely gobsmacked and delighted. On Tuesday, the England squad trained at Chelsea and had a practice match against the full Chelsea team. Dennis played for the England team for the whole first half. After the break, Haynes replaced Dennis. Walter Winterbottom was watching intently as the Fulham player got involved. After ten minutes Haynes pulled up suddenly clutching his right leg, after treatment he hobbled back to the dressing room. The match ended 4-4 - Haynes was out of the team and Dennis was in. Johnny had a badly strained right leg. Talking about the loss of the Fulham man Winterbottom said: "It gives us an opportunity to learn to play without him."

Dennis was obviously pleased to be back in the international side again. It meant Dennis's first cap for 16 months and only his second for England. It also meant that Jimmy Armfield, the Blackpool full-back, would captain England in the absence of Haynes. United's match against Aston Villa was now postponed because of a new ruling by the FA leaving Villa boss Joe Mercer, seething. "The League seem to be making all kind of concessions," he told reporters.

Dennis told reporters that he reckoned he had done a good job for United by getting selected. "United have Bobby and myself down here in London, and Noel Cantwell, Maurice Setters, and David Herd injured. I only hope I manage to play as well for England as I have been playing for United," he told them.

Flops! That's World Cup New Boys John Fantham, Ray Pointer and Dennis Viollet

So screamed the bold headlines of the *Daily Express*. All the other newspapers were just as scathing. The Express reporter, Clive Toye, wrote: "Bobby Charlton saved England's blushes by scoring twice to save England from shame and humiliation against the brave amateurs of Luxembourg as 33,000 Englishmen whistled and jeered their disgust. Every jeer, every shrill shriek, was aimed at England's show of shame - a fumbling, bungling performance of men who want to wear the white shirts of England in the World Cup finals in Chile next year. I fear England will show only the white shirt of surrender if they rely on this team next month against Portugal. Even Walter Winterbottom, the England manager could hardly believe how badly he missed Jimmy Greaves, Johnny Haynes and either Bobby Smith or Gerry Hitchins. Dennis Viollet, Ray Pointer and John Fantham were a world away from the sort of success a Third Division team would have expected against the crude collection of losers from Luxembourg.

"Only Charlton, Peter Swan, Ron Flowers and Bobby Robson looked their class. The biggest cheer was reserved when Luxembourg scored from a free kick 15 minutes before the end. By that time England had scored four. By comparison to the applause that greeted Luxembourg's goal, England's scores were greeted with the polite murmuring reserved for a despised visiting team."

Ray Pointer scored the first goal. A couple of minutes later Brian Douglas sent Pointer away and Paul Steffen, the Luxembourg goalkeeper failed to hold his low cross. Dennis, quick as a flash walked the ball into the net without a defender anywhere near him. Bobby Charlton scored

England's last two goals with thunderous shooting. The reaction to Dennis's second cap for England had almost certainly ensured that it would be his last. Not one newspaper excused his performance and with the opposition so weak there were few extenuating circumstances to call on.

Dennis's dismal run continued. On his return to first team duty against Arsenal, the Gunners shot United to pieces (5-1), Dennis scoring United's solitary goal. Bolton hammered United 3-0 at Old Trafford and a 3-1 defeat followed at Sheffield Wednesday, Dennis again scoring United's consolation. Both David Herd and Albert Quixall were dropped for this game and played for the reserves against Huddersfield in a 2-0 victory for the Reds' second team. It was around this time that a certain George Best was starring in United's junior sides.

Jimmy Hill, the bearded Fulham forward who, along with Cliff Lloyd, was instrumental in the abolition of the maximum wage, was talking about retiring and managing Coventry City. He had just published a book on his thoughts of how football should be played. Dennis Viollet featured very prominently in Jimmy's book. Hill felt that Dennis and Johnny Haynes should play together in the England team along with Jimmy Greaves, giving England an inside forward trio to match the famed Hungarian line-up of Koscis, Hideguti and Puskas. Still, following Dennis's recent performance there seemed little prospect of this happening.

David Herd was still missing from the first team when on the November 11th 1961 Dennis played what would turn out to be his last League game for United, against Leicester City at Old Trafford, in front of just 21,567. The match ended 2-2 with Dennis and Johnny Giles scoring. The following day's newspaper reports did not make pleasant reading for Dennis. They described him as being slow and missing dozens of goal chances, clearly his form had suffered after the England game. The following Monday night Dennis found himself playing in the Manchester Senior Cup final at Old Trafford. United, fielding a near full team, lost 1-0.

Dennis had been dropped before, of course, but his absence from the first team now looked a little more permanent. Under Busby, players were often give a run out in the reserves if their form had dipped, just as Bill Foulkes had done for 11 games the season before. Dennis had no real reason to believe that he couldn't fight his way back into the first team through sheer weight of goals in the reserves.

However even regular reserve team action seemed beyond him. What is certain is that until his sudden departure from the club, Dennis was never considered again for the first team. Even a centre-forward injury crisis couldn't prevent Dennis's inevitable transfer. Nobby Lawton was now selected ahead of him if a replacement was needed in the first team forward line.

On Saturday January 13th 1962, Dennis pulled on the red shirt of Manchester United for the very last time when he turned out for the reserves against Blackpool reserves. A 2-1 defeat was not the kind of finale Dennis would have chosen after such a glittering and momentous career at Old Trafford.

Farewell United

The departure of Dennis from Old Trafford still mystifies supporters from the period - like the recent Jaap Stam saga, it was so sudden and unexpected that it shocked supporters.

Football had undergone some big changes during the past year. The maximum wage had been abolished in 1961, and players were re-negotiating for higher wages with their clubs, so there may have been issues with certain players demanding inflated wages. However this does not seem to be the case with Dennis. He was now 29 and had spent thirteen very happy years at the club he loved. Though out of the first team since November and upset at not being able to regain his first team spot, he seemed quite happy to bide his time and wait for the opportunity to regain his first team place.

Dennis clearly had no idea he was about to be transferred as he had opened a small business, a record shop called the 'Dennis Viollet Record Bar' in Manchester. Unfortunately the business was not a success. It opened in 1959 and was closed following Dennis's move to Stoke City. Nevertheless it showed he had little intention of leaving.

There is a story that persists to this day that the first Dennis Viollet knew about his transfer to Stoke was while he was at home one night. The phone rang and Dennis answered it. Tony Waddington, the Stoke City manager was on the line. "Hello Dennis," said Mr Waddington. "Don't bother reporting to Old Trafford for training tomorrow, make your way down here to Stoke because I have just bought you from United."

In Dennis Viollet's unpublished autobiography this is what he himself had to say: "One night while sat at home watching television, the phone rang. 'Hello,' I answered, it was Tony Waddington, the Stoke City manager. He told me he had spoken to Matt Busby and he had been given permission to sign me. Can you imagine how I felt? I never spoke for a few seconds, Tony could sense that I was shocked and asked if I would mind if he called to my house straight away? I readily agreed.

"When Tony came he explained that he had negotiated a fee for my transfer with Matt and as long as I had no objections the deal was done. Obviously he told me the terms and they were quite good. However, my mind was in turmoil, but I shrugged my shoulders and turned to Tony. 'Right,' I said, 'this sounds great, where are the forms? I'll sign for Stoke.' And he signed me for Stoke City. And that's how I left Manchester United and headed for the Potteries.

"After the Stoke manager left my house, I felt a sudden emptiness come over me, my mind was in a daze with lots of thoughts running through my mind. I picked up the phone and dialled Matt Busby's home number. The Boss's Scottish tones came over the line. Yes, he told me, Tony Waddington had been on to him. Matt then said he was sorry he hadn't mentioned things to me but he had been rather busy. Further conversation as far as I was concerned was rather pointless and I hung up quickly, although politely. I have said many complimentary things about Matt Busby in this book and I don't think I have told anything but the truth about an exceptional man in football, possibly the best manager the game has every seen. But I will never forgive him for the heartless way in which he handled my leaving Old Trafford.

"It felt to me as if I had become like an old pair of boots to Busby that could be flung in the corner and ignored. Was I asking too much for Busby to say: 'This is the situation, Dennis. Stoke City want you. How do you feel about it?' Oh, Busby was nice enough when it came to the final farewell, but that didn't mean very much to me. I remember as I replaced the receiver after speaking to him I saw in my mind's eye a young team standing round Busby and listening to his every word. Now those words seem hollow."

The Stoke City manager, Tony Waddington, had played for Manchester United as an amateur a few years before. He was getting together a team of experienced professionals for his Stoke team. Stoke had been watching Dennis for weeks and Waddington believed that Dennis would fit in perfectly with Stanley Matthews' inspired revival of Stoke

City. Unbeknown to Dennis, the Stoke manager had already discussed Dennis's position with Matt Busby and was ready to offer United a substantial sum of money for Dennis. "Dennis is an astute and intelligent player, and if I can come to terms with United I will be delighted to bring him to Stoke," Mr Waddington told the press.

If Stoke did sign Dennis they would be able to field a forward line which included three internationals: Dennis, Stanley Matthews and Jackie Mudie.

On Monday January 15th 1962, when the press heard of Stoke's interest they asked Matt Busby about Dennis's position. He told them that Stoke City had approached him about Dennis sometime ago but at the time it didn't go any further. However, he said that if Stoke inquired again about Dennis, he would put their offer before his board and discussed it in the usual manner. "I cannot say what the position would be," he told them.

Significantly, Dennis was not chosen for that evening's re-arranged league game against Aston Villa despite an injury to first choice centre-forward David Herd. Dennis had been playing at centre-forward for the reserves and it was thought that he would be an automatic replacement for Herd, if only as a short-term measure.

Incidentally Albert Quixall played at centre-forward against Aston Villa and was himself injured leaving United with a player crisis at centre-forward, yet Dennis's transfer still went ahead.

The following day, Tuesday, Dennis had been transferred to Stoke City for a fee of just over £25,000. But although he was stepping down a division he had doubled his wages. He was now on £70 a week before bonuses and it was reported that he and Matthews were the highest-paid players in Division Two, while it was believed that Dennis had signed a two-year deal with the Potters.

It was all done and dusted in record time. Obviously Dennis, who had his business interests in Manchester, wasn't certain if he would live in Stoke or stay in Manchester and commute to his new club. It was reported that he and his wife Barbara would go looking at some houses in the Stoke area over the next couple of days. Tony Waddington told reporters: "We shall not insist on Dennis living locally. The club will be quite easy on this matter, if Dennis decides to continue living in Manchester, Stoke will raise no objection. He can travel each day for training."

The Stoke City boom had begun when Stanley Matthews was signed in the October 1961 and over the following three months Stoke's attendances both home and away had doubled, their debts had been halved and they had the money to buy Dennis from United. After Dennis joined Stoke the membership of the supporters' club increased tenfold and the club avoided relegation.

It was reported in several newspapers that Dennis's would earn more at Stoke in a season than he would by being in United's first team. It was said that United's first teamers would only reach the level of Viollet's wages if they were drawing near-capacity crowds of more than 50,000 or playing two matches a week in front of big crowds. Dennis said that while it was a blow to leave United after thirteen years, "I had been in the reserves for quite a spell and I shall be earning a lot more money with Stoke."

A Hasty Exit

So why did Dennis leave United so suddenly? His departure mystified many United supporters, particularly the lack of any official tribute from the club to a player who had served United so faithfully either side of the worst disaster in the club's history. There was no mention of his transfer to Stoke City in any of the United match programmes for the rest of the season. No public good luck wishes to him from the manager or staff of Manchester United, it was as if Dennis had never played for the club.

Eric Baggaley, boyhood friend of Dennis is as mystified as the rest of us: "I often wondered just why Dennis Viollet, this magnificent footballer, then still aged only 29 and United's record goalscorer, had been so easily let go by Matt Busby in 1962. I know that Dennis was very hurt at the way things were done, learning in a phonecall from Tony Waddington that he had been transferred to Stoke City for £25,000. Nothing had been said at Old Trafford about the possibility of a transfer."

Eric goes on to say that there have been many theories and rumours that Dennis's nightclubbing had ruffled feathers in the boardroom. There was also tittle-tattle about Dennis's business interests and the pressure he was under following the breakdown of his marriage. Certainly other coaches and players have since been forced from Old Trafford because their off-the-field activities sat uneasily with United's often pious board and management.

Then there was Dennis Viollet's often outspoken views on the treatment of the United players who survived Munich, in particular those who could not resume their footballing careers. Dennis was the elder statesmen in the United team and was regarded as a spokesman for the team, as typified by his visit to the Unemployment Office with Wilf McGuinness at the height of the threat of a Players' Strike.

The argument about his pay could also have come into consideration. Was he, as a recently capped England player, requesting a pay increase to which Matt Busby objected? Was he raising the question of a Testimonial, which the club found unwelcome? Was it a matter of Matt Busby simply making one of those tough executive decisions football managers frequently have to make? It is hard knowing when and how to break up a successful team in order to launch plans for the next winning team.

After all, in order to introduce Dennis Viollet, Billy Whelan, David Pegg and his other young Busby Babes into the Manchester United first team in the 1950s, Matt Busby had to drop and then 'off-load' such Red Legends as Dennis's idol Stan Pearson. Jack Rowley, Johnny Aston, Charlie Mitten, Johnny Carey and other luminaries of the 1940s all left the club in this period. After Munich, Busby created the 1959-60 record-breaking attack trio - Albert Quixall-Dennis Viollet-Bobby Charlton, a combination many commentators wanted to see selected for England. Busby let Dennis go in January 1962 and Quixall followed less than two years later.

In that 1961-62 season, other players like Alex Dawson were also transferred. Dawson had been sold to Preston North End just a few months before Dennis moved to Stoke. Ronnie Cope and Warren Bradley also left for other clubs. Perhaps Busby's football brain and those of his scouts and advisors, were already planning a strikeforce featuring David Herd, Denis Law and George Best to complement the now legendary fixture Bobby Charlton. Perhaps these brains were working on the 'dream team' to mount an all-out assault on the 1968 European Cup, to end the decade on a high after the low of 1958? What was certain was that Dennis did not fit into these plans. However even if this was the case, why was Busby so cold in disposing of someone he claimed to be one of the greatest players he has ever managed?

Nevertheless, although Dennis was hurt, he did not bear any long-term grudge or feelings of animosity towards Matt Busby. United fans can only wonder what a forward line featuring Law, Best and Viollet would have produced.

Another factor, as has been discussed elsewhere in this

book, was that Dennis was a loner. He went by himself to do his nightclubbing and other enjoyments and never encouraged other players to go out socialising with him. This image might have been regarded as self-indulgent to United's management and board. Busby liked his teams young, fresh and obedient - Dennis knew his own mind and, at 29, could take liberties few others at the club would contemplate.

Yet his team-mates liked Dennis immensely. He was as unselfish as a person as he was as a player and there does not appear to be any kind of maliciousness attached to his departure.

United's form had clearly dipped since that remarkable first season after Munich. The team looked jaded and Busby knew his ultimate aim - to compete and win in Europe - was getting away from him. On purely footballing terms history has proved Matt Busby right. On a personal level however, the transfer, like others before and since at Old Trafford, was carried out in a shoddy, underhanded manner.

Another aspect to Dennis's departure was the arrival that season of David Herd. Dennis had looked forward to playing alongside his schoolmate but in the end they only made a handful of appearances together. It was somewhat ironic then that Herd should have in effect replaced his schoolmate as Busby's numberone choice centre-forward.

Dennis was also badly affected by the press reaction to his performance for England against Luxembourg and this clearly affected his form and confidence in a United team that had itself lost form and confidence.

However, Dennis's sudden and reluctant departure from the club he had joined as a boy turned out to be a lifesaver as far as his career was concerned. No longer dependable Dennis, he was now expendable Dennis. But he became a superstar in the Potteries, Matthews in particular responding to his cunning style of play.

At the time of Dennis's departure from Old Trafford, Harry Gregg was out injured. He had undergone several operations and was away from the club for a few weeks following an illness in his family. When he returned, Dennis had gone to Stoke. Still he doubts there was any malice in Dennis's departure. "Matt Busby loved Dennis, and I'll tell you something else, Matt loved the ground he walked on," said Harry Gregg. "Dennis and myself were good mates and I can say with all honesty that Matt worshipped Dennis, he let him go for one reason and one reason only - because he went a little too far when enjoying himself. It wasn't because of his lack of ability, because Dennis was still a young man and had bags to offer as he proved at Stoke where I joined him a short time later but Dennis's social life made it difficult for Matt to keep him."

Dennis was later to experience a small taste of the bitterness and difficulty of disappointing players' hopes as a manager. He called his brief flirtation with management at Crewe Alexandra in 1971 his "greatest mistake", and he knew how difficult the job of a football manager could be and knew it wasn't to his liking.

In the years following his departure from Old Trafford, Dennis often went to visit Matt Busby and always spoke well of his mentor, both privately and in public. He clearly had a great deal of respect and admiration for Matt. Dennis was a tolerant and forgiving man, although he was quite adamant in refusing anybody whom he felt had deliberately set out to hurt him, any opportunity of doing so a second time.

Of the enduring lessons he learned from the death of his friends and from his own survival in the Munich Disaster was that life is a precious gift to be enjoyed and shared to the full, every day. Life is valuable and important - it is to his credit that he gave neither time nor effort to bitterness or spiteful vengeance as he embarked on a new stage in his career away from United.

Hello Stoke City

Stoke City were near the bottom of the Second Division table when Tony Waddington re-signed the inspirational legend Stanley Matthews in October 1961. The great England and Blackpool player was more than happy to return to his first club and home town. Matthews' return created a great deal of excitement for the people of Stoke and within no time the attendance figures for home games had improved dramatically.

Stoke City are the second-oldest football club in the world still in existence, after Notts County, and were one of the original members of the Football League back in 1888. A proud club, the late fifties had not been kind to them but the enthusiasm that Matthews' re-signing created brought capacity crowds to the Victoria Ground.

Manager Tony Waddington believed that age was no barrier to players who had looked after themselves throughout their careers. He also knew that you could not put a price on experience, that's why he signed Matthews, Jackie Mudie and Dennis Viollet, and later players of the calibre of Peter Dobing, Maurice Setters, Roy Vernon, Jimmy McIlroy, George Eastham, Harry Gregg, David Herd, Gordon Banks and Alan Hudson.

"When I joined Stoke I was really impressed by the burning enthusiasm within the club," remarked Dennis, shortly after he left United. "The first day I was at training, Tony Waddington took my arm and told me to come and meet Stan [Matthews]. Tony told me that I would find the great man a lovely person. You have to understand that I had only met him a few times before becoming his team-mate. Of course, I had heard a great deal about him from people in the game but I didn't know him on a personal level. Stan, like all players, had his critics, but I found him the most astonishing and brilliant player I ever met in my whole career."

Dennis made his debut for Stoke City away at Bristol Rovers on the January 20th 1962, helping his new team to a 2-1 victory. The Stoke fans took an instant liking to the former Manchester United player. Matthews did not play in this game but he returned for Dennis's second appearance and his first at the Victoria Ground. While the Stoke players were changing into their kit, Dennis was sitting on a bench looking at the floor as if in a world of his own. His friend, journalist Alec Johnson, was allowed into the dressing room. He walked over to Dennis and asked what was wrong. Dennis later told Alec that he was in complete awe of Stanley Matthews, the thought of playing with him filled him with panic.

"I don't know what the reason was but when Tony Waddington announced the team on the Friday after training and Stan was selected as playing on the right wing, I suddenly became apprehensive, and that night I couldn't get off to sleep. I kept tossing and turning and I had never suffered like this before a game. I wondered how I would gel with the great man. I had no need to worry though, Stan was wonderful to me."

Later, when Stoke City played Luton Town, Ronnie Cope was Luton's centre-half. He recalls Dennis going straight over to him and asking him if had settled down in Luton, then he asked: "How's the family Copey?" The truth of the matter was that Ronnie wasn't happy at all in Luton. Dennis told him he would have a word with Tony Waddington but Stoke were well served at that time with defenders and nothing came of it. Ronnie also remembered that when he left United in 1961 Dennis was the only person who wrote to him wishing him well at his new club. "Dennis was a very special person," added Ronnie. "He was always ready to help anyone by deed or encouragement."

Ray Wood was playing for Huddersfield Town when Stoke City played them. Ray said it was lovely to meet him again. "After all, we had both been members of a special club with some unique characters as our team-mates." Ray described their meeting: "Obviously we greeted each other like long-lost friends," said Ray. The first thing he asked about was my family, and was I happy. He himself was happy, really happy at Stoke, and he told me how generous Tony Waddington was to him. Dennis told me that Tony told Dennis to write down on a piece of paper, the wages he wanted. But added, 'Don't overdo it Dennis.' He didn't, but it was like an open cheque and he appreciated being treated like that. He was settled and contented. We had a few drinks after the game and a few laughs, it was lovely."

Stoke finished eighth in Dennis's first season but despite high expectations, the 1962-63 season, Stoke's centenary, started badly. A home defeat to Leeds United was quickly followed by four draws and then another defeat, this time to Swansea City. A 0-0 draw to eventual runners-up Chelsea saw the start of an improvement which continued when Bury visited the Victoria Ground at the end of September. A crowd of 24,480 saw Stoke triumph 2-0. Dennis was now partnering Stanley Matthews with Jackie Mudie at centre-forward.

Former Wolves defenders Eddie Clamp and Eddie Stuart had also joined Stoke and they brought a bit of steel into the defence and the new tactics in midfield and defence became known to supporters as 'Waddington's Wall'. These two ex-Wolves players would constantly rib Dennis. "Are we giving you forwards the cover you require," they would laughingly ask Dennis. This was in reference to Dennis's newspaper article a few years before when he had suggested that Wolves were a 'powerhouse' team who relied on big, tough, powerful defenders. It was all taken in good heart by the players.

Waddington has to be praised for the wonderful job he did for Stoke, bringing vastly experienced players together and the tremendous team spirit he built. Stoke went on to win the Second Division championship that season. Dennis finished with 23 goals from 37 appearances and Stanley Matthews was awarded his second 'Footballer of the Year' trophy.

Allan Philpott played in the same Stoke City team as Dennis. One day outside the Victoria Ground, the milkman was making his daily delivery. Dennis waited for the milkman to go inside the club offices with the crate of milk and in a flash, Dennis had whipped a crate off the float and, unseen, stowed it in the boot of Allan Philpott's car. Out came the milkman, checked his float and found a crate missing. He was furious and started asking questions. Dennis pretended to be helpful and keeping a straight face, said to the milkman: "It was him," pointing to Allan. It went quiet. "Have a look in the boot of his car,:"said Dennis. Within seconds the milkman and Allan figured out who the real thief was and they all had a good laugh about the incident. "That was Dennis the practical joker," laughs Allan.

The following season, 1963-64, saw Stoke back in the First Division for the first time since 1953. Dennis couldn't wait for December 1963 when Stoke came to Old Trafford to play Manchester United. Stanley Matthews was winding down his career by this stage and appeared only nine times all season. Meanwhile United were putting together another wonderful team and hammered Stoke 5-2. Dennis Viollet's old schoolboy friend David Herd opened the scoring for the Reds, with Peter Dobing, the former Manchester City player, and John Ritchie scoring for Stoke. Dennis had a good game, but the other Denis on the pitch, United's Law, who had taken over United's number ten jersey, proved to be the star of the game. Law had been sent off recently and announced his departure for his yearly Christmas sabbatical by blasting in four goals. Law was aiming to take Dennis Viollet's Manchester United goalscoring record and by the time of the return match at Stoke's Victoria Ground in April 1964 he had scored 28 from 29 appearances.

Unfortunately Law missed this match and it was Dennis Viollet who played the starring role. He scored Stoke's second goal from a corner, taken by the magical former Burnley and Northern Ireland forward Jimmy McIlroy, as the Potteries side scored a convincing 3-1 victory over Dennis's old club. Stoke performed well and finished the season by getting to the final of the Football League Cup, drawing 1-1 in their first game at home to Leicester City, and losing the second leg 3-2.

Eric Skeels had just been promoted to Stoke's first team and the Potteries side were in London for his debut. The night before the game the team was located in a London Hotel, and after their main meal, the players were told to relax and be in bed for 10pm. Eric was feeling uptight and nervous about playing his first game. Dennis noticed this and while they were having a walk around the hotel garden, tried to ease young Eric's nerves.

After talking to the lad for about twenty minutes, Dennis could see that he was still edgy. "I don't think I'll sleep a wink tonight," blurted out a very worried Skeels. "Oh yes you will," responded Dennis. "Come on, were going a walk out of here." And off they went. After walking for a while Dennis marched Eric straight into a nearby pub, told him to sit down and went to the bar, returning with two pints of lager.

"Here, get that down you," Dennis told the youngster. Eric was mortified. He knew they were not supposed to drink so near to a game, and feared the wrath of Tony Waddington. But Dennis told him to stop worrying and ordered another couple of pints. Then, after a few more drinks, Eric had a big grin on his face and felt happy and relaxed. Dennis took him back to the hotel, saw him safely into his room and retired himself.

The next morning at breakfast Eric walked over to Dennis and told him he had slept like a log. "Thanks Dennis, I felt smashing after those drinks," he said.

Dennis was really enjoying himself and liked the relaxed atmosphere of the Stoke City club. He was playing with older, but vastly experienced players like himself and the spirit was great. All the players seemed to get on well with each other and manager Tony Waddington rarely put pressure on his players. He knew they had all been around and could play top-class football so he left them to it.

The following season, 1964-65, Stoke played host to United early in the season, and quickly ran into injury problems. Full-back Tony Allen finished the game limping out on one wing and then Jimmy McIlroy was also hurt and finished up on the other wing. There were no substitutes in those days of course, so Dennis dropped back to wing-half and gave a fine performance. United's right-half was Pat Crerand, and it was from two of his usual probing passes that United secured a 2-1 victory.

Stoke were paired with Blackpool in the third round of the FA Cup that year but the match had to be postponed for 48 hours due to the icy weather. By the time the game was eventually played, the draw for the fourth round had been made and the winners would meet Manchester

United. Dennis was delighted. This was an added incentive for Dennis and he scored twice against Blackpool in a 4-1 victory. Now for his dream tie against United. Though he was quite happy at Stoke, Dennis was still hurt by his hurried departure from Old Trafford, and loved nothing better than showing his old club what a mistake they had made when they sold him so suddenly.

"Line up and I'll sign for you all"

Avid Stoke City fan Dave Bronfield vividly recalls the days when he and some of his pals wagged school to go to Stoke's Victoria Ground to get some of the players' autographs. Dave was one of the smallest lads there, and always found himself at the back of a long queue of lads pushing and shoving. By the time it came for him to ask for autographs the players had usually stopped signing because of the hustle and bustle and the youngsters shouting and beseeching the players. One day, when Dennis Viollet appeared, the rush and crush seemed even worse because Dennis had quickly established himself as one of Stoke's favourite stars.

The kids surged forward thrusting their books and pictures in front of him. "Don't push and shove," said Dennis in a clear but firm voice. "Just line up and I'll sign everything for you all." Dave Bronfield said that no schoolteacher was ever able to make him and his pals snap to attention and obey as Dennis did. True to his word, Dennis stayed and signed for all the young fans, right through to the smallest lad at the back of the queue. Many years later, in a letter to Dennis's wife Helen, Dave wrote that this memory had stayed with him all his life and that, in all probability, Dennis could never have fully appreciated just how happy he had made a little 12-year-old boy feel on that day.

Dennis was very aware of young football fans, as his visits to various Boys Clubs, schools' prize-givings and award ceremonies attests. In a photograph taken at Paulden's department store in Manchester you can see the pleasure on Dennis's face as he signs autographs, and the expressions of awe and admiration on the faces of those youngsters.

On March 31st 2000, Dave Bronfield, along with Helen Viollet and friends and family, were invited guests at the unveiling of Dennis Viollet Avenue, close to Stanley Matthews Way, beside Stoke City's magnificent new Britannia Stadium. In a speech Dave repeated his precious boyhood memory of Dennis the man and added: "The most important big-name signing that Stoke City ever made has to be Stanley Matthews, but the best player signed - the one who contributed most to this club's success - was quite definitely Dennis Viollet."

Maurice Setters was also now a Stoke City player, having been sold by Matt Busby in November 1964, the year United went on to win the League championship for the first time since Munich. But the United old boys would require every last bit of skill and energy to take Stoke through to the next round of the FA Cup as they embarked on three games in eleven days - one a League match and two FA Cup ties - against Matt Busby's men.

The first game ended in a 1-1 draw at at Old Trafford while the Cup-tie at Stoke was a dour, hard-fought scoreless affair out of which neither side emerged with a great deal of credit. The two stars, Viollet and Law, both missed chances they would normally have put away with ease. The replay at Old Trafford turned out to be another tough and bruising encounter. Setters was tackling as if his life depended on the outcome and several times the referee had to have words with him. Following so many encounters in such a short period, and the presence of a number of United old boys in the Stoke team, there seemed to be a lot of 'needle' and tension in all three games. Unfortunately for Dennis,

TOP: *Dennis and Helen are married on September 29th 1969 in Manchester.*
BOTTOM: (LEFT) *Dennis during a stint as coach of Preston North End in 1970 and* (RIGHT) *appearing for the Baltimore Bays in 1967*

ABOVE: *Dennis, Jack Crompton on his left, Alan Ball senior 2nd from end at a Jack Coggan Fund Raising game at Stalybridge in 1970 in aid of the family of a Blackpool Police Officer shot dead while on duty.*

BELOW: *The happy couple in the early 70s.*

DENNIS, HELEN AND RACHEL
(BORN 1972) AT VARIOUS
STAGES OF THE SEVENTIES.

CHRISTMAS 1975: *Helen,
Dennis, Rachel and tinsel.*

NATURAL BORN FOOTBALLER:
*Dennis always claimed Rachel had a better right foot than him.
Here she demonstrates the art of passing before an NASL game*

DENNIS AND 'THE GIRL': *Dennis was delighted by Rachel's progress on the tennis court, and was so committed to her success that he sold various medals and memorabilia to pay her expenses. Rachel became British Ladies' number one in 1996*

COACH VIOLLET:
Dennis's reputation as a coach grew alongside Noel Cantwell at the Boston Teamen. Dennis was appointed Head Coach in 1983 when the Teamen joined the American Soccer League and the city of Jacksonville won its first (and only) professional sports championship.

Dennis was later voted Coach of the Year and, as holder of both an English FA Coaching badge and an American Coaching license, Dennis was appointed Staff Coach to the Florida Youth Soccer Association.

Clockwise from top right: *Dennis accepts the key to the city of Jacksonville in May 1998 for services to soccer in the US.* Middle *Dennis with a baby kangaroo, at his home in Jacksonville and before a game.* Bottom: *Dennis with the youth teams he coached Orange Park Raiders* (left) *and a member of the Sharks* (right).

MEETING THE LADS AGAIN: *The Munich survivors at the Olympic Stadium May 1997.*
BACK ROW: *Harry Gregg, Jackie Blanchflower, Ray Wood.*
FRONT ROW: *Bill Foulkes, Dennis, Sir Bobby Charlton, Kenny Morgans and Albert Scanlon*
This was Dennis's last outing before he learnt of his serious illness

HAPPY MEMORIES: *Dennis shares a joke with Jimmy Murphy* (ABOVE) (LEFT) *and Kenny Morgans* (RIGHT) *at a testimonial dinner*

DENNIS SYDNEY VIOLLET 1933-1999

United got the only goal of a best forgotten game, his old schoolmate David Herd the scorer.

In April, there was a glitzy testimonial game for Stanley Matthews, who was now of course Sir Stanley! Dennis got to know the great Sir Stanley during their time together at Stoke. Dennis always spoke highly of Matthews, telling friends what a beautiful, down-to-earth person Stan was. "Well, what do I call you now?"asked a smiling Dennis shortly after it was announced that Matthews was to be knighted. "Do you want Sir Stan or Sir Stanley?" Matthews looked at Dennis and said very matter of factly: "Don't blooming well start all that nonsense. You've called me Stan ever since you've known me and that's good enough for me now!" Dennis said there were no airs or graces about the living legend. He admired him immensely, not only for being a truly great footballer who looked after himself, but for being so helpful during his spell in the Potteries.

In the 1965-66 season another wonderfully talented insideforward joined Dennis at Stoke. Ex-Evertonian Roy Vernon was, like Dennis, a gifted schemer and goal scorer. In this season Stoke drew twice with United, 1-1 at Old Trafford and 2-2 at the Victoria Ground. Dennis played 36 games but scored only six times. The following season, Stoke thrashed United 3-0 at the Victoria Ground. The teams then met each other in the fourth round of the FA Cup at Old Trafford, and poignantly, this would be Dennis Viollet's final appearance on his old stamping ground, fifteen years after his debut.

He was now playing right half for Stoke but was powerless to stop his former team winning 2-0, with Denis Law among the goals. United would of course end the season as champions and being a Manchester lad, born and bred, Dennis was delighted that his old club had regained some of their former glory by being back at the top.

By this time Dennis was well into his thirties and his career was coming to an end. After a great deal of thought he decided that he would retire at the end of the 1966-67 season. Just as at United, he had played in several positions for Stoke and appeared in over 200 league and cup games, scoring 66 goals. Ironically, Dennis's farewell for Stoke City was a 3-1 victory at the Victoria Ground on 29th April 1967 against Leicester City, the team he played in his final first team appearance for United. He was well appreciated by everyone connected with Stoke, so much so that Stoke granted Dennis a testimonial match against England's 1966 World Cup team, in which Nobby Stiles and Bobby Charlton played.

Dennis was touched by this wonderful gesture by the club. For although Stoke City were by no means a wealthy club, they had no hesitation in granting a player who had been at the club for just five-and-a-half years such a tribute. It made many people wonder why other more wealthy clubs couldn't treat their players in this manner, especially after giving them the best years of their career.

Alan Wallace was a schoolfriend of Dennis who played in the same St Margaret's Central High School XI in the late 1940s. In 1967, when Stoke arranged the testimonial match for Dennis against the England World Champions, Dennis made Alan one of his invited guests. He told his friend: "You were there at the start of my soccer career, and I would like you to be there at the end of it." Allan was touched by his friend's invitation but this was typical of Dennis Viollet, he never forgot the people he knew before he became a famous footballer. Helen Viollet remembers fondly that Dennis gave Allan his fullest attention, introducing him to people and showing him the same warm friendship shown to the other more famous personalities present.

"I was delighted to be invited to Dennis's testimonial,"

said Alan. "He wrote me a letter telling me he was delighted I had accepted his invitation to be at the game. He took me into the England dressing room and introduced me to every one of the players. He also took me into the Stoke City dressing room and did the same thing. He treated me like a king. I often think of Dennis. As we grow older and we treasure our memories of when we were younger, I can still picture him scoring all those fabulous goals for St Margaret's. These memories never fade to me, Dennis Viollet was a caring and true friend. I am still proud to tell people that Dennis was my friend."

The testimonial match was arranged for the May 23rd 1967 and a 17,000 strong crowd gave Dennis a right royal send-off. The two teams gave the fans a great deal of fun and served up a wealth of football as the 7-5 scoreline in favour of the World Cup team suggests. Dennis scored and was carried off on the shoulders of his Stoke City team-mates.

So, having inspired Stoke City and successfully led them back from the Second Division in his first season (1962-63) to compete well for a further four seasons in Division One Dennis Viollet, abruptly off-loaded by Manchester United as 'surplus to requirements', was retiring. Having appeared in 182 league games, scoring 59 goals and now at the age of 33, he was leaving England for the New World and a new life in football. The second half of Dennis's life was to be spent in various locations on both sides of the Atlantic, but Dennis was always deeply involved in football.

During his time at Stoke, Dennis and Bill Asprey became quite close friends. Dennis called his team-mate 'Billy'. "He was the only person throughout my life who ever called me 'Billy'," said Bill. "I came from Dudley in Wolverhampton, where Duncan Edwards was born. During the middle 1950s I often went to Manchester for a night out. I got to know the other United lads through Duncan and they were marvellous company. The first time I actually met Dennis was one Saturday night in the Continental Club in Manchester, Dennis and Bobby Charlton were on stage singing a duet. It was great! Tommy Taylor also liked a singsong as well. All those lads they called the Busby Babes were characters and wonderful company. Those were unforgettable occasions which I shall always remember with fondness.

"When Dennis came to Stoke, we hit it off straight away. He was a lovely fellow, down to earth, always ready for a bit of fun. As a player he was like a latter-day Michael Owen. He scored goals so easily and without any fuss. His technique was first class and the way he read situations during a game was uncanny. During his time at Stoke I never once saw him get his name taken by a referee, or even warned for that matter. He relied on skill and a brilliant football brain. There are so many memories of Dennis that I wouldn't really know where to start. What I can tell you was that I never once heard him talk about anybody in a derogatory sense, never! A great, great footballer, and a tremendous friend and human being!"

Jimmy McIlroy, the former Burnley, Northern Ireland and Stoke City inside-forward, was a team-mate at Stoke. Jimmy, who Sir Matt Busby regarded as: "One of the greatest scheming insideforwards of my time," has fond memories of Dennis Viollet the footballer and person.

"Dennis Viollet's nickname was 'Tricky' and I never knew whether it was a result of his football skills or his lifestyle. I had watched Dennis play for Manchester United during the Busby Babes era, when manager Matt Busby excited the football world by fielding a team of highly-talented youngsters that threatened to dominate the English game - only to be tragically lost to us by the Munich Air Disaster. Dennis was in the Sanyi Kocsis-Just Fontaine- Jimmy

Greaves class as a goalscoring inside-forward."

Jimmy McIlroy was a disciple of the Matt Busby philosophy on football and said the composition of Manchester United's wonderful pre-Munich team made a soccer immortal of Matt Busby because that side, which he felt certain would have dominated English football for years, had the perfect blend of so many varying virtues. "Each player's talents were utilised to the full, while their weaknesses were treated as of little importance," said Jimmy. Warming to the subject of Dennis Viollet, he continued. "Dennis survived the crash and afterwards became one of the finest strikers in the Football League. He possessed the essential gift all natural goalscorers require - an icy coolness in front of goal. It was something I lacked because I was much cooler in possession back on my own six-yard line. It was only when I joined Stoke City that I really got to know the man. Dennis was one of manager Tony Waddington's shrewdest signings and he quickly became a favourite at the Victoria Ground.

"In analysing Dennis's skills it must be said that it is difficult to single out one that could be described as brilliant or world-class. His strength lay in the fact that he was a superb all-round striker. He was nippy, without being lightning fast, good but not brilliant in the air. His awareness of situations was first class and there weren't many in top class football who could find the net as consistently from half-chances. On top of all this he was a nice person. There was nothing nasty or vicious in his play, in fact I cannot ever recall Dennis being involved in a single vengeful tackle. I admired the man immensely and I was honoured to have played with and against this talented footballer."

Sir Stanley Matthews was another great admirer. Talking about how Tony Waddington signed Dennis, Sir Stanley said: "Tony Waddington was a cagey fellow, and he used my name to bring other experienced players to Stoke City.

Dennis Viollet joined Stoke three months after Tony secured my signature. Other First Division clubs wanted to sign him but Tony got him to join Stoke for a very reasonable fee. Dennis Viollet was a bargain! Good inside-forwards are born with their gifts and without doubt Dennis was blessed. He was a superbly gifted player who could also score goals. He possessed a clinical and imaginative football brain, boundless energy and all-round technical ability. There are no players like him around now, though I see some similarities in the play of Teddy Sheringham. Sheringham, like Dennis, is an uncomplicated provider and more than occasional goalscorer, sometimes maligned and often underrated, Sheringham's admirers, like Dennis's, are usually to be found among his fellow professionals. Teddy Sheringham gears his play to the good of the team and shares with Dennis that most enviable of reputations, being a players' player. Dennis knew when to hold the ball and when to release it. More importantly, who to release it to. Dennis never made a pass simply to get himself out of trouble or to hand responsibility to a team-mate. Every pass was constructive, a creative arrow that would, in a split second, turn defence into attack. His speed of thought was tremendous. Rarely, in all my years of playing football, did I ever come across such a quick thinking player. Dennis Viollet made the ball do the work. That he did so well for Stoke City was down to him, of course, but also because of the seasoned players about him. Dennis found teammates whose anticipation could match his speed of thought and ability to change plans. He was a truly wonderful player and, to my mind, much underrated."

"When Dennis joined Stoke, he played mainly in midfield," said his friend and former United colleague, Noel Cantwell. "Being the clever footballer he was, he was as comfortable and confident playing in that position as he had been up-front. He did very, very well for Stoke City. Even from midfield he was a fantastic taker of goals because he was so light-footed. He was not one for shouting and bawling and remonstrating with referees, he rarely got noticed. But other professionals knew his true greatness. Dennis was good at so many things on the field of play."

A fitting tribute?

Upon hearing that Stoke City had given Dennis a testimonial game after only five seasons with their club, many Manchester United supporters were shaking their heads in disbelief at their club's treatment of their former players. Of course times have changed and footballers today are amongst this country's highest earners. They now take an agent, accountant and solicitor with them when negotiating for an increase in their wages or a transfer to a new club. To most older supporters loyalty doesn't seem to be a word in football anymore. But there also appear to be a larger number of modern day players receiving prestigious and rewarding testimonial games.

Why are modern players given this extra money when they are on much higher wages than their predecessors? To the average working-class football supporter who is asked to shell out their hard-earned cash for tickets for these games, it seems like nothing more than greed. Manchester United's record on this matter is a cause for concern among supporters.

In 1953 United gave Tom Curry, their first team trainer, a testimonial, followed by Johnny Aston senior in 1956. However these were the only pre-Munich players or officials granted testimonials by United. Johnny Aston was a great club man, as a player, coach and scout. He had been struck down with the dreaded disease of that period, TB. Everyone from the board to supporters, agreed that his was a worthy cause. But it was 1970 before another testimonial was awarded when long-serving stalwart Bill Foulkes was the recipient. Then, like the number 53 bus, there came a spate of testimonials. 1972 - Bobby Charlton, 1973 - Denis Law and Tony Dunne, 1975 - Paddy Crerand and Alex Stepney, 1981 - Sammy McIlroy, 1983 - Martin Buchan and 1986 - Lou Macari. Indeed in the years since, there has been at least one testimonial a year, some well attended, others not. In most circumstances the supporters vote with their feet, although the nature of the opposition and the timing of the game can be crucial.

But what of the Munich survivors? For some reason only known to the club, the survivors and their families had to wait until forty years after the crash before a testimonial match was organised to help them out financially. And, in reality, it wasn't the club who gave them the money, but the hardcore of United supporters who paid for the tickets to make the occasion such a huge success.

United's board have since attempted to correct many of the oversights that caused so much bad feeling between the Munich survivors' families and the club and while it is certainly true that you can't hold the present board responsible for the actions of its predecessors forty years ago, the fact remains that Bill Foulkes and Bobby Charlton aside, none of the the Munich survivors were offered a testimonial despite their assistance during the most difficult years in the club's history.

What next Dennis?

Having ended his English professional career with Stoke, Dennis moved to America where he played for the Baltimore Bays in the North America Soccer league (NASL). Quite a few older players from Britain, Europe and South America were ending their active playing careers in this new and exciting environment. George Best, Franz Beckenbauer and even the great Pele played in America later but Dennis was one of the first, arriving in April 1967 and staying until September 1968.

He returned to England and signed for his long-time Manchester City rival and close friend Ken Barnes who was managing Witton Albion in the Cheshire League. He had turned down various coaching jobs including the Malaysian national XI and instead chose to play for Ken for £10 a week from January to August 1969. Dennis then had a successful spell playing for Linfield in Northern Ireland, winning another medal when he helped Linfield win the Irish Cup in the 1969-70 season.

On a personal note, Dennis's first marriage to wife Barbara had been all but over for some time and in August 1969 their 17-year marriage ended in divorce. A month later, on September 29th 1969, Dennis married Helen Greeph, at Jackson's Row Register Office in Manchester.

In 1970 Dennis was drawn into coaching. He loved helping teach younger players the skills of the game and his coaching had become more and more important to him. He joined Preston North End and stayed with them until he was appointed manager of Crewe Alexandra for the 1971-72 season. Though Dennis was later to become a fine coach, on his own admission he wasn't cut out for the British style of football club management. He later admitted that "my greatest mistake was becoming a manager." It was in his brief role as a manager that he saw football from the other side of the fence. He hated telling players they were not going to be retained or explaining to youngsters that they wouldn't make the grade. These kind of decisions used to upset him a great deal and he decided that if he was to stay in the game it would most probably be as a coach.

Just before embarking on his journey to America, Dennis called to see his friend Jack Coggan at his tailor's shop in Stalybridge. Jack was busy organising a charity football match to be held at Bower Fold, Stalybridge Celtic's ground. Dennis offered his services and Jack accepted gratefully. It was around this time that the newspapers were full of stories about rioting hooligans, fights on the pitch and clubs at loggerheads with players. The general public were becoming used to reading about football in a negative sense.

In fact, the general public rarely got to hear about the good deeds and charitable work most players willingly did for worthy causes. They were often accused of being money grabbers, when in reality the players were more generous than most people gave them credit for being. The evidence of Jack Coggan's forthcoming charity game bore ample testimony to this. All proceeds from Jack's match were being donated to a fund opened to assist relatives of the late Blackpool Superintendent Gerard Richardson, of the Lancashire Constabulary. Superintendent Richardson had been shot down in cold blood by a gunman evading arrest.

Because of Dennis's involvement players like Harry Gregg, Johnny Morris, Charlie Mitten, Bill Foulkes and Bobby Noble offered their services. Eddie Hopkinson, the former Bolton and England goalkeeper, put his name down as did Ken Barnes and Malcolm Allison from Manchester City. Matt Woods, of Everton and Stockport County fame, and Neil Franklin, the former Stoke City and England centre-half and George Smith, the Birmingham and Stalybridge Celtic player also committed themselves. From show business came Freddie Garrity of Freddie and the Dreamers, journalist Peter Keeling also turned out, as did with David Duffy from Granada Television.

The match was billed as Jack Coggan's XI versus Stalybridge Divisional Police XI. Prince Philip sent his best wishes, as did Sir Matt Busby, Frank O'Farrell and Joe Mercer. Everyone had a great deal of fun and £600, a substantial sum of money was raised. Bobby Charlton agreed to give out the medals and Cilla Black accepted the cheque on behalf of the fund.

Dennis and the players were in fits of laughter when big Harry Gregg, after winning 16 international caps in the Home International tournament, besides umpteen others against foreign opposition declared himself the team centre-forward. "I would have won twice as many caps if I had started playing centre-forward earlier," said Harry. Dennis and the other players stifled their giggles, as Harry told them how he wanted the ball delivered to him. Jack Coggan was delighted with the game. He said Dennis was, as always, a great ambassador for professional football and players. "He was up to his eyes in sorting out his new life in America," added Jack, "but dropped everything to play in this charity game. All these players were wonderful, caring people."

American Odyssey

In 1972 Maryland and the Baltimore Bays club asked for Dennis's services once more. This time Dennis, Helen and baby daughter Rachel, born on the February 11th 1972, decided to make the States their home. As coach of the Bays, he moved with them to Washington DC in 1973 where they became Washington Diplomats in the NASL. During his four years with them he achieved the status of 'runner-up' in the Coach of the Year Awards.

In 1978, Dennis moved to Boston to join the New England Teamen organisation. He coached the team with former Manchester United captain and friend Noel Cantwell. The club was based first at Foxborough and then moved to Jacksonville, Florida in 1981. Dennis was appointed Head Coach in 1983 when the Teamen joined the American Soccer League and the city of Jacksonville won its first (and only) professional sports championship. Dennis was also voted Coach of the Year and, as holder of both the English FA Coaching badge and the American Coaching License, Dennis was appointed Staff Coach to the Florida Youth Soccer Association.

His numerous soccer camps attracted young boys and girls aged 10 and under through to high school players aged 18. The move into College and University soccer was a clear progression and Dennis took full control of both men's and women's programmes at Jacksonville University in 1990. His drive and enthusiasm for good football played with 'dignity and class' never diminished.

Noel Cantwell, talking about his partnership with Dennis in America said: "I hadn't seen Dennis for a few years. The next time I met up with him was after I had been offered a job in Boston. Phil Woosnam, one of the very first British coaches to go to America, advised me to take it. I knew nothing about American soccer and I thought to myself, who can I get to help me? I thought of Dennis and he became my assistant coach. We got things moving and won the Eastern Division and I was voted Coach of the Year by the national press over there, but Dennis did as much of the coaching as I did, so to all intents we were joint coaches of the year. He was brilliant in every respect. Our families became very close and we spent a number of years together in the States. It was the most enjoyable relationship of my life, a lovely man with a beautiful, loving family."

"I Have my team photograph and my memories. I don't need the rest."

Rachel was becoming quite proficient at tennis as a schoolgirl and teenager. The development of his daughter from British Junior Grass Court Tennis Champion (14 and under) in 1986, gave Dennis immense satisfaction. And as Rachel got older she went from strength to strength, advancing to ever-higher quality competition. In 1996, despite a defeat to Martina Hingis in Round Two at Wimbledon, Rachel became Britain's Number One woman player.

Proud parents Dennis and Helen were delighted. Young Rachel was also good at soccer. It was obvious she had inherited some of her father's silky skills, focus and determination. Nevertheless, as she matured it became clear that tennis was her forte. Dennis loved playing tennis with her, and continued to encourage her developing skills. Coincidentally, the great Sir Stanley Matthews, Dennis's former team-mate at Stoke, also saw his prodigious ball skills reflected in his child's tennis ability. Stan Matthews junior played at Wimbledon and gained a national ranking for Britain - Rachel would do the same.

Tennis equipment and the frequent competitions and tours were proving expensive and stretched the Viollet family finances to the limit. Dennis didn't play his football in the days of mega earnings and was still working hard, earning his living as a soccer coach, long after his playing days were over.

Like Bill Foulkes and so many others, he had come to the conclusion that, if his ambitions for his family were to be realised then his medals, prizes and trophies had to be sold. Rachel's tennis success now meant more to him than his own past glories. He told Helen what he had decided. "Oh, Dennis, are you sure?" Helen asked him, looking at his Football League Champions medals, FA Cup Final medals, European Cup souvenirs, England caps, Manchester Evening News Footballer of the Year Award and other memorabilia. "I have my team photograph and my memories. I don't need the rest," Dennis told his wife.

The team photograph Dennis spoke about was a framed black and white picture of the Busby Babes. The picture was his pride and joy. This was the team in which he starred and with whom he had won back to back Division One Championship titles in 1955- 56 and 1956-57. It was the team so cruelly denied the then elusive League and FA Cup Double in those seasons.

The first double had been ruined by the infamous shoulder- charge by Aston Villa's Irish international, Peter McParland, which broke Ray Wood's cheekbone and forced United to struggle with virtually ten men and a make-shift goalkeeper in Jackie Blanchflower. The second double was wrecked not only by the Munich crash, but by yet another so-called shoulder-charge by the rampaging Nat Lofthouse, the Bolton centre-forward, who bundled Harry Gregg, United's goalkeeper and Munich hero, into the net in the 1958 FA Cup final.

Eventually Helen and Rachel reluctantly agreed with Dennis's idea of selling his medals, caps, and awards. They arranged, however, to take some nostalgic photographs, with Rachel wearing one of the England caps and sporting Dennis's 1958 Wembley FA Cup Final shirt, with its symbolic and emotive phoenix rising from the ashes. The *Manchester Evening News* Footballer of the Year Award marked Dennis's performance and goalscoring record in 1959-60 and was presented to him by Sir Matt Busby. This trophy was bought by Manchester United plc.

Did Dennis peak too soon?

Peter John lived in Parkside Road, near the Viollet family home in Clinton Avenue, Fallowfield and regularly drank with Mr Viollet senior in the nearby Parkside pub. Dennis would pop in on occasions to have a drink with his father, and Peter became a close friend. "My ex-wife's two brothers, Mark and Bill Scholes were close friends of Dennis and through them I got to know him quite well," recalls Peter.

Later Peter would meet and have a drink with Dennis at the dances held at Belle Vue and the Ritz. Through Dennis, Peter became friendly with Duncan Edwards, Albert Scanlon, Wilf McGuinness and the other United players. "Dennis had fantastic balance," recalled Peter. "I've seen him, from a standing position, hop onto a garden wall that stood about four foot high, one-footed without falling off. We thought it was easy until we attempted to do it and would inevitably fall off the thing. Billy Williamson, the former Manchester City player, said Dennis was the greatest player in the United forward line. 'Mr Electric' Billy called him. In the former City's players opinion, Dennis was a goalpoacher good enough to be rated with the best in the world."

After Dennis went to America, Peter lost touch with his friend, but on Dennis's visits home, the two old pals would meet up. "Dennis had his haunts, he was a real Jack the Lad," remarked Peter. After having a few drinks in the city centre, Peter would get a taxi to the Starlight Room, a classy nightclub in Didsbury. Peter would meet up with Dennis and Ken Barnes, the former Manchester City player, would often be chatting with Dennis. Singer Karl Denver would also join the company along with Alec Johnson, Dennis's journalist friend. They had some hilarious times and spent some never-to-be-forgotten nights.

It was a relaxing time for Dennis and he and Peter would usually be the last left drinking and chatting away. While sat on their own, Peter often noticed Dennis holding his head in both hands. "What's wrong Den?" he'd ask his pal. Dennis would tell him that he was suffering violent headaches. Peter would advise him to go to a doctor and have it checked but Dennis would quickly dismiss the thought. Peter always maintained that the headaches Dennis suffered were as a direct result of the head injuries he had sustained in the Munich disaster.

On another occasion when Peter and Dennis were having a quite drink they got talking about Jimmy Murphy. It was a great topic of conversation. Dennis thought highly of Jimmy as a coach and as a warm, honest person. It was no secret to Dennis that the great Jimmy Murphy, whose coaching skills developed many great footballers for Manchester United, was on record as believing that the 'best years' of Dennis's career came before the Munich disaster of February 1958. Jimmy always spoke highly of Dennis and loved the Viollet brand of football but often wondered if Munich had affected him much more than anyone, especially Dennis himself, had realised. Jimmy often reckoned Dennis had suffered some kind of late reaction to the crash.

Certainly, Dennis had extraordinary success as a teenager, playing for and captaining the Manchester, Lancashire and England schoolboy teams. Then, after signing for Manchester United, the decade between 1947 and 1958 saw him blossom through the junior ranks and eventually replace the established Old Trafford legend, and Dennis's favourite player, Stan Pearson. Dennis starred in the back-to-back League Championship winning seasons (1955-6 and 1956-7) and enjoyed great success in United's first European campaigns, scoring 13 goals in his 12 games - a strike rate never likely to be equalled.

Of course Dennis was not the same after the Munich disaster, who could have been? Wilf McGuinness said that he himself, although mercifully not in the crash, was never the same again after Munich. But Dennis miraculously recovered from injuries that surgeons thought would put an end to his sparkling career. Importantly, the accident also deprived him of the support and camaraderie of the Busby Babes, lads who had grown up and matured together. He returned from the horror of Munich to play in a United team bereft, through death or injury, of so many truly great players: Roger Byrne, Duncan Edwards, Eddie Colman, David Pegg, Mark Jones, Billy Whelan, Jackie Blanchflower, Johnny Berry, and his close friend and striking partner Tommy Taylor. If the truth be known, Dennis never really got over their loss. So how could things ever be the same for him again?

In the 1958 FA Cup final at Wembley, Dennis appeared to be a ghost of his former self. Although one can appreciate the eagerness of both club and players to see him take his place in the team, especially since injury had kept him out of United's FA Cup final team the previous year. Nevertheless, the general consensus of opinion among esteemed football writers was that during the period 1958 to 1962, Dennis enjoyed notable success as the brains and inspiration of that formidable post-Munich inside-forward trio of Quixall-Viollet-Charlton.

During those years, not only did Dennis replace Jack Rowley as United's all-time leading League goalscorer, netting 32 goals in 36 games (1959-60) but he also gained the national recognition (albeit belated and miserly) of two England caps. Between 1962 and 1967 he continued a fine career as player and captain of Stoke City and led them to promotion from the Second Division in 1962-63. His 'swansong' as a player was thus lengthy and noteworthy, still playing at First Division level and blending his magnificent skills with other Stoke heroes - Sir Stanley Matthews, Maurice Setters, Jackie Mudie, Jimmy McIlroy and others. So what can we call his 'best years'?

Many people close to Dennis firmly believe that away from football, the best years for Dennis Viollet were not only post- Munich, but post-Manchester United because he was able to move further away from the 'ghosts' of his traumatic experience at Munich and on towards developing his coaching and training techniques. After Stoke City he embarked on a new career doing something that was very dear to him, helping others to love the game of football and to play it to the best of their ability. Many believe the 34 years of his life spent with Helen and their daughter Rachel and his coaching career in America were the happiest. Not least because he was able to encourage Rachel's tennis career and see her not only qualify for Wimbledon in 1996 but, despite defeat by Martina Hingis, become Britain's Number One woman tennis player.

It is doubtful whether this personal happiness and professional fulfilment would ever have been possible in Manchester or anywhere else in England. The 'best years' for Dennis were to be found in his adopted home with his new family and career.

Meeting The Lads Again

One day in April 1997, Helen was busy working on the switchboard at the office where she worked in Jacksonville, Florida. Although always busy, she welcomed either Rachel or Dennis phoning her. On this particular day she took a call from Dennis and he sounded extremely excited. "Helen," he said, "listen to this letter that's just arrived." He read it out to her.

"UEFA is proud to have Manchester United FC as a member of the European footballing family and to Dennis, personally, we say: 'You are one of the gentlemen who have made this club great and contributed to the development of European Football.'"

Vaguely Helen remembered thinking that Dennis's voice was sounding different these days. It wasn't as strong, thinner somehow, and when he read out the letter from UEFA inviting him, along with the other surviving members of the 1958 Munich air disaster, to attend the European Cup final between Juventus and Borussia Dortmund, he became quite emotional. It was the reference to him as one of the gentlemen of European Football which appeared to have the greatest effect on him.

"I don't think I can get away, Helen, it's the middle of the season."

"Den, you've got to go, all the rest of the lads will be there, and I'm sure Louis will understand," Helen quickly replied.

Louis Posso was Dennis's boss, the owner of the Jacksonville Cyclones. Originally from Colombia, Louis was understandably very proud to have Dennis managing his team and although it involved an extremely hectic flying itinerary it was worked out that Dennis could attend that wonderful re-union, which also heartbreakingly turned out to be the last for him. The tumours growing under the scars from the head wounds he had sustained in the Munich crash in February 1958 were beginning to take their toll, although at this point Dennis had not been diagnosed.

When he arrived in England he met up with his old friends and former United team-mates, before they all left for Munich. Dennis stayed with Ken Barnes at his Macclesfield home. Early one cold brisk morning, Ken's wife looked out the window and saw Dennis standing at their front gate dressed only in his shorts, staring blankly into space. Mrs Barnes quickly woke her husband and Ken slipped on his pants and a top, and walked out to Dennis.

"Morning Dennis," said Ken, not knowing what was wrong. Dennis looked vague and lost. Ken said to him: "It's too cold out here Dennis, why don't you come inside and have a cup of tea and some breakfast?" and he gently led his pal back inside the house. Ken knew something was drastically wrong but Dennis left Ken's house and went to a hotel near Ringway Airport where Harry Gregg and Albert Scanlon were also booked in. None of his old pals had an inkling that all was not well.

The receptionist told Harry Gregg that Dennis was already booked in but had nipped out with Helen's mother. A short time later the phone in Harry's room rang and as he picked it up he instantly recognised the voice.

"Hiya Greggie," shouted Dennis. "Hello Tricky,"replied Harry. After some small talk Dennis said he was having a shave, then he would go up to Harry's room. Harry was a little surprised when he saw Dennis. He had no inkling that anything was wrong with him.

"He was always an immaculate dresser, was Tricky,

well groomed with the knot in his tie always perfect," said Harry. "When I opened the door I looked at him and thought God, Dennis Viollet! I couldn't believe it. He had an old American pullover on. He looked untidy, not scruffy but untidy. Very unlike the well-groomed debonair man I knew. 'You're looking great Greggie,' said Dennis. 'You're looking great Tricky as well.' And I thought to myself 'who's the biggest liar?' We arranged to have a meal with Ken Barnes and his wife."

The other United players had left on an earlier flight, Dennis and Harry got delayed so flew from Manchester to Stuttgart where they had to take another flight to Munich. While waiting for their connecting flight Dennis was wandering all over the airport and Harry was wondering what was wrong with his pal. "We had no German money," said Harry. "He kept going walkabout and I said to him to keep close because we should get the call to join the aircraft at any moment. Dennis asked me where the toilets were and I pointed them out to him. He handed me his case, ticket and passport and headed for the exit. I stopped him and told him he couldn't go down there laughing and joking. When the flight was called I couldn't find him. I went to the personnel desk and asked if they would page him over the tannoy system, which they did several times. The plane was held up for the two of us, but there was no sign of him. I was told by the airport officials that I would have to board the flight immediately and leave Dennis's passport with them. I eventually met up with Albert Scanlon, Ray Wood, Bobby Charlton, Jackie Blanchflower, and the other lads. I asked them if they had noticed anything wrong with Tricky in Manchester? They said no, though Ray said he kept going missing. I told them there was something wrong with Tricky Viollet.

"Later that night, some of the UEFA officials told me

Dennis was in his room. They wanted to wake him but I told them to let him sleep, but the following morning I saw him and asked him where he had vanished in Stuttgart. He laughed and said he went to a nightclub around the corner. It reminded me of the snowbound runway at Munich and the deep gash he had on his head.

"One final thing I would like to say regarding Dennis. I have said it before and I'll repeat myself. I do not use the word 'great' lightly. There's too many film stars in the world like John Wayne who never fought in the war and ended up with more medals than the people who actually won it. But when talking about Dennis Viollet I use the word 'great' with every sense of the meaning of the word. He had frightening talent, a great, great player and one of the best friends a man could wish for. God bless him!"

The Cup Final took place on the May 28th 1997. Exactly one month later, on June 28th, while making what appeared to be a routine recovery after surgery, Helen received a call from the hospital informing her that Dennis was very ill. He had suffered bleeding to the brain and within twenty-four hours he was undergoing a second operation to remove a blood clot. Although this procedure was performed successfully, it left Dennis with what is called 'left side neglect.' The man whose renowned footballing skills many attributed to his incredible sense of balance would spend the rest of his life in a wheelchair.

The first indication that something was wrong with Dennis had come in January 1997. The Viollets had rented a small apartment for a couple of months after Dennis had resigned from his position as manager of the Richmond, Virginia team which he had coached very successfully for two seasons. Louis Posso had decided to move his soccer franchise, The Tampa Bay Cyclones to Jacksonville. The Viollets had, despite Richmond being a beautiful city, missed Florida, so decided that as they still owned property in Jacksonville they would accept Louis' offer for Dennis to manage the team. Unfortunately the tenant renting their home had a year's lease, meaning they couldn't move home until February.

Pre-season training had started and one day Dennis remarked to Helen that he had been feeling light-headed during practice. "I've got to drink more fluids," he told her, dismissing it as he always did. However, one evening after getting up from the table he staggered forward. Alarmed, Helen asked Dennis what was wrong. "I keep getting dizzy spells along with a sweet smell and deja-vu sensations," he told her.

On another occasion, after suffering these spells, he told Helen he thought he saw some of the players who died at Munich. He also said that he saw Duncan Edwards and spoke to him. Helen suggested that he should make an immediate appointment to see the doctor. "I will if I don't feel any better," was his familiar response. "Besides, we have to wait for our new insurance to take effect." Later Helen said she wished she had been more insistent that he seek medical advice but the symptoms passed after a couple more bouts and despite her continual unease, Helen went along with Dennis's theory that it was, he was sure, nothing more than a virus. Someone at the office had had similar symptoms, he told his wife and in March, a month before the start of the season, he told Helen that he felt "as fit as a butcher's dog."

March 1997 was the calm before the storm. Life was exciting and held much promise for the months ahead. Preparations were underway for the start of the season in April and an exhibition game was scheduled with DC United, the Major League Soccer champions from the nation's capital. This was to be played at the impressive new Alltel Stadium, built for the city's American Football league team, The Jacksonville Jaguars. There was to be a special surprise presentation to Dennis that night. It had taken a great deal of careful planning, subterfuge and secret phone calls to make sure Dennis knew absolutely nothing about it.

Somewhere over the years Dennis had misplaced his England blazer. Normally this kind of thing was of no concern to him but having only played twice for his country its loss was something he regretted considerably. Having mentioned it a few times to a good friend of the Viollets, Claude Bass, he had decided to do something about it. With contributions from many people in Jacksonville who knew Dennis and had benefited from his soccer knowledge over the years and with the help of Helen's highly organised cousin Norma, who lived in London, the problem was solved. A replica England blazer, complete with the England badge of three lions and decorative gold buttons was obtained.

It was an exciting evening. Professional soccer was returning to the city. Apart from all the young people playing in the area, their parents and coaches and there were many fans who remembered the Tea Men, the first soccer franchise in Jacksonville. When the Lipton Company decided to move the franchise from New England to north Florida, Noel Cantwell became head coach and Dennis his assistant. When Noel and his family returned to England, Dennis took over his position.

It is hard to describe the really close friendship between the two men. It was a rare kind of relationship especially in an arena as competitive as professional sport which tends to spawn so much jealousy and mistrust. Noel and Dennis had a unique friendship. Their years of working together overflowed with camaraderie and trust based in all likelihood on the bond that had been formed during their time together at Manchester United. There was success on the field and there was also disappointment. There were hours of discussion, agreement and disagreement, but mainly there was laughter, much laughter and there was love, because to know Dennis Viollet and Noel Cantwell was to love them.

Youth and college soccer players, their coaches, parents, fans, local businesses and the media, from both New England and Jacksonville took the Irishman and the Englishman to their hearts.

Noel was there that night at Alltel Stadium, when Dennis was presented with the blazer and made his thank you speech. It also gave Dennis much pleasure to announce Noel's presence to a wonderful reception from the fans and have them share the occasion. When Dennis tried on the blazer it fitted him perfectly, but sadly he was never to wear it again.

A few months after he died, Helen took down the few special clothes of Dennis's which she could neither bear to look at or part with and she packed them away. The England blazer alone still hangs in the closet. To Helen it would always be a symbol of not only the appreciation of a community but of the re-union of two men who were lucky enough to have experienced the true meaning of unconditional friendship.

A few months before Dennis was diagnosed with a fatal illness, Dennis would be regularly found watching the Jacksonville Dolphins and attending the Graduation ceremonies of his pupils and charges with great pride. For years he would have as many as seven University teams under his command and, whether on speaking engagements or taking coaching courses, 'Coach Viollet' was acclaimed as an ambassador of 'good soccer' wherever he travelled in the US.

The City of Jacksonville also honoured him with a special citation for services to soccer and awarded him the Key to the City in May 1998. This was indeed a great honour and Dennis was rightly proud. An extract from the Official Citation accorded to Dennis read as follows:

"Whereas Dennis Viollet has, for nearly two decades, been one of the leading forces for the popularisation of soccer in Jacksonville. And whereas Coach Viollet's career in Jacksonville began in 1981, as assistant coach, and later as head coach of the Jacksonville Tea Men who won the NASL Championship in 1983 and Mr Viollet was named NASL Coach of the Year.

"And whereas after the demise of the NASL and a time in private business, Coach Viollet shifted his coaching talents to the Collegiate level, becoming head coach of the Jacksonville University Soccer in 1990.

"And whereas Coach Viollet has been one of the vital forces for the popularisation of soccer in the United States in general and in Jacksonville in particular, and has contributed immeasurably to Jacksonville's standing in the soccer community.

"Now, therefore, be it resolved by the Council of the City of Jacksonville that the Council hereby honour and commend Dennis Viollet for his outstanding career as both player and a coach of soccer at Collegiate and Professional levels, and for his immeasurable contributions to the status of soccer in Jacksonville. The Council extends its best wishes for his continued success."

This was followed by the presentation to Dennis of the Key of the City of Jacksonville.

On March 10th 1999, a very moving ceremony took place at Jacksonville University. Dennis was by now very ill and in a wheelchair which was something he hated, of course. Many coaches and friends were present and they said that Dennis Viollet was an inspiration to them in so many ways. They admired him tremendously and felt honoured to have met, worked with and been influenced by him. Though these people were from different walks of life who had enjoyed many different forms of contact with Dennis they all spoke of his humility, dignity, integrity, sense of fun, concern for others, zest for life and his power to communicate a love and enjoyment of football. These warm compliments were just as important to Dennis as the official recognition of his contribution to the development of football in Jacksonville and the US as a whole. The founding of the Dennis Viollet Tournament, Cup and Scholarship at Jacksonville University, all speak eloquently of the high regard in which he was held in the US.

The Greatest Test

When Bill Asprey heard of Dennis's illness, he was working in the Middle East. Bill immediately jumped on a plane and flew to Jacksonville. "I was shocked when I saw him," he recalls. "Dennis was very ill but his face lit up as I walked over to where he lay. I felt like crying, but composed myself. I sat next to him and talked to him about some of our hilarious escapades and he smiled weakly, he was tired and weary. Before I left, I put my arms around him and we embraced. He said: 'Thanks for coming Billy.' I loved Dennis Viollet as a close and cherished friend. God bless him!"

When the *Manchester Evening News* published a story concerning Dennis's illness and explained the crippling cost of his medical treatment, Manchester United and Stoke City supporters rallied round and through the internet, a fund was organised. Many people, even at this time, are under the impression that Manchester United didn't contribute any financial help to the Viollet family.

This, we are happy to reveal, is misleading. Helen said that United did help with Dennis's medical expenses after she wrote to them for help. UEFA also helped as did the managers' guild. "They were wonderful," said Helen.

Albert Scanlon was heartbroken upon hearing of the seriousness of his pal's illness. "Before we flew out to Munich for the European Cup final, I had a meal with him and he seemed his normal self. From first getting to know him in the 1950s he was always on the move, couldn't sit still. He asked if I fancied going to a nightclub in the city centre for a few drinks. We had to be up for 5am so I said I didn't think it was a good idea, then he disappeared. I couldn't get off to sleep, the bed was too high and I was tossing and turning. I kept looking out of the window and seeing the lights on the runway. Then suddenly the phone in my room rang and this startled me. 'Who is it,' I asked. 'Hi Scanny. It's me, Dennis, do you feel like going into Manchester?' he said. I looked at my watch it was just gone 4am. 'Do you know what time it is?' I asked, quickly telling him. He said goodnight and hung up.

"In Munich he was forever going missing. Something was obviously wrong with him and I was concerned. On the flight home I closed my eyes and the pictures of Dennis Viollet at his peak came vividly into my mind's eye. What a great player, he was an inside-forward of the old school with complete control of the ball. A lovely, fluent mover, so fluent he was always in automatic drive. He was a consistent goalscorer, too, at a rate beyond most modern strikers. He was great in the opposition's half. He scored all types of goals, he could pass short or long, it was no trouble to Dennis, and his body swerve and balance were envied. On top of all this, he had elegance. He wasn't the greatest defender but his many other assets made up for this. He was a footballer apart, he combined just about everything that is good in football. He was born with the gift of exceptional acceleration. He was a tough little feller as well. Although he was only skin-and-bones, many a defender came out of tackles with him aching. Dennis would certainly be in my six best ever Manchester United players. I will always have fond memories of Tricky Viollet. God bless him!'

After the *Manchester Evening News* article appeared, quite a number of readers wrote to express their sorrow and support. "How sad to read about Dennis Viollet - 'Dennis the Menace' as he was known was a wonderful player, a great goalscorer and a joy to watch. Like the late Jack Rowley, Viollet was truly a legend at Old Trafford," wrote 'Old Red Devil' from Shaw in Oldham.

"Dennis Viollet and his wife Helen were friends of mine. Dennis would get anybody a match ticket and would not take any money for it. He would sign autographs until he had cramp and then sign some more with his other hand. I think the nice things being said about him now, should have been said earlier, it would have meant a lot to him," wrote a Mr Smith from Bury.

When old chum Noel Cantwell heard about the seriousness of Dennis's illness he flew over to Jacksonville. "I went to see Dennis about six months before he died," recalled Noel. "He went through a really tough time. But as ill as he was he still had a wonderful sense of humour. When I walked into his home he was upstairs having some kind of treatment. When he was told I was down stairs he hobbled down the stairs with a male nurse helping him and it took him ages to get down. Once he sat down he was moving his left foot slowly, trying to keep the circulation going. I said jokingly: 'Dennis, your left foot isn't very good!' but he immediately shot back with: 'It's about as good as your right!'

"Even when he was ravished with pain he still had his sense of humour. We loved him, God bless him. When you

think how good a footballer he was and only got two caps
- it's a crime. He went about his job in such a quiet way. He
was brave and loyal, never got into trouble with referees or
officials. I have to smile when I look back at some of the
pranks we got up to. We had some great, momentous nights
out, both in Manchester and in America. He was a genuine
guy who would never betray your confidence."

Karl Smith, mentioned earlier in this book, left Manchester
to live in Blackpool. Karl was a frequent visitor to Bloomfield
Road, Blackpool's ground. While in the hospitality suite
after one game he got talking to Barry Martin, Blackpool's
left full-back. Barry told Karl that although Blackpool had
good players such as Jimmy Armfield, Roy Gratrix, David
Durie and the rest, whenever they played against Manchester
United when Dennis was in the team they found it hard to
cope. "He would be worth millions if he was playing today,"
said Barry. Over the years Karl also met Liverpool legend
Roger Hunt and asked him his opinion on Dennis: "He
was unique as a player. A one-off, simply brilliant!" He also
met former England goalkeeping hero Gordon Banks and
asked him the same question. Gordon told Karl that Dennis
was a fantastic signing for Stoke City and a fabulous friend.

On another occasion, Karl was having a drink after a
game against Oxford United and spoke to Dennis Smith,
the up-andcoming Oxford manager. Karl overheard Mr
Smith tell his players to drink up and get onto the coach as
he was in a hurry to get going. After excusing himself, Karl
told him how much he had admired him as a player and
mentioned his hero Dennis Viollet. The Oxford manager
stopped and told Karl: "I was in awe of Dennis Viollet" and
proceeded to speak to Karl for over half an hour about his
hero. It was quite obvious his admiration was genuine. "I
don't know what his players, sat waiting on the coach, must
have thought!" said Karl.

One evening, while reading the *Manchester Evening News*, Karl read a story about his hero being quite ill and struggling with the crippling medical bills. Karl was heartbroken and decided to write to Dennis to offer support and mention his adoration for his boyhood hero. A few days later he was delighted to receive a letter from Helen thanking him for his letter and inviting him to Jacksonville if he was ever over in Florida. Karl couldn't resist a chance to meet his hero. Karl was married by this time, so he flew to Florida with his family, drove through the forest fires that were raging in the area and arrived at the Viollet home in Jacksonville.

"What a great thrill it was for me and my family," said Karl. "We spent a day with Dennis and Helen, he was so modest. I asked him why he didn't play in the 1957 FA Cup final and he explained that he had a groin strain. I told him I was there when United played Aston Villa in the Charity Shield and trounced them by four goals, Dennis scoring two. We left and I still remember the warmth and happiness we received, knowing that I had met one of the cornerstones of Manchester United, a true legend!"

Another Manchester United fan who heard of Dennis Viollet's illness and financial predicament was Paul Windridge. Paul set up a Dennis Viollet Fund for which the Viollet family were extremely grateful. In the mid-1980s Paul's daughter, Eliza, became a dyed-in- the-wool United follower and begged her father to take her to watch them play at Old Trafford. After one of their regular jaunts to the Theatre of Dreams Paul and Eliza wandered past the players' entrance when Paul spotted a familiar face. They stopped briefly, not wanting to intrude, shook the man's hand and wished him well. He smiled graciously and said "Thank you." It was the briefest of encounters and as they walked away Eliza asked her father who the man was. "Dennis Viollet," he told her, adding he was one of the best inside-forwards to have pulled on the red shirt of United.

Over a decade later, their paths crossed again, but on this occasion the circumstances were different. In 1997 the news of Dennis's condition had prompted IMUSA (the Independent Manchester United Supporters' Association) to put together a package to send over to Dennis and Helen in Jacksonville. It was a sort of 'get well and thanks for the memories' type package for a player who will always be synonymous with the best of United. Paul's contribution was an original drawing of Dennis in action and the whole package was sent over to America with his best wishes for a man who graced Old Trafford until his untimely departure in 1962. A few days later, Paul's phone rang. It was Helen calling to say a heartfelt thank you. From that moment on Paul received regular updates on Dennis's condition. Consequently, Paul was able to relay the news to Dennis's many admirers around the world.

In June 1998, Paul, his wife Karen and their children, Alex, who was then 13 and Gina, who was 8, visited America to celebrate his 50th birthday. The plan was to spend a few days in Florida and then drive north through Georgia to Carolina. The fact that this route took the family right past Jacksonville was no co-incidence, so a brief stop-over to visit Dennis and Helen was also on their agenda. Two days before reaching his half-century Paul and the family spent the morning in the beautiful old town of St Augustine before taking the short drive to the Viollet household in Jacksonville. That afternoon the Windridge family sat in the sundrenched Viollet living room chatting with Helen as though they had known each other for years. Dennis had been delayed at physiotherapy so Helen took the opportunity to make sure they were aware that his appearance may not have been quite as expected. In actual fact the tumour had altered his facial appearance, but his body was as strong as ever. Paul vividly recalled looking at Dennis's arms as he sat in the wheelchair and imagining them protruding from a United shirt just as he remembered them from the times he watched him play.

By this time Dennis was not the communicator of old. He found it difficult to hold his attention for very long, but despite these problems he was still the same Dennis - his character unaltered by the awful circumstances. Paul had already decided not to stay too long for fear of over-tiring him, but one story they told seemed to amuse Dennis greatly. The family had been recommended to spend the previous night in a hotel owned by a Viollet family friend. It was slightly more upmarket from those they had been used to and this extended to the variety available at breakfast that morning. It was the stuff of dreams for a certain young man! The extensive range of doughnuts on display were just too much for young Alex. He resolved to sample as many as his voracious appetite would allow as they recounted the story of just how many he had consumed, Dennis smiled knowingly , looked over towards Alex and nodded his approval. A commendation from the man for pushing the art of doughnut eating to the realms of belly-aching piggery!

Paul spoke very little about football and Manchester United to Dennis, but more about life. They were now firm friends and not just passing acquaintances outside Old Trafford on a cold and wet Saturday afternoon. Although Paul's actual birthday was still a couple of days away for him it had come early by meeting his hero Dennis Viollet. "I only wish there could have been many more of them to share."

John Heilperns was a top feature writer for *The Observer* newspaper for years. He has interviewed LS Lowry, Prince Charles, Noel Coward, Sir John Gielgud and numerous other celebrities. John offered this tribute to Dennis.

"When my friend Dennis Viollet was coaching in America, we both went to see his wife Helen play soccer in Boston for a Sunday team called the 'Green Machine'. 'You've got to see this,' said Dennis. I had known him since we met in the Shakespeare pub off Market Street in Manchester during the 1960s when he was first dating Helen, my childhood friend. In the glorious days of the Green Machine, I was living in New York and turned up eagerly in Boston to watch her play on the right wing. You should have seen Dennis's face. 'Go for the ball,' he yelled at her from the line, laughing his head off good-naturedly. 'Don't just stand there looking at it!' At that, Helen seemed to charge off after the referee for some reason. The ref looked nervous. 'What's she doing?' I asked Dennis. 'I think she's sending him off!' he replied.

"Life was always fun with Dennis around. He made it fun, looking almost studious, innocent. Helen knew this better than anyone, of course. They were married for thirty happy years, together for thirty-four. Soccer players of all ages are boyish by nature. 'Snapper' as he was nicknamed in America, was young even in middle age; quick-witted, snappy, full of mischief. He was born in Moss Side and knew that I had always been a Manchester City supporter, which accounts for the permanently pained expression on my face. 'Oh dear,' he'd invariably say when we met, 'I see the Blues lost again.' He was a folk hero in an era when soccer stars earned little more than the fans crowding the terraces. He had no regrets. He played because he loved the game. He was the most selfeffacing of men.

"One afternoon, I was watching him coach his soccer camp for youngsters in Jacksonville and this little kid with this huge soccer ball must have been about eight or nine years old. Dennis was kneeling down as the lad listened earnestly to his advice - he talked to him as an equal. On another occasion, he had gone with Helen to visit the British aircraft carrier HMS Hermes, which was holding an open day at the Mayport naval base. He enjoyed it; it was like being in England. He was having a beer with some of the crew, who were not even born when he became a legend, when one of the midshipmen suddenly exclaimed: 'I cannot believe it, I'm sitting here having a drink with Dennis Viollet!' But Dennis looked as if he wanted to dive under the table. He was a modest man, disliking anything showy or flash. He was dressed neatly and invariably in the same outfit, like a ritual, with his blazer, grey trousers and wellpolished shoes, which gave him a timeless air. He wasn't tall, about 5ft 8in or so, which helped his agility and quicksilver speed. He had noticeably small feet, size seven and a half, which gave him his lightness and extraordinary balance - and his lethal right foot.

"Sometimes he would barbecue for us on the small patio of his Jacksonville home. He carved a chicken the way he carved up defences; meticulously slicing through. As a player, he possessed the deadly certainty of a cool assassin. He never played to the gallery - that would have been too flash. Whenever I saw him in those great traumatic local Derbies with Manchester City and the ball was at his feet, I thought with a sense of dread, oh no. He would make a goal seem inevitable and glorious. Stanley Matthews said it was like a spotlight shining on him. Defences just couldn't read him. When Dennis Viollet had the ball in the penalty box, all you knew was that within seconds, perhaps before you were even aware of it, the ball would be nestling in the back of the net. He actually defined the essence of the game for me. I asked him what he thought the game was all about. Who could even begin to attempt an answer? This is what he said: 'Soccer is a game of great simplicity and beauty in which one side tries to score more goals than the other.'

It was so beautifully, laughably simple! Or so he made it seem. Only a great, unpretentious artist would see the great English game of soccer that way. He ought to be in the Oxford Dictionary of Quotations.

"He mentioned Munich to me only once. It was something I would never have asked him about, but it was the anniversary of the disaster and he wanted to talk about it a little. He said they should never have got on that plane a third time. He blamed the ice on the wings. He was haunted by one particular memory. He remembered staggering from the wreckage and seeing the body of Roger Byrne thrown clear of the plane. He was his closest friend on the team and at first he thought he was still alive. 'There wasn't a mark on him,' he said. 'It was if he was sleeping,' said Dennis.

"We do not know the suffering that visited the heroes and survivors of Munich but America gave Dennis a new life. He said the proudest day in his life was when Rachel graduated from the University of Miami. Judging by his grin all that day, we can believe him. He adored her. She had only to walk in the room and his face would light up. Rachel played tennis for England but she used to play soccer too. He used to say that she had a better right foot than him! We all miss him, all his friends, all his fans, everyone. Dennis Viollet's name will be remembered wherever soccer is played. His talent was kissed by God! But anyone who knew him was lucky. We were glad to be in his company, glad to be his friend and join in the laughter. We loved him."

When Dennis Viollet's friend and personal soccer idol Pele heard about Dennis's illness he immediately wrote to him in Jacksonville:

Dear Dennis,

I heard recently of your illness and wanted to share some thoughts with you. I know your illness last year came as a blow to your family, just as the Munich air crash did 40 years ago. Just think of the recovery you and your Club made from that night in Munich. With God's help I know you can do the same and I will pray to Him to help again now. Beyond your name as a great footballer, your reputation as a true sportsman reaches far and wide. We look forward to seeing you healthy again soon and active in our beloved sport of football.

Your friend,
Pele

The Final Whistle

At precisely 3 o'clock on the afternoon of Saturday March 6th 1999, the final whistle was blown on the life of Dennis Viollet. It ended all the pain and suffering for a very, very brave man. Dennis was 66. The two tumours co-incidentally appeared under the two scars inflicted in the Munich airplane disaster. The boy from Moss Side, Manchester, had played football in 40 different countries and graced the sport for close on five decades. As player, coach and human being, he had lived a full, rich and enriching life. The many tributes paid to him since his death have all affirmed how much he was respected and loved inside and outside the world of football. Wherever and however you met or knew Dennis Viollet, you never forgot him. He was one of those very special people whose contact made a deep impression on your life, an impression which time will never diminish.

In March 1999, some of Manchester United's biggest names were present in the Old Trafford stadium which they had helped make into the 'Theatre of Dreams.' The occasion was a unique memorial service and the sad farewell to a true Manchester United legend. The service was conducted by the Reverend Howard Entwistle, rector of St Matthew's Stretford. Johnny Morris and Charlie Mitten, members of United's brilliant 1948 team were there, as were Bill Foulkes and Albert Scanlon, both survivors of the Munich air disaster. John Doherty, one of the first Busby Babes, was also there along with Noel Cantwell, Maurice Setters, Nobby Stiles, Denis Law, David Sadler and Shay Brennan. Former Manchester City players who were friendly with Dennis also attended: Ken Barnes, Roy Little, Paddy Fagan and John Williamson. Sir Bobby Charlton sent his respects. They all recalled the good times and remembered a truly remarkable footballer who had no airs or graces before, during or after his playing career had ended. A sincere, genuine and wonderful human being right to the end.

Helen brought her husband's ashes back to Manchester to be scattered in the goalmouth at the Stretford End of the Old Trafford ground. Helen told guests: "Dennis requested that you were to smile and think of the laughs and the good times you spent together, and not mourn." Reverend Entwistle told them: "Though the death of Dennis was sad, it was not a solemn occasion-and that was something Dennis would have wanted. Let us be thankful for his life."

Dennis had told Helen just before he died: "Let people come to the funeral in their shorts and bright dresses, but tell them to have some fun." However, for all that, there were plenty of tears too as the ashes were laid in the evening sunshine at the silent stadium. Denis Law added: "Dennis Viollet was a direct, precise goalscorer, and very good at that. But most of all he was a good person."

On March 31st 2000, at another ceremony at Stoke City, soccer stars, civil dignitaries, relatives and friends turned out to celebrate the opening of Dennis Viollet Avenue, leading to the Britannia Stadium. Helen and Rachel were joined by the Lord Mayor, Reg Booth, club officials and former Stoke City players including Gordon Banks, Jimmy O'Neill, Terry Conroy and Jackie Marsh. In a short speech, Helen Viollet said: "I cannot begin to tell you how wonderful this is and what it would mean to Dennis. He would probably say: 'Why me? It wasn't just me; it was all the team!'"

A tribute from Sir Tom Finney OBE

Just before the completion of this book, Sir Tom Finney, possibly one of this country's greatest football ambassadors called to apologise for his being late in replying to our request for any little anecdotes concerning Dennis. Sir Tom's wife was not too well - we all hope and pray she gets better soon.

"Dennis Viollet was vastly underrated and never quite received the credit that he deserved. When I say underrated, I mean by members of the press and the general football supporters. However, he certainly wasn't underrated by Matt Busby, Jimmy Murphy and the players and staff at Old Trafford, I can tell you. They were forever singing his praises whenever we met which was quite often in the 1950s and 1960s, and several times after we had retired from active participation.

"Playing for Preston in the 1950s we had many tussles and confrontations with Manchester United, the fantastic 1948 FA Cup winning team who went on to win the First Division championship and later the famous Busby Babes team of the middle 1950s. Dennis made his debut in 1953 and quite a lot of the older players helped him through his early games. Players like Jack Rowley, Johnny Aston, Allenby Chilton and Stan Pearson eased his transition from reserve team to First Division football. Those wonderful players would tell him where and when to run and release the ball. They would praise him when he did something good and give him a gentle rollicking if he did something wrong. Mind you that Busby Babes team was something special and Dennis made them run smoothly. Yes I know the likes of Roger Byrne, Tommy Taylor, Duncan Edwards and Eddie Colman were exceptionally talented, but it was the willowy Viollet who made the team function. 'When

Dennis is on song, the team runs like clockwork,' Jimmy Murphy would say.

"Dennis was a remarkable player, a goalscorer supreme, a mid-field schemer and on occasions a dazzling right-winger. A pure footballer! Looking at him you would never imagine him to be a professional footballer playing against big, tough, rough hard men. He was so slim and weighed about nine stone, but he was a naturally gifted player. His balance was unique and he could dribble with the best of them. He could change direction while in full flight and go past defenders with ease. His acceleration from a standing position was simply breathtaking. His goals were an added bonus for United, and what a scorer as his goal ratio and record proves.

"I always thought he deserved a lot more caps than the two he received near the tail end of his Manchester United career. But that was one of the sad things about the game in those days. Dennis was among the top inside-forwards of the 1950s and to an extent the early 1960s. After Munich, Matt Busby moved him from inside left and played him at centre-forward. At first the trio of Albert Quixall-Dennis Viollet-Bobby Charlton didn't gel, but because of his immense talent Dennis made it work and what a fabulous trio they turned out to be.

"Like many others in football, I often thought England could have benefited from selecting all three together, it was certainly worth a try. Having said all that, Dennis had a wonderful career in football. After all, think of the many players who would have given their right arms to play in that Busby Babes team.

"I met Dennis on quite a few social occasions and found him to be a good sort. Always polite and courteous but also ready for a good laugh even if sometimes the joke was aimed at him. Stan Matthews used to tell me how easy he found it playing with Dennis when they were together with Stoke City. Stan would tell me that the ball was played perfectly to the spot where he wanted it and, he said, Dennis was always running into space to receive a return pass. To conclude, I hope this book will give readers a chance to learn something of a player who rarely received the publicity his efforts deserved because of his quiet disposition on the football field. There were not many better judges of a player than Matt Busby and Jimmy Murphy and to them Dennis was a football artiste and captain supreme."

The Final Word

In April 2000, Les Scott wrote a wonderful tribute to Dennis entitled 'Talent in bloom at the Victoria' in the *Sentinel Sunday Sport* newspaper.

"It was a fitting ceremony attended by his immediate family, former team-mates and those who simply wanted to pay their respects to a gracious man and a gifted player. A new road leading off from the Britannia Stadium was named in honour of one Dennis Viollet. It was a ceremony in keeping with how he played the game. Simple and with an inordinate amount of grace," wrote Mr Scott, who went on to tell his readers that football was indeed a simple game, but those players blessed with skills to make it uncomplicated and straightforward were few. Dennis Viollet though, was one of the few.

Mr Scott then reminded his readers that Dennis was one of the original Busby Babes and a survivor of the Munich air disaster, that Dennis had signed for Stoke in January 1962 as part of Tony Waddington's rebuilding programme. "As with all rebuilding structures, one requires varied talents. The physical strength of labourers and hod carriers, the swiftness and eye to detail of brickies but, above all, a creative mind to conceive the design. Stanley Matthews was the talisman of

Stoke City's championship side of 1963. The likes of Eddie Stuart and Eddie Clamp provided the physical strength but in Dennis Viollet, Tony Waddington found his architect." He wrote about Dennis being born in Manchester in 1933 and how he joined Manchester United as a junior in 1948, the year in which Matt Busby's first great United team of Carey, Rowley and Pearson beat Blackpool 4-2 in that classic FA Cup final.

"Stan Matthews had his swansong at Stoke City, and Dennis Viollet was his perfect conductor. At the time, the Victoria Ground on a Saturday was like Dickens' Mrs Fezziwig, 'One vast substantial smile' and with good reason. The wonder was not the blend and balance and tactical resource of a side that had the oldest average age of any team to win a championship in English football. Conversely, for all their seasoned years, it was their freshness of approach, joyfulness of mind and physical resilience. The fetching and carrying legs came from Bill Asprey, Tony Allen, Eric Skeels and Keith Bebbington. The physical presence came from Stuart and Clamp. The mercurial wizardry from Matthews, McIlroy, Mudie, Radcliffe and Viollet who, full of the joys of enjoying their football again, danced like young foals in pasture.

"Viollet was icy cool and resolute throughout the season's hottest fires. An architect-in-chief who, apart from having a natural eye for goal, played a role now long since forgotten in football, that of schemer. It took Stoke seven games to register their first win that season. It came against Charlton Athletic, a resounding 6-3 win in which Viollet scored four. His goals were gems of their kind, revealing a sense of timing and position as uncommon as it was innate. Viollet possessed a willowy suppleness of body, whipcord endurance, fleetness of foot and alertness which the still modern, professional approach to football demanded. That he had grace there is little doubt. Yet, for all his panache, he dodged and dummied, twisted and turned with consummate ease to send bewildered defenders madly along false trails."

Sir Stanley Matthews said of Dennis: "There were moments in games when the ball came to Dennis and it was if a spotlight had fallen on him and every other player was in his shadow. Your eyes were drawn to him as he engineered first space to work in, then proceeded to conjure up his own special brand of magic. Only when the ball had left Dennis's feet did you see the opening as the ball glided across the turf just in front of one our galloping forwards for the course of the game to be changed. Short pass, long pass, low pass, high pass, it mattered not one jot. Whatever it was, it was always the right pass when it came from Dennis."

Les Scott mentioned that opposed to his time at Old Trafford, when Dennis moved to Stoke City, he became more of a tactician and creator of goals than a goalscorer, as his tally of 66 goals in 207 appearances indicated. But for all that, he was Stoke's leading scorer with 23 in their Championship season. What a season it was. As Stoke pushed for promotion, the crowds rolled up. Over the Easter period, a total of 134,923 spectators saw Stoke's three holiday games. A staggering 66,199 turned up at Stamford Bridge to see the promotion win over Chelsea. At the Victoria Ground, crowds in excess of 30,000 were common. When Stoke kicked off the 1963-64 season against the star-studded Tottenham team, more than 41,000 turned up at the Victoria Ground to see Viollet and McIlroy turn in absolutely brilliant performances in a 2-1 win. On their way back to London, the Spurs players discussed the game. Jimmy Greaves told Les Scott: "We were in awe of Stan Matthews, still magical in the First Division at 48, but the other name on everyone's lips was Dennis Viollet.

A player who never received the honours or recognition his considerable ability deserved."

Now that has been rectified. Thanks to loyal fan Graham Bridgwood and others, there is now a road that bears his name. A lasting and fitting testimony to a great player, one as modest as the flower that also bears his name.

This Poem was written by Geoffrey H Galley for Helen in honour of Dennis.

Though I am sad to leave you
Though fate may seem unkind
There is no sorrow in my heart
As I leave this life behind

Fortune has dealt me a shorter term
Than three score years and ten
But I have lived a thousand lives
In the hearts of other men

For I have shared and treasured
The precious gift of few
I have known the pleasure and the pride
Of boyhood dreams come true
I have tasted the thrill of victory
In the course of battles run
I have soared aloft on the roar of the crowd
As another goal was won

And if as they say a life is rich
With one single friend alone
How great is the wealth of a man with friends
Whose number is never known

I think of the comrades I have loved

Whose lives were cruelly stilled
Weep for them, weep not for me
My life has been fulfilled

Oft I have dined at the feast of joy
I have tasted the sweetest wine
And who can say that he has shared
A love as deep as mine

And so farewell, yet do not grieve
Think of me for a while
Beyond a tear I'd rather be
Remembered with a smile

Afterword

Dennis played a season for Linfield in Belfast. He would fly over for the game and back again the same evening. We were living in Wythenshawe at the time and one Saturday night after the match, Den arrived home with a young Irish boy who had missed his flight and was going to spend the night at the airport.

"I couldn't leave him there, could I?" he said to me. The boy, of course, stayed overnight. He was a shy lad who left his veg and just ate the meat and potatoes! Dennis dropped him off the next morning at the airport, making sure he was able to get a flight out.

The reason I relate this incident is not because of its specific content, but because it was typical of the way Den lived his life. Never, ever did he think of himself as a star. Two sayings of his come to mind which epitomised his whole attitude to being a professional footballer: "So, I'm a footballer, what does that mean, except that I am lucky to be doing something I love and am getting paid for it." The other - and how significant it is today: "We are nothing without the fans." This is a philosophy Den lived by through his entire professional life.

I was delighted when Brian and Roy decided to write this book, and at some point I hope there will be a second one, 'The American Years'. There are two very distinct chapters in the life of Dennis Viollet. Firstly the one chronicled here by Brian and Roy and all who have contributed. The glamour years of schoolboy 329 glory; of Manchester United and Stoke City; the horror of Munich and Den's own way of dealing with it; of his life in Manchester and his affection for the people and the city of his birth which never diminished. This is certainly chapter one. Chapter two is the twenty six years spent conveying to Americans of all ages, backgrounds and abilities, his concept of what 'soccer' is really all about. This is a story that should also be told because only in the telling of those years is it possible to grasp the true concept of Dennis Viollet the man.

It will be three years on March 6th 2002 since Dennis was taken from us. The manner of his dying, and the indescribable pain of the events in the last two and a half weeks preceding his death is not something to dwell on in my contribution to this part of Den's story. For myself, I continue to miss him every minute of every hour, of every day, but always am aware of how fortunate I was to have shared a life filled with love and laughter for so many years.

Helen Viollet
October 2001

Dennis Viollet
Complete Statistical Record

Manchester United 1949 - 1962
Debut: v Newcastle Utd (A) 2-1, 11th April 1952
Last Game: v Leicester C (H) 2-2, 11th November 1961
Dennis made 294 appearances scoring 179 goals

BY COMPETITION AND SEASON

Appearances (goals)

Season	League	FACup	Europe	Other	Total
1952-53	3 (1)				3 (1)
1953-54	29 (11)	1 (1)			30 (12)
1954-55	34 (20)	3 (1)			37 (21)
1955-56	34 (20)	1 (0)			35 (20)
1956-57	27 (16)	5 (0)	6 (9)	1 (1)	39 (26)
1957-58	22 (16)	3 (3)	6 (4)	1 (0)	32 (23)
1958-59	37 (21)	1 (0)			38 (21)
1959-60	37 (32)	2 (0)			39 (32)
1960-61	24 (15)	1 (0)		2 (1)	27 (16)
1961-62	14 (7)				14 (7)
TOTALS	261(159)	17 (5)	12(13)	4 (2)	294(179)

Goals/Games ratio: 0.611 - United's 4th highest ever

England Caps (2)

1959-60	Hungary (A)	F	0-2 (0 goals)
1961-62	Luxembourg (H)	WC	4-1 (1 goal)

Scoring Records

Goals per game ratio

Player	Goals	Games	Ratio
Charlie Sagar	24	33	0.727
Tommy Taylor	131	191	0.686
Ronnie Burke	23	35	0.657
Dennis Viollet	179	294	0.611

Highest United goalscorers

Bobby Charlton 249 (199 league)
Denis Law 237 (171 league)
Jack Rowley 211 (182 league)
George Best 179 (137 league)
Dennis Viollet 179 (159 league)

Scoring Feats

Four Goals in a game:

(1) 1956/7 Anderlecht (H) Won 10-0

Hat-Tricks (8):

1954/5	Chelsea (A)	Won 6-5
1955/6	West Brom (A)	Won 4-1
1956/7	Preston NE (H)	Won 3-2
1957/8	Workington (A) (FAC)	Won 3-1
1958/9	Leeds Utd (H)	Won 4-0
1959/60	Nottm Forest (A)	Won 5-1
1960/1	Burnley (A)	Lost 3-5
1961/2	Burnley (H)	Won 6-0

Record Breaking Season - 1959/60

West Brom (A) 2
Luton Town (H) 2
Newcastle Utd (H) 2
Everton (A) 1
Chelsea (A) 2
Blackpool (H) 2
Leeds Utd (H) 1
Nottm Forest (A) 3
Tottenham H (H) 1
Burnley (A) 2

Leicester City (H) 2
Birmingham C (H) 1
Arsenal (H) 1
Preston NE (H) 1
Wolves (A) 1
Blackpool (A) 2
Sheff Wed (H) 2
Fulham (A) 2
Fulham (H) 1
Sheff Wed (A) 1

32 goals - 16 Home - 16 Away

Stoke City 1962-67

Debut: v Bristol Rovers (a) 2-0, 20 January 1962
Farewell: v Leicester City (h) 3-1, 29 April 1967
Dennis made 207 appearances scoring 66 goals

BY COMPETITION AND SEASON

Appearances (goals)

Season	League	FA Cup	Lge Cup	Totals
1961-62	13 (5)	0 (0)	0 (0)	13 (5)
1962-63	37 (23)	1 (0)	1 (1)	39 (24)
1963-64	32 (10)	3 (2)	6 (1)	41 (13)
1964-65	34 (13)	3 (2)	3 (1)	40 (16)
1965-66	32 (6)	1 (0)	5 (0)	38 (6)
1966-67	33+1 (2)	1 (0)	1 (0)	35+1 (2)
TOTALS	**181+1 (59)**	**9 (4)**	**16 (3)**	**206+1 (66)**

Index

Holand, Roy 196
Holden Ray 21-2
Holland, John 10
Hopkinson, Eddie 173, 280
Hotel Metropole, Belgrade 144
Howard, Peter 150, 153
Howe, Don 168
Huddersfield Town FC 51, 57-8, 60, 62, 66, 72, 76, 79, 232, 252, 265
Hudson, Alan 263
Hungary 65, 84, 97, 232-4
Hunt, Roger 300
Hunter, Reg 189, 225

Ipswich Town FC 134, 162, 249
IMUSA 302

Jack, David 198
Jackson, Harry 27
Jackson, Tom 153
Jacksonville Tea Men 296
Jacksonville, City of 296-7, 299, 301-2, 304-5
  DV presented the key to 296-7
John, Peter 285
Johnson, Alec 1-2, 108, 264
Johnson, Mike 6
Johnstone, Bobby 193
Jones, Mark 15, 18, 31, 33, 34-6, 45, 56, 61, 66, 73, 82,

99, 115, 127, 136, 138, 140, 142, 148, 151, 161, 166, 177, 223, 287
Juventus 114

Keeling, Peter 281
Kelsey, Jack 136
Kerr, Andy 216
Kevan, Derek 186
Kilmarnock FC 57-8
King, Dave 229
Kocsis, Sanyi 275
Kopa, Raymond 6, 110, 112, 212-4
Kwiatowski 92

Law, Denis 29, 104, 115, 235, 236, 241, 259, 271, 277, 308-9
Lawton, Nobby 188, 224, 253
Lawton, Tommy 78
League of Ireland 90, 196, 212
Ledbrooke, Archie 16, 153
Ladley, Roy 20
Leeds United 69, 199, 201, 265
Leicester City FC 125, 130, 210, 221, 240, 243, 252, 267, 272
Leivers, Bill 229
Lewin, Derek 169
Lewis , Eddie 35, 43, 72

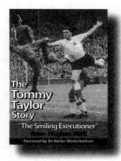

'The Smiling Executioner'
The Tommy Taylor Story
by Brian Hughes MBE
£8.95 - 268pp - over 50 photographs
"Magnifico" ALFREDO DI STEFANO
"Tommy Taylor - how could I forget him, he was the greatest centre-forward ever!"
TOMMY DOCHERTY

Starmaker

298pp · 24pp photographs · £16.95
by Brian Hughes MBE
Foreword by John Charles
Introduction by Nobby Stiles

When Jimmy Murphy arrived at Old Trafford in 1946 he was greeted by the ruins of what had once been one of the wonders of pre-war Manchester. The stadium was a bombed-out wreck while the players trained on a patch of dangerous gravel not fit for a modern day car park and the club reeled from the embarassment of playing their 'home' games at Maine Road. By the time Murphy packed his bags and left Old Trafford for the last time, Manchester United were world-famous: they had been conquered by and then conquered Europe, raised the profile of English league football to a degree unimaginable before the war and touched the hearts of millions in the process.

Sir Alex, United and Me
by Andy Pacino
Foreword by Sir Alex Ferguson
350pp - £8.99

The tale of one fan's remarkable relationship with Manchester United's legendary manager is told in this often humourous account of Fergie's tricky early years

Order by Credit Card 0161 872 3319

The King

Denis Law, Hero of the Stretford End
by Brian Hughes MBE
ISBN: 1901746356 - £17.95 - 421 pp
'The Greatest Thing on Two Feet'
BILL SHANKLY

Denis Law was hero and villain all rolled into one. His high-octane performances made him a Boys' Own hero to many. He was a player capable of incredible feats of skill and power - all carried off with the knowing smile and villainous touch of a Piccadilly pickpocket. To Mancunians, this son of an Aberdonian trawlerman became part of the fabric of the city; first as a dynamic frontman for the Blues and later as an all-action hero at Matt Busby's United.

In the latest of his biographies of former United greats, Brian Hughes traces the Scot's transformation from unlikely looking teenage footballer to the world's pre-eminent striker. Law's progress up the football ladder was prolific. The bespectacled youth who joined Huddersfield in 1955 didn't look much like a future world star but Bill Shankly's first reaction to his performances on the pitch were telling - 'he's a terror', said the then Huddersfield boss.

But if Denis' subsequent transfers to Manchester City and later Torino confirmed his status as football's rising star, his arrival at Old Trafford in 1962 confirmed him as a phenomenon. The Reds £115,000 swoop secured a player of huge influence both on and off the pitch. For 11 years his personality dominated the thoughts of United fans as Lawmania gripped the city until his shock transfer to the Blues in 1973.

Thus the stage was set for the ironic denouement in April 1974 - Denis' backheel consigning United to Second Division football and the Law legend to immortality.

'Out of the Void'
The Story of Primal Scream
by Brendan Yates
Published October 2003
ISBN: 1901746364 - £10.99 - 260pp
'From leather-clad rock icons to Ecstasy popping ravers, Primal Scream have appealed too and appalled their following in equal measure'